Saving Childhood

Saving Childhood

PROTECTING OUR CHILDREN
FROM THE NATIONAL
ASSAULT ON INNOCENCE

Michael Medved and Diane Medved, Ph.D.

HarperCollins*Publishers*
Zondervan

HarperCollins books may be purchased for educational, business, or sales promotional use. For information please write: Special Markets Department, HarperCollins Publishers, Inc., 10 East 53rd Street, New York, NY 10022.

FIRST EDITION

Designed by Nancy Singer Olaguera

Library of Congress Cataloging-in-Publication Data
Medved, Michael.
    Saving childhood : protecting our children from the national assault on innocence / Michael Medved and Diane Medved. —1st ed.
        p.   cm.
    ISBN 0–06–017372–6
    Includes bibliographical references and index.
    1. Children—United States. 2. Children and adults—United States.
3. Mass media and children—United States. 4. Child rearing—United States. 5. Innocence (Psychology)   I. Medved, Diane.   II. Title.
    HQ792.U5M43   1998
    305.23'0973–dc21   98–11850

98 99 00 01 02   ❖/RRD 10 9 8 7 6 5 4 3 2 1

For our children, Sarah, Shayna, and Danny

*who allow their adoring parents to share the joy
and significance of childhood innocence*

In the sun that is young once only,
Time let me play and be
Golden in the mercy of his means . . .

. . . it was all
Shining, it was Adam and maiden,
The sky gathered again
And the sun grew round that very day.
So it must have been after the birth of the simple light
In the first, spinning place . . .

And nothing I cared, at my sky blue trades, that time
    allows
In all his tuneful turning so few and such morning
    songs
Before the children green and golden
Follow him out of grace . . .

—DYLAN THOMAS, "FERN HILL"

The world is so full of a number of things,
I'm sure we should all be as happy as kings.
            —ROBERT LOUIS STEVENSON, *A CHILD'S GARDEN
            OF VERSES*

Contents

Acknowledgments

When we began collaborating on this project two years ago, a number of worried acquaintances warned us of potentially dire consequences to our relationship. Marriage involves enough daily stresses and strains, they argued, without husband and wife making a foolhardy effort to balance their contributions and define their roles as coauthors of a demanding book. Yes, we'd written eleven previous titles combined, and respectfully reviewed one another's manuscripts, but we'd never before shared formal responsibilities as we did here. As it turned out, the process proved unexpectedly pleasurable, and caused no discernible damage to our marriage. In fact, we conclude with only intensified mutual respect and affection. This happy surprise is due in no small part to the friends and associates who help us in all aspects of our complicated lives.

Our grateful association with our literary agents, the father-and-son team of Arthur and Richard Pine, spans more than two decades. Michael recommended Richard as an agent to Diane as part of our first conversation, within minutes of meeting. We have also enjoyed productive partnerships with our insightful editors, Hugh Van Dusen at HarperCollins (who's worked on two Medved projects) and John Sloan at Zondervan (who's handled three). Our lifelong friends Denise and Judd Magilnick of Santa Monica provided crucial research and helpful suggestions, as did our honored associate Lissa Roche of Hillsdale College. David Altschuler offered advice and encouragement, computer whiz Robert Brownell interrupted his triumphal progress at Microsoft selflessly to solve mind-numbing problems at all hours of the night, while Michael's crack radio show producers Jeremy Steiner and Dan Sytman provided the daily support that allows such literary and other efforts to flourish. Judith Wachs, together with Deb and Dale Leyde, proved such splendid friends and such a generous blessing to our kids that those children happily survived their parents' occasional distraction. Our neighbors Rabbi Daniel and Rebbetzin Susan Lapin (and their seven children) taught by example and, along with Yarden Weidenfeld of Toward Tradition, shared too many mutual challenges to be specifically enumerated.

Our families offered unflagging support, particularly our parents Stanley and Genevieve Edwards of Westlake Village, California, Renate Medved of Los Angeles, and David and Yael Medved of Jerusalem. Michael's brother (and prior coauthor) Harry Medved has always been indispensable to all our endeavors—he even lived with us during the first four years of our marriage. Our children (who ultimately displaced him), Sarah, Shayna, and Danny, though not overlooking the irony that their parents devoted so much attention to other people's childhoods, nonetheless provided the impetus for this project and continue as the light of our lives. We also must thank the wonderful staff of the King County Library System Answer line, ever-available and ever-helpful.

Finally, it is with great affection and enormous gratitude that we acknowledge the invaluable, efficient, and consistently cheerful support of our brilliant and absolutely irreplaceable administrative assistant, Alexis Prida. With her dedicated and exhaustive efforts she makes our work possible. She is a daily blessing to the Medved family and, indeed, to everyone fortunate enough to encounter her.

Diane and Michael Medved

SECTION 1

The Assault

1

Childhood Crashed and Burned

To Frighten and Corrupt

In every corner of contemporary culture, childhood innocence is under assault. The very idea of parental protectiveness has been overwhelmed by relentless pressure from a society that seems determined to expose its young to every perversion and peril in an effort to "prepare" them for a harsh, dangerous future.

From the bleakest ghettos to the most privileged suburbs, families face the same fears. We worry not only about what might happen to our kids on the way to school, but about what values they will learn once they get there. We're concerned not only with the threat of physical assault, but with the emotional and moral battering that our children endure from peers and the media. In short, we feel powerless to counteract the implacable social forces that push our own flesh and blood to grow up too soon—and too cynical. We may shower youngsters with every sort of material blessing and glitzy diversion, but we can't seem to give them the greatest gift of all—a secure, optimistic, and reasonably sheltered childhood.

Nihilistic messages that frighten and corrupt now come at our kids from so many directions at once that childhood innocence barely stands a chance. Consider:

In Philadelphia, a four-year-old keeps squirming away when embraced by a favorite uncle who'd come for his weekly visit. When asked by her puzzled relative what's wrong, she tells him that her nursery school teacher warned her against any adults who "touch her too hard." If he persists in squeezing her, she tearfully informs him, she'll have to call the police.

In New York City, a ten-year-old kisses his parents good-bye in the morning and goes off to his exclusive (and outrageously expensive) private school. When he comes home that evening following some after-school adventures with his best friends, he proudly displays a small silver ring inserted into his newly pierced nose.

In Dallas, a three-year-old returns from play group to regale his disbelieving parents with an earnest, straight-faced singing and dancing rendition of "Mama's Got a Great Big Butt."

In Salt Lake City, a first grader begins compulsively throwing away her previously cherished dolls, much to the horror of her parents. It takes several hours to get an explanation: her teacher showed the class that the world was so bad—and so crowded—that nobody should have children. The sensitive and solemn little girl didn't even want to *pretend* to raise babies of her own.

In suburban Kansas, the local school board abruptly terminates an elderly and popular crossing guard who's worked without complaint at the same intersection for nearly twenty years. A few suspicious parents had expressed their worries about his affectionate attitude, and occasional hugs, to his favorite children. The officials can hardly risk the threat of scandal or a lawsuit.

And in our own home, in the winter of '94, our younger daughter, Shayna, joins her excited kindergarten classmates for an after-school field trip to the botanical gardens. As these neatly uniformed parochial school kids squeal and giggle in the backseat of a van, the adults listen to the hourly news on the radio—which includes a graphic description of Lorena Bobbitt cutting off her husband's penis and throwing it out the window of her car. Hearing this, our daughter covers her ears in horror and begins sobbing uncontrollably, soon joined by two of her frightened classmates.

Admittedly, these anecdotes represent relatively minor upsets in a world scarred by youth violence, widespread substance abuse, teen pregnancy, and adolescent suicide. Nevertheless, such small examples illustrate the depth—and breadth—of the problem: today, even the most conscientious and protective parents feel helpless when it comes to shielding the innocence of their children. Moreover, this careless cultural assault on the innocence of small children can be directly connected to the development of more dangerous behavior in maturing adolescents. An abundance of evidence suggests that one of the reasons today's teenagers are more frequently troubled and tormented than young people of previous generations is that their parents, teachers, peers—and even the shapers of popular culture—adopted a novel and radical approach to child-rearing in their earliest years.

In her prophetic 1981 book *Children Without Childhood*, Marie Winn powerfully develops the argument that civilization has recently shifted its fundamental attitude toward nurturing the young. She writes that "the change has occurred so swiftly that most adults are hardly aware that a true conceptual and behavioral revolution is under way, one that has yet to be clearly defined and understood. . . . Once parents struggled to preserve children's innocence, to keep childhood a carefree golden age, and to shelter children from life's vicissitudes. The new era operates on the belief that children must be exposed early to adult experience in order to survive in an increasingly complex and uncontrollable world. The Age of Protection has ended. An Age of Preparation has set in."

In 1981, that "Age of Preparation" remained too new to properly analyze its impact on real-world kids. Seventeen years later, however, it should be possible to determine whether this fresh dispensation has succeeded in its own terms. Has this revolutionary, and purportedly realistic, approach to childhood helped children cope with the challenges of contemporary life? For all the current emphasis on preparation, are today's kids actually well prepared?

Statistical indications are hardly encouraging.

Item: Since 1960, the rate at which teenagers take their own lives has more than tripled; by 1995, 14 percent of all those who died between the ages of fifteen and twenty-four died at their own hands. According to the Centers for Disease Control, in 1993 a horrifying 8.6 percent of high school students had attempted suicide in the twelve months preceding the survey. The U.S. Department of Health and Human Services reports more than 500,000 such attempts each year—or nearly 1,400 every day.

Item: "The fastest growing segment of the criminal population is made up of children," notes former Secretary of Education William Bennett. Since 1965, the juvenile arrest rate for violent crimes has tripled (with more than 100,000 annual arrests). Approximately seven teenagers die each day as murder victims; more than 20 percent of all high school students carry a knife, razor, firearm, or other weapon to school on a regular basis.

Item: Between 1992 and 1995, use of marijuana nearly doubled among eighth and tenth graders; 52 percent of seventeen-year-olds say that they "know someone who sells illegal drugs"; 86 percent of teenagers in Los Angeles County agree with the statement "marijuana is everywhere." In 1995, the University of Michigan's Institute for Social Research completed a national survey showing that 50 percent of all twelfth graders (and 40 percent of tenth graders!) have used some illicit drug, including LSD, inhalants, stimulants, barbiturates, cocaine, and crack. According to the study's chief investigator, Lloyd D. Johnson, this is "a problem that is getting worse at a fairly rapid pace."

Item: Today, 51 percent of girls and 67 percent of boys have intercourse before age eighteen (compared to 35 percent and 55 percent in the early 1970s). About 3 million teenagers—about one in four of those with sexual experience—acquire a sexually transmitted disease *every year*. The rate of unmarried teenagers getting pregnant has nearly doubled in the last twenty years, and today, 30 percent of all births are illegitimate. By the end of the decade, according to the most reliable projections, 40 percent of all American births and 80 percent of all minority births will occur out of wedlock.

If the purpose of the preparation model of childhood is to ready our kids to confront the challenges of adolescence and young adulthood, it can only be adjudged an appalling failure. The disaster is so obvious that one can only wonder at the unshakable determination of so much of the educational, psychological, and cultural establishment to press on with the new approach, regardless of its consequences, extending the assault on innocence to ever-younger victims, all in the name of equipping them for the future. This stubbornly impractical insistence fits George Santayana's classic definition of fanaticism, which, he writes, "consists in redoubling your efforts when you have forgotten your aim."

As if to remind us all how far we strayed from our original aims, and to focus urgent new attention on the ongoing attack on old-era notions of childhood, the horrifying and officially unconnected deaths of a pair of small girls became two of the most pondered and publicized tragedies of recent years.

Two Little Girls

In April 1996, seven-year-old Jessica Dubroff, with her beaming father at her side, climbed into her red booster seat aboard a Cessna 177B in Cheyenne, Wyoming, for the second leg of what was supposed to have been her triumphant journey as the world's youngest cross-country pilot. Instead, minutes after takeoff in blustery sheet-rain, Jessica, her father, and a flight instructor crashed on a residential street, sending all three to a fiery death.

Eight months later, six-year-old beauty princess JonBenet Ramsey was found brutally strangled and sexually assaulted in the basement of her parents' Boulder, Colorado, home the day after Christmas. Immediately, photos of the child, in makeup and showgirl costumes, prancing in suggestive poses on the stage of beauty pageants, flashed across the country in magazines and on the TV news—bringing public outcry about a world where toddlers as well as teens are immersed in adult affectations.

The deaths of two bright and beautiful children naturally provoked waves of national sorrow, but America also felt profoundly shocked by circumstances that would not only allow but encourage youngsters to leap prematurely and destructively into adult roles and responsibilities.

Both cases highlight a paradoxical fascination in our society with precocity. On the one hand, we find it irresistible in its oddity.

On the other, we intuitively protest and mourn the loss of precious and irretrievable innocence.

Reporters gathered eagerly when Jessica Dubroff's father called them to cover each stop of her planned journey. They abetted and supported the youngster's effort, though there was not even an official record to break. In fact, Jessica's dad, Lloyd Dubroff, fifty-seven, had inquired of the *Guinness Book of Records* about his hope of recognition for Jessica and discovered that Guinness had dropped their "youngest-pilot" category. That didn't deter him from proposing the journey to his daughter, who had been taking flying lessons for only four months, earning flight experience of just thirty-five hours.

Jessica embraced her dad's plan but, like a typical seven-year-old on a long ride in a moving vehicle, fell asleep during the first leg of the flight, precluding the possibility of any distinction as a cross-country pilot. That didn't diminish her father's ambitions, however, and Mr. Dubroff scheduled several national press conferences, including the final one that lingered on as the storm outside worsened. Wendy Shalit in the *Weekly Standard* asked, "Why was Jessica wearing a cap that said 'Women Fly,' when no woman, only a little seven-year-old girl, was flying that day? . . . Pushy parents have existed from time immemorial, but social pressure to protect children—particularly young girls—also existed to check the egos of parents."

In the case of Jessica Dubroff, that ego remained on display even after the crash that killed her. The little girl's mother, Lisa Hathaway, told the *Los Angeles Times:* "Clearly, I would want my children to die in a state of joy. I would prefer it was not at age 7, but God, she went with her joy and her passion, and her life was in her hands." In her distinctly New Age home, Ms. Hathaway prohibited candy and children's books as inappropriately childish indulgences and instead encouraged her little girl to begin as soon as possible to pursue adult notions of liberation. "I did everything so this child could have freedom of choice and have what America stands for," she declared. "Liberty comes from . . . just living your life. I couldn't bear to have my children in any other position."

The result of this attitude, and the father's media-driven dreams of glory, brought little Jessica Dubroff ultimately to the driver's seat of her doomed Cessna, in a position that utterly contradicted fundamental conceptions of childhood. A seven-year-old little girl should be able to rely on others for her basic needs and protection, while the pilot of a plane asks others to depend on her.

"An adult with 35 hours is just about ready for a 100-mile trip," flight instructor John Vandevort told the *Los Angeles Times*. "In Jessica's case, they were going to go 7,000 miles. That's not a training event. That's an adventure. An adult adventure."

JonBenet Ramsey also captured worldwide attention for unchildlike activities. In the week of January 20, 1997, shortly after her death, readers gasped at the sultry glare of the perfect rose-lipped girl who occupied full pages in *Time* and *Newsweek* magazines. They sighed at the glitter-crowned child on the cover of that week's *People* magazine, with its article boldly headlined "Lost Innocent." And they felt riveted and revolted by tales of her beauty-queen mother's ambitions for the lovely child, which juxtaposed sweet childhood with an almost tawdry show-biz exhibitionism. For JonBenet, learning to read was combined with lessons on how to purse her lips, parade in sophisticated clothing, and arrange highlighted hair and harsh makeup.

"Her death illuminated the peculiar world of child pageantry," said *Newsweek*, "which enlists thousands of girls below the age of 12, plus an equal number of mothers and grandmothers, supporting a nationwide industry of contest promoters, costume designers, grooming consultants and publishers." Psychologist William Pinsof, president of the Family Institute at Northwestern University, conducted extensive studies showing that participation in child beauty contests often results in drug addiction, eating disorders, and depression in puberty. "You end up with hollow children and narcissistic parents," he says of pageant participants.

A *New York Post* article by Steve Dunleavy concludes, "There's no question in any investigator's mind, in any veteran law enforcement officer's mind, in my mind—that little JonBenet's persona and appearance had a lot to do with her shocking death." That tragedy is especially uncomfortable because it creates unnatural and opposing pairings—innocence and seduction, childhood and death. JonBenet's posed pout, splashed like a coldly calculated fashion model's smirk across so many magazine covers, both captivated and disturbed us because of this paradox—rightfully producing anger and an inevitably inchoate call to action.

On one point, however, virtually all observers agreed: both tiny victims had been pushed by their own parents to grow up too fast. Rather than acting as guardians against life-and-death pressures (like piloting an airplane) and exploitation (like parading for judges on the basis of appearance), they saw themselves as facilitators of the next generation's unfettered fantasies.

Basking in the limelight as a pilot and a princess are more adolescent stunts than adult activities. Parents may justify such endeavors as "natural" (and therefore praiseworthy) little-girl desires; the children were "just doing what they wanted to do, and we were proud of them," said the apologists. But without parents pushing them, what child would *invent* such activities?

Sure, kids dream of flying airplanes—but "when I grow up," not *now*. Sure, little girls play dress-up and parade in front of a mirror—but they're using Mommy's shoes and lipstick and are practicing for the day when the women's size 8 high heels actually fit. The full story of JonBenet Ramsey's demise may never be known, but regardless of who murdered the girl, there is little doubt about who murdered her innocence.

In these two heartbreaking cases, the parents were essential "enablers," turning their own immature make-believe into dangerous reality. They undoubtedly got a charge out of their children's adventures, and rationalized away any misgivings by insisting that unencumbered children naturally know best.

For JonBenet and Jessica, perhaps the essential problem went beyond the parental pressure to leave childhood too soon; in both cases their parents' obsessive fantasies served to deny them childhood altogether. The earliest years in a young person's life once required responsible adults playing the role of benevolent authorities, putting fences around their children not so much to keep the kids in as to keep the intrusive, abusive world out. Now those parents have changed direction, eschewing fences as prisons and proclaiming the menacing world "necessary reality" rather than peril. Gone is the safety of early life, and the security of loving parental enclosure. And with that protected space to grow goes that special time we define as childhood.

The sad stories of the Dubroff and Ramsey families highlight several essential aspects of childhood's disappearance. For one thing, the two cases show the way defenders of a new approach to parenting can make the paradoxical claim that they assault childhood for the sake of children.

Grim Truths, All at Once

Meanwhile, at least one powerful source of this assault makes no claim whatsoever of altruistic intentions. The masters of mass media insist on their right to the pure pursuit of profit, and only shrug at the possibility that children might be wounded in the crossfire.

Neil Postman of New York University emphasizes the role of television in *The Disappearance of Childhood*. Where adults once could ease children into the "secrets" of maturity, the tube presents them with the grim truths from the earliest ages, and all at once. Even benign situation-comedies of the '50s were bracketed by real-life headlines touting "The News at Six"; images of accidents, murders, wars, and scandals flashing into living rooms slashed the power of parents to shield their children's sensitivities.

At the same time, with families pressured for higher income and women urged to take advantage of newly opened opportunities in the workforce, a fresh emphasis in parenting emerged. David Elkind, in his classic *The Hurried Child*, says that this culture of "fast-lane" striving forced a focus on gaining an edge in the marketplace. Parents want their children to have the greatest advantage in order to succeed—the best prep schools, the finest colleges, and ultimately the most lucrative and prestigious careers—and so encourage them to read at earlier ages, earn the most awards and the highest grades and scores. School programs and the media play into parents' desires to escalate early achievement, causing children in modern competitive homes to rush out of childhood and into debilitating symptoms of stress.

Too often, social and economic tides inexorably erode the values that parents seek to live and impart. When parents are asked how raising children today is different from a generation ago, they reply "there's no respect," reports Dana Mack in *The Assault on Parent-*

hood. "And by this, they do not only mean that children no longer have enough respect for parents. They mean also that the larger culture no longer supports the family as an inviolate unit engaged in a crucial and worthy task—the task of child-rearing." Ms. Mack carefully details the means by which our culture undermines parents' traditional roles, but offers the hope of a "new familism" through which mothers and fathers can reclaim their authority (via such methods as home schooling and inventive work scheduling) and renew their spirits.

Home Truths

Even homes that have already taken advantage of such strategies face an uphill, everyday struggle against questionable but all-conquering messages that can penetrate the most cunningly designed protective strategies. Our own three children (Sarah, eleven, Shayna, nine, and Danny, five) attend Jewish religious schools and have lived their entire lives in a home that is proudly TV-free. Nevertheless, at the dinner table some four years ago our oldest suddenly floored us with a bizarre question.

Chewing on her brown-hair braid, with her large eyes wet and worried, our then seven-year-old wanted to know how soon she would start to bleed. Taken aback, her mother asked the obvious question. "Where did you hear about that?"

"In my book," Sarah replied.

"What book?"

"The one I checked out at the library today," Sarah answered. "It's called *Are You There, God? It's Me, Margaret.* What's all this about girls and blood?"

A quick examination of the volume in question, written by acclaimed children's author Judy Blume, revealed that the teenage heroine's first period is indeed an important element of the plot. Our little Sarah took home this book at the recommendation of a kindly neighborhood librarian who noted our child's precocious reading level and felt that her religious bent would help her connect with Blume's spiritual themes. It clearly never occurred to her that intimate details of menstruation might well shock a reader in second grade.

"You want to know about girls and blood?" Diane told her queasy daughter, suddenly aware that all her training in psychology had abandoned her. "It's nothing you have to worry about right now, honey. And by the way, could you give me that book?"

And with that spare response, Sarah learned that some topics remain inappropriate for a seven-year-old girl; she became more forcefully aware of that world of "things that you will learn about later." And she respected it. In fact, in more recent years, explanations of pending anatomical changes have been received less than enthusiastically. For her, ignorance is cherished bliss; of her own volition, Sarah prefers to resist mature realities until they are unavoidable.

In this spirit, our self-described "bookworm" endorsed a protective policy we developed jointly for future visits to the library. Before she checks out a book and brings it home on her own, she'll look at the copyright date to make sure it was written before 1960. We've discovered the hard way that work from these earlier days can usually be better trusted to portray childhood the way Sarah feels it should be—with issues and problems of the sort girls typically and appropriately confront: who will be friends with whom, how to earn spending money, mastering a two-wheeler, or planning a surprise birthday party. In Sarah's unsophisticated world, teachers and parents are authorities, little brothers are pests, and girlfriends are accomplices.

And sisters can be friend or foe. One of the most charming—and normal—entanglements is Sarah's relationship with her sister, Shayna, who is two years, four months, and a day younger. Here's the poem Sarah wrote for her school newspaper:

> *Sisters fight,*
> *then reunite.*
> *Not long can they stay mad.*
> *Sisters can be*
> *the best company,*
> *No better you ever had.*
> *After you fight*
> *(then reunite)*
> *Oh boy! Are you both glad.*

And *we* are glad that our daughters are consumed with such "old-fashioned" occupations—we work diligently to allow them space to flourish. We've been told that we are disadvantaging, and perhaps even *abusing* our offspring by enfolding them in our values and a (temporarily) rose-colored view of the world. After all, shouldn't the youngsters be properly *prepared* for the rough and threatening experiences that lie ahead in adolescence and beyond?

Such arguments miss the mark by underestimating the imperial reach of contemporary culture. In even the most isolated outposts of this country, and especially in our news-saturated home, it's hard to escape the sad tales of JonBenet Ramsey and Jennifer Dubroff—not to mention every shocking detail concerning Lorena Bobbitt, O. J. Simpson, Timothy McVeigh, and even Princess Di and the president of the United States. We don't want to contribute even *further* to the encroachment of life's menacing, sordid, or sad circumstances by adding specific warnings, dire stories, and terrifying images of "what might happen to you if. . . ."

Ward Cleaver Is Dead

The basic arguments against our policy with our own kids and our position on children in general are so obvious and commonplace that we can recite them by heart.

Ozzie and Harriet, we're repeatedly told, went off the air more than thirty years ago, and today's kids can hardly count on Ward Cleaver to guide them. Indeed, 27 out of 100 children live in single-parent families; drugs and gangs are not just clips on the evening news but facts of life in even middle-class neighborhoods; mothers can buy hair-sample drug tests at the corner dime store. Kids arrive for kindergarten fed on *Sesame Street* warnings about "uncomfortable touches" and armed with a fingerprinted "stolen child" identification card. Your kids may come across a smattering of similarly naive offspring of a few intact families, but just by looking around they learn that theirs is a charmed life that could crumble at any time; that a lot of their peers see their dads only on weekends, if they see them at all. It seems ridiculous to propose turning back the clock: analog timepieces are gone forever, and the digits just keep flipping forward. So the popular wisdom concludes that kids *need* their warnings and preparation. The dangers they face are real, and most experts insist that advance knowledge is the only way to cope with such menace.

But the depressing realities of the world don't negate our view; they reinforce it. The fact that children's lives may be bleak or miserable doesn't mean they need reassuring and warmhearted messages less—it means they need them *more*. No child of divorce wants to see a movie about another miserable kid whose parents are fighting. No normal seven-year-old wants to be told that Mommy and Daddy may be "bad guys" abusing dangerous substances—like the beer or aspirin some teachers ask them to search out in their homes. When educators and parents plant in children the idea that they should anticipate danger at every turn, fear and suspicion become the officially endorsed daily posture—crushing childhood's delicate spirit.

Few parents realize that this demoralization is being foisted upon their children, and upon themselves as guardians of their children's welfare. Worse, they seldom acknowledge the extent to which their own attitudes and behaviors contribute to the problem. At the same time, all parents want to do whatever it takes to give their offspring the best chance for a hopeful and rewarding life. It's a whirlpool of forces sucking kids and their mothers and fathers into a maelstrom of confusion, frustration, and helplessness, blending their roles and cracking the chain of command.

The result is demonstrated in the wealth of research on the loss of that special set-aside time we understand as childhood. Each scholar reaffirms the problem and contributes his or her own special twist. Neil Postman lays major blame on television; David Elkind adds the culprit of competition; Dana Mack sees these and other social forces ripping away parental authority, and sympathizes. We agree that there's a collusion of factors, adding that we might also look critically at the generation that has inspired these changes—our own "baby-boomer" cohort, with its perpetually self-absorbed and adolescent worldview. As Pogo famously declared: "We have met the enemy, and he is us." Facing this responsibility is the first step in fighting back against the encroachment on the innocence of our nation's children.

Sounding the Alarm

And that is what this book is all about: letting parents see that they *can resist* the popular but destructive philosophy they're unthinkingly buying into—and ultimately perpetrating. We hope to sound the alarm that families, teachers, clerics, and neighbors are often unwittingly attacking something precious, killing something irreplaceable. And in killing innocence, they could actually set up a self-fulfilling prophecy, *creating* the ominous world they try to prepare their youngsters to survive.

In the first section of this book, "The Assault," we describe the four ubiquitous factors that, under the banner of benevolent preparation, work to destroy innocence. They include *the media, schools, peers,* and *parents themselves*. These factors weave the fabric of every child's life; they are so fundamental as to be the *sources* of the child's personality—yet in our present national climate they may actually choke off youngsters' healthy development and stuff them with fears, terrifying scenarios, and pessimism about the future. In considering the way each of these influences operates in today's world, we examine both the *what* and the *why*; not only describing what such forces do to our kids but exploring why they do it.

In the second section of the book, "The Defense," we offer parents concrete means to counteract the assault and guard the three basic components of childhood innocence: *security, a sense of wonder, and optimism*. At the moment, our society seems to be obsessed with the importance of "self-esteem," but we argue that as significant as it may be for children to believe that "I'm a great kid," it's even more crucial for them to believe that "It's a great world." If feelings of gratitude and hope and appropriate awe at our astonishing universe aren't instilled in childhood, chances are they will be denied for a lifetime. We hope to inspire parents to take practical steps and to speak clearly to their children—and to others—about the importance of protecting and even, in some cases, restoring these precious characteristics of childhood.

The need for such a conversation, in our kitchens and in our culture, is pressing and urgent. But before we can structure an effective defense, or mount any meaningful counterattack, we must first come to terms with the fundamental nature of the assault.

The Assault on Innocence by Media

TV and the Ubiquitous Assailants

Out of the Mouths of Babes

As usual, the television season of 1990 opened with great fanfare. The CBS network heralded a new comedy series, *Uncle Buck*, based on a successful 1989 movie starring the rotund and lovable funny man John Candy.

In one sense, it turned out that the show deserved all the hoopla. When the big night came, a national uproar began within thirty seconds of its opening scenes. "The show was denounced by critics and viewers because the uncle (who inherited the kids following the death of his brother) was a lazy, immature, cigar-smoking, drinking slob," recall Tim Brooks and Earle Marsh in their survey of the medium.

But a disgusting leading man (played by Kevin Meany) was not the only reason why *Uncle Buck* put viewers in shock: "within the first moments of the show's debut, 6-year-old Maizy enters the house and yells, 'Miles! You suck!'

"When questioned why, she responded, 'He called me a freckle-butt, but I don't have freckles on my butt! They're beauty marks!'"

The bad taste of the words themselves caused a reaction, but what really drew the public's outrage was that these words were spoken by a *six-year-old girl*. Both reviewers and TV fans agreed: it's bad enough that children must observe *adults'* ubiquitous plunge into crude dialogue, but TV execs lower the cultural level for everyone when they broadcast to all ages this kind of coarse-ness—emitted by one not yet old enough to read.

Would anyone take notice now? Doubtful. Such language is everywhere—on TV, in movies rated suitable for young viewers, in "literature" aimed at tender ages, on billboards designed to catch even the smallest eyes. Nowadays, six-year-olds can get away with saying anything. After all, they're well prepared to face a crude and cruel world.

Can't Escape It

The limits of propriety are so lax and flabby—harmfully so—that even a six-year-old can't escape the taint. Parents concerned for their children must be constantly alert because *the media's assault on innocence is ubiquitous and comes on several fronts.*

Television is the most potent and pervasive offender. With screens now as tall as an ostrich and twice as wide, television dom-inates the world of whoever inhabits a room. And with the boob tube now so inexpensive, there's no need to endure conflict over who watches what. There's the white swivel TV in the kitchen, the set in each of the kids' rooms, the little model for the workshop, and don't forget the deluxe set with WebTV in the parents' boudoir. No consumer selects these images as desirable, but they get swal-lowed into consciousness anyway. The impact of this invasion is profound—redefining norms, creating slang terms, presenting the negative but not the positive side of reality with the daily news.

That newscast brings with it lots of horrifying statistics. We see the crimes, watch the trials, see the tears of the victims. Floods decimate towns, earthquakes level villages, wars slash families. We confront unavoidably the most trying and heart-wrenching aspects of reality, and not only in our circle, in our town or state. We're also fed the worst aspects of reality around the world, with terrorists exploding market squares and fires ripping through faraway forests. Snow in the most remote corner of the Alaskan tundra was dampened with tears as Princess Diana was laid to rest, her life's details brought into consciousness via satellite, as if she were a sister. Our relatives in Israel express their opinions to us via satellite-fed phone line about the not-so-private life of our president.

TV forces on us unceasing numbers—studies that show everything from the likelihood of cancer to the percentage of illiterate adults. Often, newscasts present the worst picture to shock, to stir adrenaline, to make us angry and discontented, in the lauded pursuit of "pushing the envelope." We see everything and gain an encyclopedic scope of knowledge and statistical savvy never possessed by any generation before.

But perhaps the most frightening statistic of all is this: the average individual watches twenty-four hours of television per week.

Twenty-four hours per week! The average schoolchild under twelve—overprogrammed and "hurried" with sports, computer, homework, and social life—watches twenty-one hours, forty-nine minutes per week. Imagine: at the end of the usual life span, the average person will have endured more than ten uninterrupted *years* of television, day and night, with no breaks for the potty, no sleep, no work, no school. Ten years of staring at a cathode-ray tube, looking at images that for the most part one doesn't control and never chose.

That's more hours than anyone will ever spend working. More hours than all the schooling one could receive through a graduate degree. Certainly far more hours than most people get to enjoy their families, their hobbies, their leisure. It's more time by age five than a child will spend talking to his father in a *lifetime*.

That's why we've divided this topic into two chapters. Media are plural. There are many types, and they enter into view and consciousness in every aspect of our lives, inescapably. We read the backs of our cereal boxes: print medium. We see billboards on the street: print medium. We hear music while we're shopping: radio, rock. The grocery store has a video section: film.

Often, while other influences harming childhood are at work, media are adding to the damage simultaneously. Peers are an important influence on kids, but one of their most significant commonalities, and indeed a basis of kids' communication, is their absorption in media. They talk about TV shows, the latest movies, teen rock idols, concerts. Parents are potent shapers of children's values, but how many homes have TV on day and night, even as parents are trying to talk to their kids? How many parents silence their carpooling children to hear the latest epiphany of Dr. Laura or Imus? How many families use their "family time" to watch a rented video together? And how many homes are stocked with TVs in nearly every room?

Media are more pervasive than any other influence because they are the conduit for understanding anything outside the building we now inhabit. And people in this mobile and isolated time crave and demand a connection with each other. Many people know Roseanne better than they know their next-door neighbors. Often a lack of real face-to-face relationships makes this yearning for media all the more acute, to the point where some people immerse themselves completely in their medium of choice, nearly obliterating the intrusion of the real world—causing "TV addiction," "talk-radio addiction," and recently, "Internet addiction." It is a pathetic indictment of our culture that media have more input in our thinking and our linking than does talking directly, with interchange and feedback, to real human beings. Think about it—how much of your day do you spend entirely media-free?

The bombardment of TV in typical American homes is constant—no one takes weekends or vacations away from the tube, as we do from school and work. The *average daily* television viewing per household is 7.28 hours. It's on in the morning, starting your day with interviews with the latest best-selling author. Then come soaps and after-school specials, game shows and endless selections on cable. Specialty channels, shopping channels, and the remote control is right there, making it easy to switch when a plot gets the slightest bit boring. Sports programming can take up an entire Sunday—"sports widows" mourn the loss of their husbands in the consolation of video-filled shopping malls. Furniture makers are now offering coffee tables with pull-down niches made just for storing those easy-to-misplace remote controls.

Even if your home's TV-restricted, your kids are not safe. When your child goes over to the neighbor kid's to play, his mom's got *her* TV on, keeping her company as she whips up dinner. The kids there most likely watch a video, something pulled without comment from a shelf where adult selections mingle with Barney the Dinosaur. Even at Payless Shoe Source, the monitor in the corner of the children's section is feeding images into those fertile brains, allowing Mom to pick out shoes and slip them on nonrunning feet, or perhaps mosey over to the other side of the store to shop for herself in peace.

Anyone who has visited an airport recently has observed the constant presence of the television. As an illustration, consider the true and involuntary experience of Diane Medved, returning from a speech in Iowa. Put yourself in her place—it could easily happen to you.

You're on the way to Seattle, waiting to board. There's a slight delay—you sit down and the voice rising above the commotion is that of a female newscaster, telling you about the latest events, the weather everywhere in the country. And then you notice the "feature," a fashion report showing models swaying down the Paris runway. Once you look upward to the screen suspended from the ceiling, the action becomes compelling.

You notice the strange colors of the clothes, the parade of young women-sticks, breastless, hipless, and what's this? They're wobbling as they walk, and it's not just because they're wearing six-inch patent-leather heels. Finally you figure it out: these ladies don't walk like normal humans trying to get somewhere. They walk by crossing the rear foot over the front foot, pulling out the behind foot and swinging it around to cross over the foot now in front. It's bizarre. But—maybe it's trendy. Does it make women look thinner? Sexier? Maybe *you* should try walking like this. You go home and tell your daughters about it. They begin tottering and weaving around the house.

Is this something worthy of several million expended brain cells? Is it harmless diversion while waiting for a delayed plane? Or is this an invasion of one's private life, intruding on one's ability to read, to think, to meditate, to observe the real world in the vicinity? Did we *want* to find out that fashion models walk like Martians? And once this strange information is impressed on our minds, do we want to be fascinated by the knowledge of this enough to transfer it to the minds of our children?

Can you escape the imposition of the media? We think not.

Suggesting that "If you don't like it you can just turn it off" is like saying "If you don't like the smog, then stop breathing."

An article on the quarter-century of research on TV by Professors Dorothy and Jerome Singer at Yale University notes that "even if a household went TV-free, the medium is so much a part of American society that, as an advertising slogan of fairly recent vintage had it, 'you can turn off the TV, but you can't turn off its influence.'"

An Associated Press piece by Calvin Woodward describes "Cafe USA," thriving and spreading to a projected two hundred shopping malls, beaming a continuous thirty-minute loop of programming to patrons in food courts. In response, Rutgers University psychologist Robert Kubey, author of *Television and the Quality of Life*, asks, "Are we becoming less able to just be by ourselves, to entertain ourselves, to be alone with our own thoughts and emotions?" No wonder he's frustrated: author Kubey expressed dismay when he "took his family to a restaurant where the TV was showing gynecological surgery. People at his gym exercised to a radio station's report on child abuse." (Hey, where's he been? This is normal life!)

Fortunately, one of the most respected moral philosophers of our time has courageously stepped forward to enlighten humanity about TV's dangers to our children. "Television is pure poison," she declares. "To be plopped in front of a TV instead of being read to, talked to, or encouraged to interact with other human beings is a huge mistake, and that's what happens to a lot of children."

So says Madonna, in a 1996 interview with the British magazine *She*. When even the most publicized idol of pop culture appreciates the pitfalls of television, surely more conventional parents see its noxious effects infiltrating their children's lives even more clearly.

Madonna is probably unaware of how long she has been assisting us in making this point. When Michael gives lectures about the impact of the media, he often likes to try a little experiment. He'll ask his audience: "How many of you have ever been to a Madonna concert?" Usually one or two in an audience of several hundred will sheepishly raise a hand.

He continues to probe: "And how many of you have gone out to purchase a Madonna CD or album?" Usually a scattering of hands go up.

"OK, and now, how many of you know who Madonna is?" Every hand shoots up, and everyone looks around approvingly. They're finally all in the same club.

"Now, how many of you chose to have that knowledge of Madonna in your brain?" The audience breaks out laughing—because there's recognition all around that few people wanted this woman in their heads. "And that's the point! I guarantee you that there are Amish kids in Pennsylvania who ride in buggies and don't use zippers who know who Madonna is!"

Television: Pervading the Day

Television is the most pervasive and intrusive medium, and even though those Amish kids don't use anything electrical, it's guaranteed that they know a lot about TV. And it's guaranteed that television is doing damage to their quality of life.

The reason is that television teaches values that are counter to the traditional virtues that the Amish—and those of any religious or ethical sensibility—hold dear. These negative values seep into the culture to influence the behavior of *everyone*—but perhaps most harmfully, serve to harden innocent babes into cynical, suspicious, and fearful young punks.

TV Is Good?

It's either the most brilliant or the most asinine advertising campaign in television history, but it's surely among the most outrageous. As poll after poll reveals that Americans consider the content of television shows beneath their standards, the American Broadcasting Corporation comes out with a forty-million-dollar campaign by the unconventional ad office of Chiat Day, housed in funky quarters in Venice Beach, California, with enormous, human-dwarfing, Claes Oldenburg–designed binoculars as part of its facade. And what did the esteemed network get for its big bucks? Yellow. A forceful mustard yellow. And a tongue-in-cheek message asserting "TV is good."

We'd read in the newspapers about the upcoming campaign, launched in the summer of 1997. We knew it was to be a brash, sassy approach, something so startling that viewers and airtime buyers alike would say, "Wow, what a daring image."

Then the campaign hit, and billboards scattered around downtown Seattle carried the signature yellow background with a few wry, absurd, or plain ridiculous words or phrases: "Scientists say we use 10% of our brain. That's way too much. TV is good." "8 hours a day, that's all we ask." "It's a beautiful day, what are you doing outside? TV is good." "You can talk to your wife anytime. TV is good." "TV is like a muscle, if you don't use it you lose it."

Good for a chuckle, maybe. But wait—what's this arriving in Michael's mail? A listener to his radio show sent the back cover of a *TV Guide*, a whole page of hilarious yet somehow pathetic assertions headed by the slogan . . . "TV is God." What? TV is *God*? Turns out that the helpful correspondent had obliterated one *o*. Reading the ad copy, it seems that his alteration perhaps provided a more accurate headline:

For years the pundits, moralists and self-righteous, self-appointed preservers of our culture have told us that television is bad. . . . They've sought to wean us from our harmless habit by derisively referring to television as the Boob Tube or the Idiot Box.

Well, television is not the evil destroyer of all that is right in this world. In fact, and we say this with all the disdain we can muster for the elitists who purport otherwise—TV is good.

TV binds us together. It makes us laugh. Makes us cry. Why, in the span of ten years, TV brought us the downfall of an American president, one giant step for mankind and the introduction of Farrah Fawcett as one of "Charlie's Angels." . . . Who among us hasn't spent an entire weekend on the couch, bathed in the cool glow of a Sony Trinitron, only to return to work recuperated and completely refreshed? . . .

Why then should we cower behind our remote controls? . . .

Let us climb the highest figurative mountaintop and proclaim with all the vigor and shrillness that made Roseanne a household name, that TV is goo.

Could it be merely typographic incompetence that made Diane leave off the final *d* when copying the previous sentence? Or are unconscious biases against the medium surfacing? To the contrary, our biases are entirely conscious.

Call us elitist, self-righteous, self-appointed preservers of our culture, but hey, TV *is* goo.

We contacted an advertising executive at Chiat Day, who claimed that the campaign was successful in its goal of getting new viewers to try the network. The agency had sought, he said, to distinguish ABC from its rivals. Certainly the mustard yellow with black lettering was eye-catching, but the campaign probably paid off most "in the industry" rather than with the public because in the community of creative competitors, novelty is good.

But that yellow sure is gold to us because it proves our point. To insist that "TV is good" is simply to acknowledge the powerfully unstoppable feeling around the country that TV is bad, very bad. In fact, that TV is the enemy, and as the prophetic movie *Network* so many years ago predicted, we're about to toss our tubes through the window with a disgusted "I'm mad as hell and I won't take it anymore!"

Evidence of national sentiment: "A Los Angeles Times Poll of 1,258 adults across the United States conducted this month . . . concluded that most people think there's too much sex and violence on television and that TV is worse than a decade ago and should be doing more to clean up its act."

There's more: "Nearly all of the 65,000 readers responding to our write-in survey say TV is too vulgar, too violent and too racy," screams the subhead in *USA Weekend*. The piece opens with the following vignette from *Grace Under Fire*, viewed weekly in mid-1995 by 28.3 million people, 5.6 million of them under the age of eighteen:

Grace: How come your daddy didn't come in and say hey?
Kid: Aw, he was in a hurry. He had a date with some slut.

Grace: Quentin! I'm going to wash your mouth out with
        fabric softener. Where did you hear that word?
  Kid: Dad's house. It was on cable.

The article summarizes its "key finding: Many viewers want to wash out TV's mouth with something stronger than fabric softener. They're especially upset that much of the unclean stuff is coming out of the mouths of relative babes like Quentin and into the eyes and ears of kids."

"Eighty-one percent of Americans think TV contributes to the decline of family values, and 46 percent of Hollywood leaders agree with that sentiment," shouts a large pull-quote in *U.S. News & World Report* (April 1996). A September 1997 *Los Angeles Times* poll found that 87 percent of respondents agree that "TV has more sex and violence than 10 years ago"—and 71 percent say shows depicting nudity or sex encourage immorality. A survey of 570 Hollywood elite found that even within the industry itself, *half* "said that TV had a negative impact on the country, and strong majorities said TV only did a fair or poor job in encouraging such things as lawful behavior, sexual abstinence and respect for police."

These feelings stand on solid ground. While much of the public expresses disgust with television's high amounts of violence, overt sexuality, and vulgarity, Americans also feel disgruntled with the entire content level in the medium. Viewers realize that programming is not only poor but in some cases evil, that it panders to— and encourages—the lowest common denominator in our culture. To paraphrase a network ad, TV is no good.

Violence Begets Violence

"A 13-year-old Spanaway boy wanted to be 'just like the stunt men on TV.' But after he asked two friends yesterday to douse him repeatedly with flammable liquids and set him on fire with a match, the boy learned a searing lesson: TV guys usually walk off the set without second- and third-degree burns. . . . "

This story, datelined September 19, 1997, from our Seattle newspaper, is just one recent example of children emulating TV with disastrous consequences. But for every horrifying case like this, TV apologists tell their own stories: "I was brought up in a house where the TV was on all day and all night and *I* came out OK." On TV's *Crossfire*, Michael debated Jack Valenti, president of the Motion Picture Association of America, who made similar remarks about his kids—and *they* turned out pretty good, too.

Anecdotal evidence isn't worth much. No one's suggesting that watching television violence is going to make everyone, or even a significant percentage of viewers, go out and try something stupid. But certainly the average child will be influenced in some ways by watching the 8,000 murders and 100,000 other violent acts the American Psychological Association estimates he will see on television before graduating from elementary school. It can't help but desensitize children to the horrors of the real thing, perhaps adding to a reluctance to help out or "become involved" when confronted with it. Watching all that injury and death contributes to feelings of insecurity and distrust of others. And lack of sensitivity and fear are both powerful destroyers of innocence.

Though no one considers one exposure to a stimulus on television seriously influential, advertisers hawking products ranging from politicians to pet food, from lozenges to luxury cars bank on the cumulative effect of repeated messages not only to nudge target groups to buy their products, but also to establish their brand as the standard of quality and value among the public at large. Only a small fraction of the millions of people who view commercials for the Cadillac ever have the resources to purchase the vehicle, and an even smaller number will be lured to the showroom and close the deal. Yet General Motors feels its advertising dollars well spent despite the proportionately few sales that result, because it not only profits from every purchase by middle-aged, well-to-do customers, but plants in the minds of younger viewers that the Cadillac is a status symbol to strive to own one day.

In presenting a steady diet of murder, deceit, and trouble-making in programming, the media sell violence and socially deleterious behavior in much the way they sell cars. Though only a miniscule percentage of consumers imitate what they see on screen, nearly everyone else uses Hollywood's messages to redefine what constitutes fashionable or desirable conduct. Repeated exposure to media images alters our perceptions of the society in which we live, and gradually shapes what we accept—and expect—from our fellow citizens. Just as General Motors benefits significantly if only a tiny percentage of those viewing its ads buy a Cadillac, our society suffers significantly if a similarly small percentage of viewers of violence are turned toward criminal behavior, harming innocent citizens and increasing our level of fear.

A *U.S. News & World Report* survey of voters reveals that 91 percent "think media mayhem contributes to real-life violence," while 54 percent of the public thinks violence in entertainment media "is a *major* factor that contributes to the level of violence in America." But only 30 percent of those with the power to control it, the Hollywood elite, agree.

As we've been saying for years, there's a huge chasm between the Hollywood clan and the American people on standards for content of programs. Media leaders who responded to a survey by *U.S. News & World Report* and UCLA (867 out of 6,333 questionnaires mailed) were asked the degree to which various on-screen actions constituted inappropriate levels of violence, with surprising results. Most were unwilling to rule out portraying fatal shootings (84 percent would show them), rape (76 percent say enacting them could be appropriate), child abuse (68 percent OK its portrayal), stalking a woman (76 percent give the nod), and fatal stabbings (81 percent consider showing them permissible). Responses revealed some glaring inconsistencies, too: whereas showing real actors involved in "a stabbing that results in death" was considered "always" inappropriate by only 19 percent of Hollywood personnel, a whopping 40 percent said that *cartoon* characters seriously injuring or killing each other was "always" inappropriate.

Any night's TV lineup confirms that the Hollywood community is generally willing to offer a remarkably graphic view of violence.

Copy-Cat Crime

But what about the raft of reputable studies concluding repeatedly that watching violent content on TV encourages children's aggressive behavior? Findings linking the two that started piling up significantly decades ago resulted in the 1972 *Surgeon General's Report on TV Violence.*

"Since then, however, the empirical evidence has grown much stronger," states S. Robert Lichter, coauthor of *Prime Time: How TV Portrays American Culture,* "leading the National Institute of Mental Health in 1982 and the American Psychological Association in 1992 to conclude without reservation that TV violence causes aggression and other antisocial behavior." Note the unequivocal statement: "TV violence *causes* aggression." It's clear and indisputable. And, we should add, contributes greatly to children's departure from what would be their more gentle inclinations. Lichter describes "the roughly 1,000 studies and reports that have contributed to this conclusion," which ranged from tracking aggression in individuals longitudinally over decades, to laboratory experiments carefully detailing changes in subjects after viewing violence, to looking at crime rates in towns before and after the introduction of TV.

One such comparison was made by researcher Brandon S. Centerwall, who reviewed homicide rates among Americans, Canadians, and South Africans for the years 1945 through 1974. During those years, "the white homicide rate in the United States increased 93 percent. In Canada, the homicide rate increased 92 percent. In South Africa, where TV was banned [until 1975], the white homicide rate declined by 7 percent."

He asks the logical question, "Could there be some explanation other than television for the fact that violence increased dramatically in the U.S. and Canada while dropping in South Africa?" and addresses it by carefully analyzing and ruling out the impact of economic growth and civil unrest, concluding, "Many factors other than television influence the amount of violent crime. Nevertheless, if, hypothetically, TV had never developed, violent crime would be half of what it is." Powerful stuff.

S. Robert Lichter, Linda Lichter, and Stanley Rothman, in their detailed historical analysis of television content from the 1950s to the 1990s, found a prime-time average of 3.6 crimes per program episode, about fifty per night. "That total would include about a dozen murders and fifteen to twenty assorted robberies, rapes, assaults, and other acts of mayhem . . . ," they write in their book. "A majority of crimes portrayed involve violence, and nearly one in four are murders. In real life, according to the FBI, violent crimes account for about 5 percent of all arrests. On television they make up 56 percent of all illegal acts."

This forcefully smashes the industry argument that their product merely reflects reality. The most dangerous spot in the country is not south-central L.A., it's not the housing projects of Chicago, or Manhattan's Central Park at night. The most violent ghetto in the United States is prime-time TV.

And the results keep coming. "Violence on television poses substantial risks of 'harmful effects' to viewers, according to the first report in a three-year study designed to be the most intensive and comprehensive look at TV violence ever conducted," declares a *Los Angeles Times* report in February 1996. The study "also concluded that the majority of programs on cable and network television contain violence, that perpetrators of violent acts largely go unpunished [73 percent of the time!] and that most violent portrayals [84 percent] do not show the negative consequences of the acts." This is from the National Television Violence Study, in which researchers assessed incidents of televised violence but interestingly chose *not* to include nightly news or sports in their figures.

Among the most potent destroyers of innocence are programs aimed at children themselves, often *loaded* with violent messages. "Mighty Morphin Power Rangers is the most violent program ever produced for young children, averaging 200 acts of violence per hour," say Debra Lebo and Sue Ann Keiser, specialists in arming teachers to combat violent tendencies in the classroom. "Children committed seven times as many acts of aggression in play after viewing one episode of the Power Rangers show, as compared to children who didn't see the show."

Another study of 204 preschool and kindergarten teachers found that 97 percent voiced at least one concern about the negative effects of Power Rangers on kids in their classrooms—ranging from increased confrontations to confusion of fantasy and reality to poor role modeling, which may even inspire nonaggressive *girls* toward more injurious behavior.

"In 1994, the Canadian Broadcast Standards Council ruled that the show . . . violated the broadcasters' code on violence," notes a *Maclean's* magazine report. Power Rangers was pulled by two networks there, though crafty Canadians could still tune in courtesy of U.S. Fox network stations. Power Rangers was also axed in Sweden after the brutal murder of a five-year-old by two other youngsters, ages five and six. The Power Rangers phenomenon, at its peak, fueled a furious fad affecting toddlers to preteens. Even our Danny, then age two, a boy who had never seen even a moment of Power Rangers on TV, received and then demanded more five-inch-high metallic "action figures." Hearing other kids talk about Power Rangers made him select the silver-masked costume for the Jewish dress-up holiday of Purim. Among kids, identification with the show made aggression "cool."

Is this an isolated case? Power Rangers is perhaps the most analyzed and publicized illustration of television's negative impact on behavior, but it is by no means an exceptional one. When deleterious results of a single TV show are so palpable that teacher and even political protests reach the level they did over Power Rangers, we need to realize that probably hundreds of more subtle instances of violent content slip by, and that cumulatively, their influence is most likely much greater than that of a single show. The bottom line: programs labeled for kids are not necessarily benign.

Pediatric News, which bills itself as "the leading independent newspaper for the Pediatrician," went so far as to urge its readers to be on the lookout for "attachment deficit disorder" and other signs of aggression from too much TV. Dr. Loraine Stern, of the American Academy of Pediatrics' Media Resource Team, added, "the effects of violent programming are too severe to be ignored." She described the confession of a boy treated for spinal cord injury after gunplay: "I didn't think it would hurt."

Apologists for live-action violence on TV have long claimed that such scenes are no worse than what children can view in cartoons. Our answer to them: *So what?* Cartoon violence, though somewhat less threatening because these are clearly drawings, is hardly a positive factor in the life of our kids. Characters who are squished by boulders and then emerge with no more than a few dizzy-whirls over their heads teach false consequences to dangerous behaviors. Characters in cartoons tend to be inordinately cruel to one another, "getting even" for all sorts of minor affronts. Just because there have always been mean-spirited and unrealistic cartoons of vio-

lence on TV—with few immediately negative consequences to children—doesn't clear them, or vindicate live-action violence.

News That Abuses

In February 1998, during the explosion of news about President
Clinton's private activities, we were enjoying a media-free Sabbath
meal with our family and a tableful of guests. We treasure the
Sabbath because for twenty-five hours we remove the burdens of
weekday life such as the phone, the radio, and every other electronic intrusion. As the meal progressed, conversation naturally
turned to the astonishing news out of Washington, published and
broadcast everywhere. As the talk became lively, discussing evidence and opinions of what may or may not have taken place in the
Oval Office with a twenty-one-year-old intern, Michael turned to
our young daughters with instinctive protectiveness and said,
"Girls, I think you have to leave the table. We're talking about the
president of the United States."

Any parent of young children has his or her own anecdotes
about the impact of the White House sex scandals on their little
ones' innocence. Waiting for our kindergartener to emerge from his
class at three-thirty, Diane heard several mothers inquiring, "How
did you handle it with *your* five-year-old?" Diane listened as they
blushingly gave their answers to the inevitable question their
youngsters posed: "What is oral sex?" Though these "soccer moms"
were politically mixed, they shared a distress over the fact they
were forced to address this with their young children. Some
blamed the president for refusing to explain and dispense with the
problem; others blamed the press for so aggressively and explicitly
reporting details. None of them had planned or desired to talk
about adult sexuality with their primary-grade children, but there
they were, placed in an uncomfortable position because for better
or worse, we live in a media-saturated society.

True stories, winter 1998:

A dad of a seven-year-old was shocked when he overheard the raft
of randy presidential jokes his son repeated to his carpool cronies.

A mother told of driving her kids home from a foray to Toys "Я" Us, where her five-year-old daughter had just purchased a new Barbie. Her son, seven, perusing the doll's box with its pictures of Barbie friends available for purchase, pointed to one with dark hair and proclaimed, "Look, Mom, a Monica Lewinsky doll!"

Our own sweet daughters, eleven and eight, and their equally sweet girlfriend gathered the two sets of parents to perform for us their own parody of "Just My Bill" from *Showboat!*: "And yet to be, taxed by he, so much money, he spends on his honeys. . . . Girls love him, because he's president, because he's just their Bill!"

We had mixed reactions to our girls' performance—while their lyrics were certainly clever, we'd rather they didn't spend their precious playtime interpreting unsavory newscasts. Unfortunately, the evolution of news-gathering has lifted our children's exposure to reporters' findings out of our control. If knowledge of Madonna is inescapable, awareness of our country's president is even more impossible to avoid. After all, he's the most important person in the world—if there's even a small problem, can we expect modern journalists to ignore it?

Nowadays, both politicians and media conspire to confuse distinctions between elected officials and Hollywood-type celebrities. Seldom do we address politicians as we once did, "the *Honorable* Senator So-and-So," partially because they shy away from descriptions that separate them from their constituents. Our national news hunger has created a symbiotic relationship: candidates seize upon the myriad of talk shows as an opportunity to present themselves, obliging the needs of burgeoning numbers of reporters for a proliferation of cable networks and people-oriented publications. The result is an unprecedented candor, almost a chumminess, that leaves journalists and show-hosts competing for a scoop free to ask candidates such personal questions as they posed to President Clinton on MTV during the campaign of 1992: "Boxers or briefs?" And the candidate answered. Once that kind of relationship was established, encouraging investigation of presidential underwear, how could the press refrain from pursuing the line of inquiry to its logical conclusion? In this era of "personalities," the loftiness of political office, no matter who holds it, has been irrevocably diminished. And with it declines the respect our children hold for our country's leaders—and by extension, the leaders of their families.

And of course, all this freely spoken discussion about extremely intimate topics blurs the line between subjects—and actions—appropriate for adults only. Even the most careful parents, who forgo discussing the sex scandals and admonish their children strongly against this type of discourse, cannot entirely protect their offspring from *other* kids' jokes, or from being in the vicinity of someone *else's* radio. Even schools' sex education curricula, diligently designed to become more specific as students mature, are suddenly obsolete when our youngest children overhear conversations about technical definitions of adultery.

A Nation of News Junkies

Real-life scandal, destruction, and brutality, on news bulletins, the evening news (often presented at 4, 5 and 6 P.M., during the dinner hour), and ads for news shows probably comprise the media content most detrimental to childhood. And yet, news is the type of programming that viewers say they watch most. The September 1997 *Los Angeles Times* poll cited above found that 42 percent of viewers asked to name their two "most-watched type of shows" cited cable and network news, and another 9 percent choose "news magazines." This compares to just 15 percent who chose network comedies and 10 percent who chose network dramas. When kids are scared by TV fiction, Mom or Dad can comfort the little ones with the reassurance that "it's not real." But when told that the murders, deceit, natural disasters, and carnage of war graphically visible before them represents reality, children's fears are confirmed and reinforced, and they learn to expect a grim, dangerous future.

"Each hour spent viewing television is associated with less social trust . . . ," writes Harvard University political scientist Robert Putnam, "while each hour reading a newspaper is associated with more." In his article in *American Prospect*, he adds, "An impressive body of literature suggests that heavy watchers of TV are unusually skeptical about the benevolence of other people."

You can't even watch an afternoon TV show without news "teases," where earnest, big-haired local news anchors excitedly spit out the most sensational and compelling headlines between commercials, in an attempt to lure viewers of earlier programming to stay tuned. Truth is, it's a tough challenge to keep news ratings up, and so the "tease" crams the most lurid shocker into its allotted ten seconds. Sadly, each "tease" is like a bullet that wounds the sensitivities of the kids waiting to see the end of their (newly designated) "educational" after-school specials.

And the whole family, simply wishing to stay abreast of current events, has been subjected more and more to descriptions of cruel and brutal incidents. An August 1997 survey of networks' nightly newscasts showed startling changes in the types of stories national sources are electing to cover. The nonpartisan, nonprofit Center for Media and Public Affairs evaluated 95,765 stories from the three network news programs broadcast from 1990 through 1996 and found—is it a surprise?—that crime headed the list with 7,448 stories, far and away surpassing the runner-up, health, with 4,055. "One out of every 20 stories since 1993 was about murder," notes an Associated Press piece on the study. "The rate of crime stories [in 1996] was triple that in the early '90s"—an alarming redirection—and, worse, "news about homicides jumped more than 700 percent."

A 1996 report in *USA Today* determined that 72 percent of that year's local news shows from around the country led off with stories of violence or disaster—living up to the rule of broadcast journalism that decrees "If it bleeds, it leads." Contrary to popular belief, this obsession can't be blamed on the blood lust and ratings hunger of unscrupulous news directors; it is a built-in, unavoidable aspect of the medium. If a father comes home at night after a long day at work and lovingly tucks in each of his five children, asking God's blessing on their slumber, that's not news. But if the same father comes home and goes from bedroom to bedroom shooting each of his children in the head with a pistol, it *is* news—and will receive extensive attention from all manner of media.

The major problem for children about the news is that it gives an unmitigatedly sad, horrific, and harsh view of the world, with only a minimal balancing positive view. The news business should more accurately be called the *bad* news business because of this unceasingly negative emphasis. Given that a crucial component of childhood innocence is optimism, any exposure to typical TV news can only have a detrimental effect.

Plus, the news that's offered is incomplete. We see the outcome without the buildup, the product without the process. Our friend, national columnist Don Feder, observes that the forte of TV news is in displaying emotional reactions to intense situations. "Where network news fails is at conveying any sense of how a situation developed," he writes. "How does a 27-year-old end up alone with a junior-high education and five kids? How have government policies and judicial decisions conspired to create a burgeoning predator population?

"One side of these stories transfers easily to film; the other does not," Feder continues. "For people who believe that national problems need to be solved through reason rather than emotion, that presents a big problem."

A Violent Reaction

Because researchers' data and viewers' complaints about violence receive lavish publicity, even the Hollywood elite concede there's a problem—and are responding. "Polls show not only that three-quarters of the public finds television entertainment too violent," Lichter reports, "but that an even higher percentage of TV station managers agree."

The *U.S. News & World Report* and UCLA survey of 867 Hollywood executives, directors, writers, and actors found that 72 percent of these industry insiders acknowledge that "the amount of violent programming on TV has increased in the past decade," and 58 percent of them have personally "avoided watching a program because of its violent content." So we have the electronic v-chip device (*v* for violence—directly aimed at helping parents screen out brutality) and television ratings that had to be revised because child advocacy groups wanted more explicit warnings. These tools, while certainly welcome, can exercise only limited influence in a society where 54 percent of kids (and 66 percent of teenagers) have televisions in their own bedroom and parents are reluctant or too busy to use monitoring aids. Besides, many parents rely on small-screen fare to entice youth to stay at home, lest other lures, like rude or punkish peers, and later, promiscuity and gangs, snare them—with even more dangerous consequences.

Raunchy and Rude: Hardening Kids, Lowering Us All

While news and dramatic violence work to make children more aggressive and insensitive, dramas and comedies with crude language, vulgar scenes, and seamy sexuality deprive them of any childlike postponement of knowledge of adult subjects, as well as the softness and sweetness that childhood once uniquely preserved.

Take the program that probably most aptly represents the youth culture, that long-term hit *Beverly Hills 90210*. It's considered totally cool to be addicted to this evening soap opera, and there are web sites devoted to savoring and recapitulating every cliff-hanging scene, like the following, from the web site alt.culture:Beverly Hills 90210.

Back at the Compound, David is waking up on the couch wondering what is taking Donna so long, and he goes into her room and we instantly go to some Satanic Mass because there are all these black candles burning and Donna is in bed in a white teddy which is ironically more clothes than she usually wears during the daytime . . . and David is like popping a tiny boner, "uh, yeh is it over?" and Donna is like, "no, it's just beginning—come here" . . . [she tries to coax him to deflower her] and David is like, "why now? I mean, what made you change your mind?" And Donna is like, "well, one part of my life ended when we graduated. And I want to spend the next part with you . . ." and then David basically climbs onto the bed and they start doing it and Donna is like, "I forgot, I have another present for you" at which point SHE REACHES OVER AND GIVES DAVID A CONDOM and Donna is like, "I love you so much" . . . and they start kissing for like two hours LIKE CUT THE SCENE ALREADY as we fade into the glowing candles about to burn the whole place down . . .

Hardly the stuff of great literature. But this run-on description doesn't even touch upon the real issue with which this program confronts young women: clothes. "In a recent study, E. Graham McKinley, a lecturer at Rider University in Lawrenceville, N.J., looked at the ways 40 girls from sixth grade to college age talked about the hit high-school soap Beverly Hills 90210," reports Joe Chidley in *Maclean's* magazine. "McKinley found that no matter what the ostensible issue, the women in the study talked about a limited range of topics: 'Hairstyles, makeup, eyebrows, clothing and boyfriends,' says McKinley. 'The show established a community of viewers who shared expertise on how women look. . . . Do we want our young women to take a deep, abiding pleasure in the idea that you are what you wear?'"

If only it were mere obsession with fashion that faddish TV shows promote! With their emphasis on the sordid and the sexual, they expose little kids with a world they should not have to confront until their teens, if they are to have a childhood. And it's a world that many adults themselves find offensive, with terms that folks endeavoring to elevate themselves even ban from their own bedrooms. In the biz it's called "trash TV" and it's available to any kids home sick from school, or left to do their homework while waiting for Mom to return.

Talk Is Cheap

Daytime topical programs have in recent years given new meaning to the bromide "Talk is cheap." When Democratic Senator Joseph Lieberman of Connecticut found his seven-year-old watching Night Stalker, a video game, he began what he calls "the revolt of the revolted." Former education secretary and author of *The Book of Virtues*, William Bennett, remarks, "It's hard to remember now, but there was once a time when personal or marital failure, subliminal desires, and perverse taste were accompanied by guilt and embarrassment. But today, these conditions are a ticket to appear as a guest on 'The Sally Jessy Raphael Show,' 'The Ricki Lake Show,' 'The Jerry Springer Show' or one of a dozen or so like them."

Don't believe it? Michael does an occasional "report from the front" on the world of TV talk on his daily radio show that illustrates just what listeners to *The Michael Medved Show* are missing during his three-hour time slot.

Here's one day's harvest (November 25, 1996):

Maury: Men who have taken paternity tests find out the results (on the air!!).

Montel Williams: A teenage girl accuses her much older husband of sexual abuse.

Bradshaw Difference: Victims of stalkers.

Jerry Springer: Women who have fallen in love with gay men.

The same day, the following story came over the news wire:

The show must go on, and "The Jenny Jones Show" does. Day after day after day. Never mind the recent conviction of Jonathan Schmitz for the March 9, 1995, shotgun slaying of Scott Amedure, who at a "Jenny Jones" taping three days before had voiced sexual designs on the unsuspecting Schmitz. Never mind the sight of Jenny Jones playing dumb on the witness stand during Court TV coverage of the so-called "talk-show murder" trial . . .

But the show must go on, and, in its sixth season, it does, showcasing life's most brazen losers:

- I let my lover have affairs while I was pregnant.

- My family won't accept my interracial lover.

- My mom had an affair with my man.

And, on another show, as if to even the score, 16-year-old man-eater B.J. boasting she could easily seduce her mother's husband . . .

"Neilson ratings from the 1994–95 season indicate that 8 million children watched one of 13 nationally syndicated talk shows on a daily basis," says an *Insight Magazine* report. Talk queen Oprah

Winfrey expressed regret for misusing her platform in a November 1995 *TV Guide* article, but Vicki Abt, a Penn State professor who criticized "sleaze talk" in a journal article, responded, "I'm glad she has changed, but it's 10 years and $350 million later. . . . A lot of what these people do is self-serving. They do the dirty deed and then they cry 'mea culpa.'"

The Media Research Center analyzed a week of daytime talk shows, with discouraging results. Four of five Sally Jessy Raphael shows "dealt with sex, with subjects such as transvestites and those who sleep with others to avenge a partner's unfaithfulness. One guest claimed to have had over 200 sexual partners; Sally asked him, 'What are your standards when it comes to women?' His reply: 'They gotta at least be breathin'.' Jerry Springer's show featured this setup: 'A 17-year-old . . . married her 71-year-old foster father. They first had sex when she was 14. They have four children. She calls him 'Dad.'"

Talk shows are likely to air any time of the day, when even the smallest children get parked in front of the tube. And the questions they inevitably ask are not necessarily going to be answered by parents. Siblings and neighbor kids might well be there to seize on the "hilarious" opportunity to play with a younger child's naïveté.

We would be remiss in discussing the descent of TV if we overlooked the impact of MTV, which enters 270 million households worldwide. When it hit the scene in 1981, it centered on three-minute music videos in which individual shots lasted no more than one or two seconds—at the time considered outrageously fast-paced. Now MTV has added other shows to the mix, including, until recently, the anything-but-innocent *Beavis and Butthead*, a title Michael prefers to refer to on his radio show as "Beavis and Friend." Action on MTV has no lead-in or warm-up. "The audience has gotten more sophisticated, and you can take certain leaps without people scratching their heads," said MTV animation head Abby Terkuhle to the *New York Times Magazine*. "It's intuitive. Our children are often not thinking about A, B, C. It's like, OK, I'm there, let's go! It's a certain non-linear experience, perhaps." Thinking "non-linearly" won't help little Kirsten get through *Little Women* or *A Separate Peace*. It doesn't help little Ashley tackle a page of math equations. It does, however, exacerbate the problem of attention-deficit disorder plaguing our schools and frustrating parents.

The "family hour," 8 to 9 P.M., was analyzed in a separate study by the Media Research Center during September and October 1995. Among the findings:

> "Vulgar language, usually unheard even late in prime time a few years back, is now constant in the 8 P.M. hour. In 117 hours of programming, 72 curse words were used. 'Ass' (29 uses), 'bitch' (13) and 'bastard' (10) were the most popular.

> "Sexual material that formerly was restricted to the 9-to-11 slot has migrated to the 'Family Hour,' where premarital sex is not only common—outnumbering portrayals of sex within marriage by an 8-to-1 ratio—but almost always condoned."

We'll spare you examples here.

Characteristics of the TV Medium That Crush Childhood

In fact, we'll spare you any more about the composition of the attack on innocence by TV and focus on how it works. Perhaps the most damaging aspect of the problem is not television's overt content, but rather the subtly imbedded between-the-lines assault on underlying values necessary for a classically carefree childhood.

Of course, most people intuitively realize this, and you often hear a nostalgic yearning for the innocent fare of yesteryear. If only the Beaver hadn't transmogrified to Beavis, folks sigh, then TV might still function as a source of harmless diversion and even of reassuring uplift. Of course, even watching *Leave It to Beaver*, *Ozzie and Harriet*, and *Father Knows Best*, which gave kids access to parents' behind-the-scenes decision-making processes, changed our view of family life, from that of participant in whatever our role was (e.g., parent, child, sibling) to an all-knowing, all-seeing omnipotence that leveled everyone to equal authority right before our eyes.

But wouldn't our lives be better if TV offered only *Beaver*-type language, more family-friendly topics, and violence that was implied rather than revealed? We might have avoided a generation of hollow-eyed mall-rats with pierced tongues and pants that bunch around their hips.

But unfortunately, this popular argument crashes head-on against a concrete wall of inconvenient recent history. The first real "TV generation," nourished on such wholesome family fare as *Ozzie and Harriet, Make Room for Daddy, The Mickey Mouse Club, The Real McCoys, Father Knows Best,* and, of course, *Leave It to Beaver* did *not* grow up as well-adjusted, optimistic, family-affirming solid citizens. Instead, many children of the sixties went more or less directly from *The Donna Reed Show* to campus riots, psychedelic experimentation, rebellious posing, love-ins, long hair, loopy politics, and all-purpose looniness. If family-friendly TV effectively implants traditional values in its eager young viewers, then how can one explain the dismissive attitude toward the nuclear family so typical of the counterculture of thirty years ago?

It is the inescapable *essence of television,* rather than a few dozen incidentally destructive shows, that undermines childhood and the values that most parents strive to pass on to their kids. When consumed in the American pattern of several hours each day, TV inevitably promotes impatience, self-pity, and superficiality.

Impatience

The most recent analyses report that the major cable and broadcast networks titillate their viewers with a new TV image at ever decreasing intervals, "to the point that we routinely absorb sequences of shots lasting eight frames, a third of a second, or less," notes James Gleick in the *New York Times Magazine* article cited above. He quotes advertising maven Tony Schwartz, who has perfected the three-second commercial: "Got a headache? Come to Bufferin," a couple of quick images and a phrase. Gleick explains, "Many of the individual shots in a commercial or a music video or even a television news segment are at or below the threshold of perception. They qualify as subliminal. Editors are conscious of this; they know that sometimes they are paring shots down to a minimal number of one-twenty-fourth-second frames—four, or two, or even one—that will leave just a sensory glimmer in the viewer's brain." This quick editing contributes in an unmistakable manner to the alarming decline in the American attention span. Andy Warhol's "fifteen minutes of fame" seem to have shrunk to perhaps fifteen seconds.

The social impact of TV's rapidly flashing images is most obvious (and appalling) in preschool classrooms. America's three- and four-year-olds seem less able than ever before to sit still for a teacher—in part because no teacher can reproduce the manic energy or protean transformations of the tube. Those teachers can, however, easily identify the children in class who most significantly overdose on TV.

"Kids reared on the fast-paced action of Sesame Street will find their science teacher 'awful dull. . . . He doesn't have a hand puppet,' says anthropologist David W. Murray," as quoted in the *Washington Times*. Teenage students' number one complaint is that their teachers are "boring," and college profs grouse that it's now the norm for students to wander the room and read during lectures "as if they were in front of a TV instead of in a classroom."

Please note that when it comes to this crucial issue of attention span, the admired and beloved Big Bird exerts the same worrisome influence as the universally (and deservedly) reviled Power Rangers. Even sympathetic researchers of *Sesame Street* worry over the way the breathlessly fast-paced show encourages restlessness in its very young viewers.

It's damage with no compensating gain: there is no evidence that such glitz helps preschoolers do well in school. Kay S. Hymowitz writes about this failure, confirmed in a Russell Sage Foundation study, and points out that *Sesame Street* content turns kids toward quick-paced video and away from books and reading as sources of enjoyment. In addition, most of *Sesame Street*'s music is original and catchy for the show and doesn't give little ones an ear for traditional or classical pieces (many of which require a longer attention span). Though one study claims that 77 percent of U.S. preschoolers watch *Sesame Street*, there has been no corresponding improvement in national skills to show for it.

Here are the dominoes toppling childhood: impatient children demand constant entertainment and receive steady external stimulation. Their imagination, like a muscle, atrophies. Where is the sense of wonder for a child with no imagination? Where is there time to explore and develop when a child is poised for a shift of scene every four seconds?

Television promotes impatience in its very structure. With most shows contained within action-packed half-hours, there's no deferred gratification or long-term perspective. In the world of TV, every sort of problem is presented and solved within thirty minutes—or, if it's a particularly formidable and complex dilemma, sixty minutes (or, in rare cases, even ninety minutes) will suffice to do the job. But childhood for a curious, inquisitive youngster doesn't fit so neatly into time packages. You can't watch a real-life caterpillar make a cocoon and hatch into a butterfly in half an hour, yet on TV nature shows, little kids watch as time-compressed cinematography makes it all flash before their accepting eyes. When children from their earliest years see quick and neat resolutions on dramas and sitcoms, it's hardly surprising that so many young Americans later feel frustrated when their personal projects—in romance, weight loss, or career advancement—fail to produce results as ideal and immediate as those they witness on TV.

The commercials that consume a substantial portion of each broadcast hour make their own powerful contribution to the sense of peevishness and unfulfilled desire that afflicts so many television viewers, including little kids, who gain a sense of entitlement about everything from sugary cereals to miniature motor cars. The very purpose of these cunningly crafted messages is, of course, to stimulate impatience—to foment an intense, immediate desire for a hamburger, an electronic toy, a beer, or a luxury car. If advertising does its job effectively, it will leave the mass audience with a perpetual attitude of unquenchable yearning for a never-ending succession of alluring new products.

Is there anything more obnoxious than kiddy materialism? Competition over faddish clothing has caused more and more school districts to require school uniforms. The tactic helps, and sends a disapproving message. But TV fosters a "yearning mentality" from babies' first exposure in the crib. Soon even in uniform-only schools, students compete to wear the most expensive shoes, the most stylish jacket, and the trendiest cap.

Self-Pity

Constant emphasis on lack and need, which form the underpinning of advertisers' messages, lead all viewers—kids as well as adults—inevitably to realize that they can never acquire enough of anything. When your fancy new computer is three months old, you realize it's outdated; when your spiky heels finally stop causing blisters, in come those chunky styles to replace them. Constant unsuccessful striving to keep up ultimately produces a perspective of self-pity and insecurity—feelings that retard childhood, even simply when exhibited by world-weary parents.

And remember, television compounds the problem with its special affinity for portraying horror and pain without a corresponding ability to explain love or heroism. Even if a news broadcast *were* determined to balance its footage of mutilated bodies and burning buildings with equal time for noble parents and dedicated teachers, which images would make the more visceral impression on a child, or remain longer in memory?

You can see the same preference for dangerous developments and bizarre circumstances in entertainment television as well. And why not, since it reflects an age-old tradition in Western culture? After all, even old Will Shakespeare focused on murders and witches and scheming villains and transvestite masquerades rather than functional families and upstanding individuals. As Tolstoy famously declared in *Anna Karenina,* "All happy families are alike; every unhappy family is unhappy in its own way." In fact, every plot line *requires* some kind of problem, or else it's a snoozer sure to pull invisible ratings or profits.

Nevertheless, the disturbing behavior in novels and plays and even radio shows of the past never enveloped an audience in the way that television does today—when an average American family keeps its set turned on more than forty-seven hours every week. Attending a Shakespeare play or even a vaudeville show was an *event*—people got dressed up and made an anticipated social occasion of the two-hour outing. Television, on the other hand, offers the phony illusion of company as it keeps people *in.* It's the Muzak in many kitchens, the guest who wouldn't go home, the relentless spoon-feeder of sounds and ideas into psyches—and its cumulative impact overpowers, weakens, and subdues.

The vast number of vivid images that pour into children's minds via TV enter their consciousness with little distinction between the factual and the fictional. Whether it's the evening news, a sitcom, a daytime talk show, a docudrama, a cartoon, or *Sesame Street*, television blurs the dividing line between reality and imagination—informing our notions of the wider reality beyond our homes and teaching us the prevailing modes of "normal" behavior. It's especially true for young children, whose concept of real vs. imaginary is not complete. Scenes of real events on TV can be so horrifying that we long to tell our children that they, too, are "only a story." But with the constant flow of one program to the next, and the snap decisions facilitated by a thumb on the remote control, we don't stop to question or separate out fact from fiction and vice versa, for ourselves *or* our children.

Producers of soap operas report that they regularly receive letters from devoted viewers who address inquiries or comments to their favorite characters—apparently not comprehending that personae they see every day on TV are actually make-believe, played by professional actors. Meanwhile, tens of millions of Americans pepper their conversations, often off-handedly, with catchy phrases or gestures from popular TV shows, making idiosyncracies of fictional characters part of their own real-life personalities.

This tension between televised "reality" and the actual lives of ordinary Americans potently prompts self-pity, especially for children. The impression youngsters take away from regular TV viewing is one of an unpredictable, menacing world, full of violence, deviance, excitement, and compelling chaos. Decades of research at the Annenberg School of Communication at the University of Pennsylvania suggests that the principal legacy of the long-standing emphasis on televised violence is the "mean world syndrome" in which all people, and more intensely children, become more fearful about both the present and the future.

If television's dangerous world leaves children needlessly frightened and insecure, it also makes them resentful that their non-TV time is vastly more "boring" than what they see on the tube. Our national epidemic of whining originates not only from TV's natural tendency for bad news to overwhelm any encouraging reports, but from the fact that most citizens remain relatively untouched by these disasters—and their quiet lives can't live up to the sense of excitement, drama, and sexual adventure that television advances as a new American entitlement. This malaise hits children, with their naturally shorter attention spans, even more severely than it does adults. And because overprogrammed parents can't minister to their children's desires, kids become increasingly frustrated. So whining begins younger and younger—and fewer parents have the patience or confidence (given their own TV exposure) to correct and redirect it.

Superficiality

We don't expect little kids to display depth of character or insight. We don't need them to advise us on political initiatives or even to select their own schools. In fact, it's a hallmark and a joy of childhood to be able to see things simply, for what they appear to be, rather than to probe beneath the surface for hidden motives or ponderous meanings.

But at the same time, we want to teach them that ideas, actions, and responses have consequences. We want them to have a sense that in some areas you must be aware that there is more than what you can see. TV undermines this delicate balance, implying that surface is everything, with little that is truly meaningful, complex, or profound.

In television, there is only the thrill of the moment, with no sense of past and little concern for the future. Venal programmers hardly deserve blame for this tendency; it is, rather, a given in a medium that by its nature emphasizes immediacy and visceral visual impact. Flashbacks in a TV drama, no matter how artfully constructed, can never compete with the power of a live broadcast, no matter how insipid. TV keeps you in the "now" partially to hold viewers over the commercial, to keep that tension poised while they sell shower scrubbers or feminine protection.

The most salient aspect of "now" is what you see at this moment—and so physical appearance is crucial. One of our family's most embarrassing moments occurred one Sabbath afternoon at our home. We were delighted to have as guests a distinguished rabbi and his wife. We had prepped our daughters, then five and seven, about the visitors, so that they could appreciate the importance of having someone with great Torah knowledge in our home. Little Danny, at two, didn't care much for the lecture. The meal went smoothly, and then we had dessert. Our guests had ice cream along with us. But afterward, the rotund rabbi had to exert himself a bit to rise from his seat. Danny, in his toddler superficiality, commented, "Rabbi, if you eat more ice cream, you'll get even fatter!"

Our daughters, thankfully, had learned not to comment on the appearance of others, and they understood also that this man's weightiness in the world was of a kind more important than simply his girth.

But in a medium where what you see is all you get, it's no coincidence that pretty people are preferred. Can anyone honestly suppose that the O. J. Simpson trials would have generated comparable interest if O. J. and his murdered wife had resembled, say, Mike Tyson and Janet Reno? The preoccupation with glamour and good looks is nowhere more painfully apparent than in the realm of TV news, where the overwhelming majority of these supposedly brilliant and dedicated professional journalists (especially the females) just coincidentally happen to be exceptionally attractive physical specimens.

Children love their mommies and think they're beautiful no matter what. But their mommies are affected by this "norm" of perfection, and kids see that. And perhaps they think, "If Mommy's not happy with her looks, then could there also be something wrong with *me*?" As TV-saturated minds grow older, constant exposure to impossible standards may lead youngsters to adopt them for themselves—sometimes with tragic results. Television, with its insistence on stunning packaging, hammers home this superficial ideal of physical perfection hardest of all.

In real life, we associate the term *airheads* with little intellectual activity, and by fostering great interest in spectacular packaging, TV makes airheads of us all. By many calculations, the most popular television show in the world at the moment is that profound and probing melodrama *Baywatch*. Its appeal can hardly be explained by the depth and distinctiveness of its characterizations; it has, rather, everything to do with gorgeous bodies abundantly displayed in fetching bathing suits. TV trains us to feel satisfied with surfaces; to focus our adoration on characters who make the most appealing visual presentation, without a thought of their ethics or accomplishments. Given the lifelong television training that most Americans experience, it should come as no surprise that most voters seem ready to forgive all misdeeds from political leaders who look cute and compassionate when they emote on the tube.

Kids fed this superficiality become even more cruel to classmates who are overweight or in other ways deviate from the ideal. Sure, kids have always been cruel. The one with glasses has always been "four-eyes" and the puny one always gets beaten up. The difference over the last couple of decades, with the loosening of TV restraint, is that now the standards are higher and the age for noticing deviance is lower. Just another way TV has made it tougher to be a kid.

Beyond the lack of complexity, beyond the misleading glamour, television emphasizes another form of destructive superficiality: an overwhelming focus on *fun as the highest human priority*.

Over the past ten years, our friend and colleague Dennis Prager has written powerfully and persuasively on the essential distinctions between fun and happiness. Fun is fleeting and unearned—a thrill ride at a theme park, an engaging video game, or a diverting half-hour sitcom on TV. Happiness, on the other hand, requires considerable effort and commitment, and in most cases proves durable and long-lasting. Fun can never be counted upon to produce happiness, but happiness almost always involves fun. For adults, casual sex may (occasionally) provide a few hours of fun, but it will never lead to the long-term happiness that a permanent marital commitment can provide. For children, a ride on Disneyland's Splash Mountain may bring screams of laughter, but once the three-minute thrill is over, there's not much to show for the two-hour wait.

Television by its very nature aspires to offer an abundance of fun but contributes nothing to lasting happiness. Consider that staple of televised entertainment: competitive sports. A child in Little League enjoys all manner of benefits—improved health and strength, a sense of personal accomplishment, lessons about teamwork and leadership, rewarding friendships. But if he invests countless hours watching basketball on TV instead, he gains nothing at all—except perhaps a few extra pounds from munching too many snacks. Sure, it's diverting and "fun" to watch displays of professional skill, but admiring the other guy doesn't teach children about fulfilling their own potential and the real-life need for practice in reaching a goal, or offer any payoff toward lasting happiness.

Watching television represents the most empty-headed, superficial sort of fun in an increasingly fun-addicted society. It is meaningless precisely because it demands so little of its viewers—in fact, physiological examination of TV watchers suggests that for the most part they are three-quarters asleep. Television steals our children's innocence when we are most vulnerable, tricking us easily because our defenses are down.

Antichildhood Values

We've looked at television content that lowers the level of discourse and concern via language, sleaze, and gore. We've looked at the medium itself, zeroing in on how the very nature of television promotes impatience, self-pity, and superficiality. Beyond even these serious affronts to innocence, we've seen how television advances underlying values that break down the fundamental bases of childhood that:

- Adults are responsible for kids.

- Kids should respect their elders.

- There are some topics children do not need to know about until necessary, which can be presented gradually and with sensitivity to the individual child.

- The world can be a friendly place.

Television is the enemy of every youngster's childhood. And yet parents pay good money to place the enemy in their family's midst, and then they plop their little ones down in front of it, directly in harm's way. No wonder the assault is so successful.

3

The Assault on Innocence by Media

The Co-conspirators

Hollywood vs. America

Nothing destroys childhood more effectively than television, because it undermines crucial values in the child's *home*, the one place that should be his safe haven. But film, print media, radio, rock music, and even the Internet amplify and reinforce the damaging content television pours into our consciousness. Together, the media create a cacophony of values so blaring that they overwhelm fundamental and cherished Judeo-Christian themes.

Michael's 1992 book, *Hollywood vs. America*, detailed the media messages that conflict with the values of the American population, generally the same messages that powerfully conflict with parents' efforts to retain their children's innocence. A sampling:

Messages *demeaning authority figures* who are closest to the child abound. In films, especially, Michael found, for example, a general distaste for and negative portrayal of clergy and religion, despite an audience that is the most religious in the Western world.

In his PBS special, *Hollywood vs. Religion*, Michael offered clips from sixty recent movies, all showing their only religious characters as crazed, criminal, or corrupt. Though *Touched by an Angel* has been one of television's top programs, TV programmers nearly always ignore Americans' profound religiosity on the rest of the dial, the rest of the time. Some facts gathered by writer Evan Gahr from a variety of studies reveal that 61 percent of TV consumers want "references to God, churchgoing, and other religious observances in prime time," 90 percent of Americans believe in God, and more than 50 percent attend church every week. Yet the industry, which claims to "just reflect reality" with its portrayals of extramarital sex, murder, and snotty kids, won't reflect the *religious* reality. Out of 1,800 prime-time hours on the networks, when researchers searched for anything from one-liners to program themes, they could only find 436 religious references.

Messages *against the family* also proliferate. Programs routinely show divorce and serial relationships as no big deal. Premarital sexuality occurs more often on television than relations within the bounds of marriage by a margin of eight to one—during the "family hour" of 8 to 9 P.M. Programs routinely suggest that promiscuity is desirable and sex easily attainable, that marriage kills passion, that glamorous Hollywood trendsetters' children born out of wedlock are chic and just as advantaged as those raised within a stable marriage.

Television also sends messages arousing suspicion of solid citizens. Michael Pack, producer of a PBS special on this subject, found that TV's favorite "heavy" is the businessman—on-screen businessmen are actually the most likely occupational group to be cast as murderers. A favorite plot twist involves a community pillar, such as a banker or teacher, leading some sort of sinister double life or surreptitiously plotting the demise of an unsuspecting victim. Not only does this confuse kids about who are the "bad guys" and the "good guys," but it plants in their minds the idea that conventional success could be phony or psychotic, thereby creating young cynics.

Another prominent message says that *our country is in trouble*, its policies imperialist and evil, and that patriotism is for the ignorant or stupid. Lichter, Lichter, and Rothman, you may recall, studied the entire history of television and found that in recent years, politicians have been second only to businessmen in their negative presentation. And ever since *M*A*S*H* featured "draftees who questioned and, when possible, subverted the military system," the media have taken every opportunity to "ridicule the boss," showing military brass in an overwhelmingly negative light. "Our content analyses found that whenever military scripts commented on back-talk, they heartily endorsed the practice," conclude Lichter et al.

Kids Still Know Best

Two more messages damage children's innocence, clearly represented in both film and television. These messages insist that:

- Children know better than their elders not only what is good for *them*, but what is good for *everyone*.

- The world is an evil, ugly, scary, and dangerous place, full of peril and deceit.

Television and film plots regularly conclude that parents are out of touch with current times, that they're impossibly stuffy and benighted, and that they have a selfish, if not mean-spirited agenda to restrict and limit the potential of their offspring. *Hollywood vs. America* argued that even wholesome, friendly, upbeat children's releases (that Michael has and would critically praise for artistic or entertainment value) can contain subtle messages that go against values most parents would want to affirm.

Lately, television boasts lots of uppity kids, like those on *The Simpsons*, *Beavis and . . .* uh, Friend, and *Married . . . With Children*. And in film, "children unchained" have become an entire genre. "Kids talking back" has evolved into just another joke, another example of "cute," from its traditional portrayal as cause for swift and stern punishment. Current stories conclude that kids don't need parents and that, in fact, the old folks inhibit their fun. Entertaining, maybe, but at direct odds with the confidence in parents kids need for a secure childhood.

Child actor Macaulay Culkin has led the way, performing in a trilogy of films whose premise is that on their own, kids are clever, powerful, and have a great time. His groundbreaking foray as the father figure of the "kids know best" genre was, of course, *Home Alone*, the 1990 hit that reminded parents never to get on a plane to Paris without counting noses. Left to fend for himself, the eight-year-old lead character, Kevin, outsmarts two burglars and does just fine. His parent-free triumph is spiritual as well as practical, since he leads a lonely old neighbor to reconcile with his estranged family just in time to enjoy Christmas.

The sequel, *Home Alone 2: Lost in New York* (1992), offers a similar Yuletide atmosphere and leaves its predecessor's violence in the dust, with lamebrained characters, ridiculous commercialism, and a setup that proves some families just can't get travel right. Once again, Macaulay Culkin shows that he can have a raft of adventures and survive them solo, even rescuing a homeless woman unable to make it without kid competence.

In 1994, the aging Culkin (born in 1980) continued his streak of snotty-kid roles, moving into the part of an eleven-year-old savior and moral guide. *Getting Even with Dad*, which was, ironically, a Father's Day release, showed dad (Ted Danson) as a petty thief and a crook, and the son has to arrange a conspiracy to help his wayward old man go straight.

Next in line is *Home Alone 3*, where long-in-the-tooth Macaulay Culkin is replaced by eight-year-old Alex D. Linz. When accidentally mailed a top-secret U.S. Defense computer chip, the young protagonist, who just happens to find himself once again home alone, foils not only four international thieves out for the reward, but reclaims the chip for the good ol' USA.

Despite this tradition, a connection to Macaulay Culkin is not a prerequisite for making films that show the triumph of kids without their lunkheaded caregivers. A stellar example of pathetic celluloid is *Don't Tell Mom, the Babysitter's Dead* (1991), the theme of which is how well the kids get on once their old-lady baby-sitter, yes, drops dead. But you don't have to wait long to see that "getting on" means "*coming* on," since within the film's first ten minutes we view liberated ten-year-olds making out and, we're led to believe, enjoying heavy petting.

One of the more surprising expressions of this parent-free, self-reliant vision of childhood turned up in 1994 in the critically acclaimed Fox television series *Party of Five*. The show portrays the adventures of the Salinger children (played by rising stars Matthew Fox, Neve Campbell, and others) who range in age from twenty-four to infancy. After their parents perish in a car crash, the kids decide to remain together as a family and to take responsibility for their own lives. Amy Lippman, co-creator of the series, told the *New York Times*, "I think what the network originally envisioned was a show more in keeping with the traditional Fox shows—kids on their own, no curfews, no rules, living a kind of wild existence though probably with some core family sensibility."

As it turned out, the characters successfully confront infidelity, racism, abortion, and alienation "hitting an emotional peak" when the teenaged brother (Scott Wolf) "descended into alcoholism and the others staged an intervention." His kid sister (Neve Campbell) goes through sexual initiation, becomes pregnant, plans an abortion, then suffers a miscarriage. Through it all, the family members cope and grow, giving one another the sort of love, support, and common sense that only the most conscientious parents provide. While praised for its emotional impact and dramatic daring, the series offered one more example of savvy, empowered kids as guides, leaders, and models, rather than recipients of parental protection and wisdom.

The point is worth repeating—when movies and television plant in children's minds the idea that they know better than their elders, youngsters discount their parents' authority and doubt that they can count on their parents to be responsible and come through. It's a quick chain reaction to feeling insecure, tense, afraid, and worried that they may have to either take care of themselves or worse, take care of their incompetent parents. When the credibility of the one anchor children have in life—that their parents will be there for them—is destroyed, kids must lurch forward to adult concerns, adult contingencies, and adult caution. Kids in movies and TV shows frequently function as the source of enlightenment and redemption not only for their fellow characters, but for all of society. This role amounts to a frontal assault on the very idea of youthful innocence, presenting children as guides rather than guided, protectors rather than protected, rendering parents and childhood itself altogether unnecessary.

Hey Kids, the World's a Horrible Place

For many years on their PBS show *Sneak Previews*, Michael and his partner, Jeffrey Lyons, included a feature called "Family Find" in which they'd recommend a movie or video the whole family could enjoy. They received many wonderful videos to review for consideration of this honor, and these often became part of our children's collection. Our daughters would squeal in delight when Michael presented them with a new offering (always as a reward for their good behavior) and they'd immediately run upstairs to enjoy their new acquisition. We remember fondly their rapture watching *Bunny Rabbit's Picnic*, filled with dancing and singing old-fashioned hand puppets, laughing and prancing to lyrics about sunshine and flowers.

We want our young daughters to have a *Bunny Rabbit's Picnic* view of the world. When we inadvertently allow contradictory messages to slip into their ears, they protest, or simply run away. For example, every Sunday we take a car field trip as a family. Naturally, we have the radio set on the Seattle talk-radio station that airs Michael's show, 570 AM. At the top of the hour, there's news—and our children immediately beg us to turn off the radio, lest they hear something—about a lost or murdered child, a natural disaster, or any act of hatred—that spoils their contentment.

Even five-year-old Danny, who's all macho boy and not averse to a good fight, wants to destroy any possibility of real evil. He dresses up as the cowboy out to kill the bad guys, and says he's a policeman who daily uses his bountiful plastic weapons to capture and dispose of robbers. In other words, he loves the imaginary violence of King Kong and John Wayne movies and make-believe shootouts with robbers only because they confirm that good always triumphs and we really have nothing to worry about.

But in recent films, and particularly on TV, the world looks grim. On screen, nearly every home is dysfunctional. Even kids in two-parent families experience abuse. It's normal for TV families to

fight, and the consensus of characters and even so-called experts on
the tube is that it's better to divorce than subject a child to a hostile
environment. Family turmoil is the grist of after-school specials,
soap operas, even sitcoms, redefining "normal" so that we tolerate
a little less harmony in our own homes.

Thankfully, portrayals of families in the media are *wrong* and
don't reflect the world real-life children encounter: 76 percent of
white children under eighteen live with two parents in the home,
and the vast majority of all families are counting their blessings.
Only a small minority of homes are *truly* dysfunctional, but talk
shows would have everyone doubt their own happiness. British
data (the best we've got) found that child abuse in a home with
married biological parents occurs rarely (compared to a risk thirty-
three times higher if the mother is unmarried but cohabiting), and
while these few cases are certainly tragedies, we need to keep their
number in perspective.

The media tend to insist that marriages and families are either
happy or they're not. Truth is, most families work pretty well most
of the time. Sometimes they work less well, sometimes better, but
there are an infinite number of constantly changing points along
several intersecting continua of relations within a family. While
even happy homes occasionally experience discord, *most* adults
seldom engage in serious arguments, and even then, the two
involved work through it and simply march on. Siblings will always
have conflicts—fighting, forming alliances, reconciling. Only in
extreme cases is this abnormal, but nowadays the media quickly
label *any* shrieks or bumps "dysfunction," making everyone hyper-
sensitive and insecure. Remember, either you're happy or you're
not.

Reasonable spouses in distress generally won't stoically accept
hostility just for the sake of the children. Instead they go for counseling and work to improve the situation—or at least go through
periods of unpleasant relations alternating with periods of stability
and even harmony. Unlike what you see on TV or in movies, in real
life complete satisfaction or divorce are not the only two possibilities in a marriage.

The vast majority of Americans know that their lives are good.
But because the media are so convincing about the world beyond

their front doors, they believe that most everyone *else* is suffering. "A new nationwide poll finds a paradox in the mood of the country," stated a *USA Today* cover story in early 1997. "Americans in modern times have rarely felt so optimistic about their own prospects. At the same time, they've never felt so pessimistic about the nation's future."

A Child's Worst Nightmare

Kids' movies promote a particularly destructive sort of pessimism by insistently playing upon every child's worst fear—loss of a parent.

In animated feature films in particular, generally aimed at viewers as young as four, mothers are more often dead than alive. This phenomenon goes well beyond the painful, much discussed deaths of protective moms in the classics *Bambi* and *Dumbo*, or the alarming murder of a beloved father in the recent mega-hit *The Lion King*. Consider such ever-popular Disney fare as *Snow White and the Seven Dwarfs*, *Cinderella*, *The Little Mermaid*, *Beauty and the Beast*, *Aladdin*, and *Pocahontas*: all feature plucky heroines with missing mommies.

Of course, much of this material has been based on classic stories and beloved fairy tales, highlighting the undeniable fact that a dead parent represents one of the nearly universal features of popular children's literature. In books as diverse as *Tom Sawyer*, *Huckleberry Finn*, *Treasure Island*, *David Copperfield*, *Oliver Twist*, *Pippi Longstocking*, and *The Wizard of Oz*, the protagonists have lost one (or both) parents. In one sense, this situation of a vulnerable, orphaned young hero or heroine represents an inevitable response to the dramatic requirements of the form. In order to create an exciting story, the storyteller must place the central character in some sort of jeopardy. The traditional assumption holds that parents will protect their children from all harm and deflect serious threats, so the easiest way to place a fictional child at risk is to remove parents from the scene. This convenient stroke also allows the young protagonists greater freedom of action and character development.

Since the loss or absence of mothers and fathers has played a prominent role in children's entertainment for many centuries, why should parents feel especially concerned about such themes in today's mass media? The basis for concern involves the ubiquitous nature of such diversion in the era of multiplexes, cable TV and video superstores. Instead of reading one book a week, or going to a move matinee every Saturday, today's media-saturated children may easily consume a dozen stories a week featuring dead parents.

Many recent films—including *Sleepless in Seattle, My Girl, Fly Away Home, Bogus,* and *Corrina, Corrina*—dwell upon the pain of such tragedies and show their devastating impact on small, wounded survivors. Each of these admirable PG-rated projects aimed at children as part of their target audience, but featured, with searing intensity, references to lost parents. Any child regularly exposed to TV and movies (in other words, any child in America) will inevitably reach the conscious or unconscious conclusion that parental death is far more common than it actually is—and represents a far greater threat to that child's world than it does in reality.

Classic fairy tales and nineteenth-century adventure yarns for kids reflected in the reality of that time when many, if not most, children in Western society experienced the death of a parent prior to reaching maturity. In helping today's youngsters cope with the emotions inevitably aroused by these stories, thoughtful parents should make clear that such accounts depict a world of long ago, and that today very few children watch their parents die before they grow up. Let the kids understand that this dramatically improved aspect of childhood represents one of the many powerful reasons to feel grateful that we live when—and where—we do.

Dreading the Future

Rather than registering such positive changes in our situation, popular culture dwells upon the darkest, bleakest aspects of both our present and our prospects. The elegantly gloomy Fox television show *The X-Files* has, by some accounts, recently supplanted the sunny, redoubtable *Baywatch* as the most popular TV program in the world. With its emphasis on doomed, blinded humanity, struggling against a conspiracy so massive it seems to include the government, extraterrestrials, demonic spirits, and the Campfire Girls, the show captures the deeply paranoid spirit of the times. Worried observers on both the right and the left warn of "hidden forces" that secretly manipulate events, plotting assassinations from Martin Luther King, Jr., to Vincent Foster, selling out our interests to some wretched cabal, leading the nation to perdition. The 1997 film *Conspiracy Theory* simultaneously mocked and validated these fears. Mel Gibson portrays a manic, mumbling nut who prattles endlessly about bizarre conspiracies of every sort, but by the movie's conclusion we discover that Gibson himself has been indeed victimized by vicious mind-control experiments conducted by the decidedly conspiratorial CIA.

With the Cold War successfully concluded and the threat of thermonuclear devastation vastly and obviously reduced, Hollywood struggles to find new sources of menace with which to thrill and terrify moviegoers—including the children who regularly flock to such frightening fare. Since the geopolitical situation appears to offer only minor threats, we now get a new wave of old-fashioned disaster movies alerting humanity to the imminent dangers of exploding volcanoes (*Dante's Peak* and *Volcano*), colliding meteors (*Deep Impact* and *Armageddon*), floods (*Hard Rain*), tornadoes (*Twister*), rampaging lizards (*Jurassic Park*, *Godzilla*), and even sinking antique luxury liners (*Titanic*).

With motion pictures inevitably emphasizing the dire threats that supposedly surround us at every turn, it's no wonder that they paint such a monochromatically grim view of our future. The mid-'60's TV optimism of *The Jetsons* or the endless *Star Trek* series seems quaint and dated—every bit as dated as the venerable visions of *Buck Rogers* and *Flash Gordon*. The new attitude of the entertainment industry views territory ahead with dread rather than delight. All the way from *Planet of the Apes* and *Blade Runner* to Kevin Costner's twin downers *Waterworld* and *The Postman*, with stops in between for sequel-heavy stories such as the *Terminator*, *Mad Max*, *Robocop*, and *Alien* movies, countless film fantasies forecast the destruction of civilization by either unceasing warfare or environmental irresponsibility. In recent decades, producers determined that they could generate more audience thrills by portraying a future of peril rather than a future of promise. These sullen projections combine with alarmist messages in the news and from the educational system to convince our kids that they one day will inherit a world significantly less pleasant or promising than the one their parents enjoyed.

Movie Messages' Ripple Effect

Now that you've read about the blatant and subtle messages pushed by movies, videos, and TV, you might think that vigilant evaluation of what you view can spare you from their impact. But of course you're not that naive.

Purveyors of both adults' and children's movies are naturally going to seize any opportunity to capitalize on their product for increased profit. Any major mall in the United States is sure to boast a Disney store staffed with friendly salespeople urging you to buy the latest merchandising miracles—thermos bottles with Hercules hurtling a spear, pencil boxes with Dalmatians parading on the lid, tutus with fairy wands in emulation of Cinderella. Across the way you'll run into a ten-foot-tall plaster Daffy Duck or a giant surfing Sylvester marking the entrance to a Warner Brothers store. Both outlets offer continuously running videos of their classic motion pictures, to spur sales and keep children inside, forcing longer shopping stints for their parents.

We don't fault entrepreneurs for seeking profit; this simply illustrates how extensively media images pervade our culture. Film details seep into our daily lives. Who hasn't used the phrase "Show me the money!" recently, probably in an *unintended* reference to the film *Jerry Maguire*? The retail store Sunglass Hut near Seattle reports bumper business selling "Predator 2" Ray-Ban sunglasses like those in the movie *Men in Black*. And "product placement" firms rake in big bucks making sure brand names like Pepsi and Lays Potato Chips get devoured by admirable characters. Manufacturers gladly ante up because they understand the way even a few seconds' exposure can register in viewers' minds—and influence buying behavior outside that big darkened room.

Does this infiltration of media commercialism assault our children's innocence? Yes and no. Much merchandising is harmless and reflects a healthy free-enterprise system. But a problem arises when wide-ranging merchandising puts content meant for adults in the faces and consciousness of unwary children.

Movie ratings, designed to help parents shield children from adult content, haven't kept a substantial number of youngsters from exposure to the violence, sex, and degradation in films. Alvin F. Poussaint, professor of psychiatry at Harvard Medical School, suggests in the *New York Times* that unless theater owners are willing to enforce ratings rules, "Congress should give ratings the force of law." He'd gone to the theater and watched a disturbing scene in an R-rated film (that's "Restricted," meaning those under age seventeen must be accompanied by a parent or guardian). But the movie wasn't the most disturbing action in the theater—it was the slap the little six- or seven-year-old girl seated between her parents received when she dared scream in fear, since she might possibly be disturbing her neighbors. Poussaint writes, "The parental non-guidance I witnessed—not to mention the unsupervised, suspiciously baby-faced '17-year-olds' seated around me—showed how ineffective this system is in protecting kids."

A content analysis by *Preview Family Movie and TV Review* of 209 films released in 1996 found that of the PG–13 films (Parental Guidance suggested; not recommended for those under age thirteen) reviewed, 91 percent had crude language, 89 percent had obscene language, and 45 percent had actual or implied sex (the company did not include violence in this analysis). Similarly, 88 percent of films rated PG featured crude language, 59.5 percent used obscene language, and 12 percent had actual or implied sex. These are worrisome statistics because usually parents feel comfortable allowing their kids to see films with any rating that includes the letter G. They shouldn't be so confident: in our experience, those famous letters PG stand not for *parental guidance*, but for *profanity guaranteed*.

While PG films may be raunchy, they tend to be far less offensive to delicate tastes than R-rated fare. Even with parents there to mediate the event, movies rated R spare no one from coarse dialogue, casual sex, nudity, and violence. Keep in mind that any parents who want to go out to a show and who don't have a baby-sitter have little choice, even if they do want to shield their progeny. Two-thirds of the 713 movies offered in 1996 were rated R (65.8 percent) while only 2.9 percent were rated G. The content analysis shows that of the 53 R-rated films from 1996 that were reviewed, 99 percent included crude language, 95 percent had obscene language, and 56 percent featured sex, half actually showing the sex act, half clearly implying it.

Children as Victims

On a sunny weekend afternoon, a proud and handsome father (John Travolta) takes his excited five-year-old son for a joyous ride on an old-fashioned carousel. They laugh together among the shiny, bobbing, brightly painted wooden horses and relish their timeless fun, totally unaware that a determined sniper (Nicholas Cage) is drawing a deadly bead on them. He actually aims at the father, but inadvertently hits the son, transforming the little body into a twitching, blood-spattered mess as the boy dies in his wailing father's arms.

This horrifying opening sequence to the 1997 summer hit *Face/Off* provided a cunning means of grabbing audience attention for a slick and critically acclaimed thriller, but also confirmed the recent collapse of a long-standing motion picture taboo. In every sort of American film, kids appear more frequently than ever before as victims of brutality and horror; Hollywood seems perversely determined to shatter the old notion of childhood as a protected period of safety, shelter, and innocence.

Just consider some of the major releases of the last few years.

- In the gross, gory, and stylish monster movie *Mimic* (starring Oscar winner Mira Sorvino), a weirdly babbling, autistic eight-year-old boy (Alexander Goodwin) develops an intense spiritual connection with ravenous, blood-thirsty, six-foot-tall insects that inhabit the sewers of New York and perpetually threaten to devour him.

- Steven Spielberg casts the spunky African-American twelve-year-old Vanessa Lee Chester as Jeff Goldblum's daughter in *The Lost World* and sends her along as a stowaway on a mission to a dangerous and mysterious island simply so she can serve as a potential snack for hungry dinosaurs. (Youngsters Joseph Mazzello and Ariana Richards served the same purpose in his 1993 original *Jurassic Park.*)

- The evil and sadistic Russian terrorist (Gary Oldman) in the deservedly popular thriller *Air Force One* not only threatens the life of President Harrison Ford's thirteen-year-old daughter (Liesel Matthews), but strokes her cheek with a potent combination of feigned tenderness and unmistakable sexual menace.

- In the rancid comedy *She's So Lovely*, John Travolta plays a prosperous but slightly unhinged building contractor who wildly brandishes a gun in front of his eight-year-old stepdaughter, after cursing at her in the most outrageously obscene terms and encouraging the little girl to relax by downing a beer.

- Most alarming of all was the spectacularly cruel and gratuitously graphic kidnap melodrama *Ransom* from crowd-pleasing director Ron Howard. Brawley Nolte (son of actor Nick Nolte) plays the bright, sensitive ten-year-old son of a self-confident tycoon (Mel Gibson). The boy is seized by a disgusting gang of conspirators (led by Gary Sinise), then bound, blindfolded, gagged with duct tape, threatened at knifepoint, starved, and tortured as he whimpers and quivers helplessly on a filthy bed.

The worst aspect of such sadistic and sickening excess is its utter pointlessness within these films: how would *Ransom* have suffered in either commercial or artistic terms if it had depicted the suffering of the little boy with more discretion or restraint? The audience hardly needs to watch the detailed abuse of a child in order to understand the desperation of his frantic parents. When viewing such scenes in recent films, it's not only upsetting to imagine the torment of the fictional children on screen, but in many ways it's even more disturbing to think of the impact on the young actors who go through the real-life experience of playing the parts. Consider the on-set experience of seven-year-old Rumer Willis in the unspeakable stinker *Striptease* (1996). The budding child star participates in numerous scenes in which her own mother, Demi Moore, sheds her clothes to bump and grind for drooling strangers while groped and threatened by the dregs of humanity. It's hard to imagine why any parent (especially one who was already receiving twelve million dollars for *her* embarrassing role) would volunteer a cherished child for this experience.

Jeopardy Without Hope

While contemporary filmmakers may seem especially eager to place kiddie characters in dangerous situations, the basic idea of children in jeopardy is nothing new. Some of the most cherished family classics in history show youngsters from time to time facing deadly peril. The Wicked Witch of the West wants to kill Dorothy (and her little dog, too), while fearsome "Injun Joe" menaces Tom Sawyer and Becky Thatcher. Grimm's fairy tales are, indeed, grim, with sorcerers and trolls and evil stepmothers constantly conspiring against innocent and sweet-tempered tots.

Nevertheless, in their most popular form these traditional tales, even when occasionally terrifying, come accompanied with sweet reassurance that children enjoy some supernatural protection and all will work out in the end. *Hansel and Gretel* (1893), the most famous opera for young people ever written, shows its two main characters lost in the deep woods, menaced by a hungry witch and noxious spirits of the night, but managing to sing a famous prayer as they fall asleep: "When I lay down my sleepy head / Fourteen angels guard my bed." Indeed, those white-robed, winged guardians then materialize on stage in an elaborate tableau, proclaiming to everyone in the audience that the little wanderers can ultimately feel safe from the ravenous witch.

In today's entertainments, children enjoy little protection—angelic or otherwise. Compared with the far-fetched and fanciful menace in old-fashioned family fare, modern threats are far more realistic (and therefore far more frightening). *Fly Away Home*, for example, one of the most charming family movies of 1996, opened with an outrageously intense and needlessly specific portrayal of a bloody traffic accident involving the little-girl heroine and her mother, in which the parent is painfully killed. The PG potboiler (and box-office flop) *Gold Diggers: The Secret of Bear Mountain* (also 1996) attempts to show two likable thirteen-year-old girls in a spirited small-town adventure in the Hardy Boys tradition, but it makes a point of showing one of the girls (Anna Chlumsky) brutally beaten and in fact scarred by her alcoholic mother's abusive boyfriend (David Keith). Even the wretched 1993 film version of Hank Ketcham's beloved cartoon strip *Dennis the Menace* showed its tow-headed tyke frighteningly assaulted by a homeless psychotic (Christopher Lloyd) wielding a knife and attacking his family's house.

Coarsening Adult Sensibilities

While some of these needlessly intense scenes find their way into movies aimed at family audiences with the apparent intention of arousing excitement among young moviegoers, many other recent scenes showing children as victims seem clearly conceived to shock adults rather than to connect with kids. Such sequences frequently appear in R-rated fare (*Face/Off*, *Mimic*, *Ransom*) that is officially limited to adults only and, in any event, bears little hope of ever bringing large numbers of youngsters to the theaters. In these situations, the purpose of such elements has nothing to do with intensifying audience identification with youthful characters on screen and instead seems designed to reach jaded grown-ups who no longer feel shocked or frightened by violence directed at adult targets.

Given the tidal wave of brutality and gore in films of the last two decades, public sensibilities have been numbed and coarsened. Like addicts who need steadily stronger doses of their chosen drug to achieve the same adrenaline rush, moviegoers who are accustomed to violent fare require constantly more alarming, graphic, and bizarre scenes of violence to receive the same thrills. Brutality against children in this sense represents a new frontier, where even generally bored film fanatics can gasp in horror.

Michael still remembers his own visceral reaction to one groundbreaking scene of that nature in the celebrated Australian import *Dead Calm* (1989), best known for introducing Nicole Kidman to American audiences. In the opening sequence, she's driving on a rainy freeway with her adorable, cooing baby when she gets involved in a traffic accident, sending the child hurtling through the windshield to its bloody, nightmarish death. This horrifyingly well-staged incident (by director Phillip Noyce) sets an overwhelmingly eerie mood that permeates the rest of the picture and its more conventional dreads. The juxtaposition of innocence, vulnerability, and sweetness with cruelty and mutilation still feels shocking and disorienting—even for pop consumers who have become notoriously difficult to shock.

Beyond the elements of surprise and sadism, why else would adults feel drawn to some of the more extreme visions of children at risk? Part of the answer may relate to an increasing sense of helplessness among American parents when it comes to protecting our own kids. The main threats children face in the real world are far more difficult to define and to resist than cinematic terrorists or kidnappers. It's emotionally satisfying to watch Mel Gibson or Harrison Ford striking back at the slimy, vicious bad guys who menace their movie kids precisely because it's so difficult for ordinary parents to take action against the infinitely more subtle perils that our children face every day. You can't readily raise fists or guns against a hedonistic culture, premature sex, teenage promiscuity, drugs, alcohol, depression, sexually transmitted diseases, pierced eyebrows, obscene tattoos, failure in school, paralyzing cynicism, or a host of other afflictions that threaten the children of today.

Even those movies that show kiddie victims who can't be rescued by concerned adults pay subconscious psychic dividends to today's worried parents. If the larger-than-life demigods who inhabit the big screens of the local multiplex can't succeed in saving their fictional kids, then how can we blame ourselves for our failures at home? In this sense, the idea that children are now impossible to protect is oddly reassuring to many parents: if they're eternally endangered in film after film, then we needn't push ourselves to achieve a level of sheltering safety that the pop culture says is impossible. Many contemporary parents may feel incapable of emulating the wise and well-adjusted example of *Father Knows*

Best or *Ozzie and Harriet*, but we can all congratulate ourselves that we do better than the despicable suburban couple played by John Travolta and Robin Wright Penn in *She's So Lovely.*

By placing children so frequently at risk, Hollywood feature films (powerfully echoed by countless TV dramatizations of switched babies and victims of kidnapping, violence, incest, or abuse) make their own powerful contribution to our national assault on innocence. Current conventional wisdom suggests that it is now impossible to protect kids, so we must instead prepare them for the worst—and some of the more distressing and realistic films showing children in jeopardy might even be welcomed as part of the process of preparation. With our increasing acceptance of violence, bad language, sexual content, and downbeat topical themes even in entertainment aimed squarely at kids, we have abandoned the ideal of childhood as a special, simpler, carefully guarded time where the young of the species can flourish and develop without frights or fears. Reasserting the importance of youthful innocence to this society is a complicated process, but on one level, at least, concerned parents need not wait for profound cultural changes. They can make an immediate difference in their own homes by conscientiously protecting their offspring—and themselves—from media images showing the cruel and needless victimization of the very young.

Speak to Me, Baby

But even something that seems merely a minor problem, like impolite language, has its consequences to childhood. Crass films that bombard adults, many of whom are parents, with so much bad language make gutter slang seem "normal," and so it easily becomes part of the common dialogue that children overhear and copy. Worse, children who themselves go to movies where they hear boorish speech think that using it makes them sound grown-up. The sensitivities of even those children whose parents strictly forbid crude language are lowered when they hear other, less supervised children—in school, in the neighborhood, at the local pizza parlor—bandy about scatological slang as if it were "cool."

Not only does it explode childish naïveté when kids inevitably ask and are told what the words mean, but, more significantly, as the general language level becomes more unrefined, so does the *content* of public discourse. Language is the primary factor that clearly differentiates humans from animals, and we could argue that being civilized means becoming less physically oriented, and more elevated and attuned to abstract concepts (like liberty, honesty, compassion, and innocence)—in other words, less like animals and more in the image of God.

We all understand this intuitively. Why is baby talk so sweet and charming? And why do we blanch when we hear a rude teenager utter profanities at a toddler? Why do college campuses have rules about what young men can say to coeds lest they feel harassed? We *know* the power of language to elevate or soil, to preserve dignity or debase. Instead of desensitizing ourselves to impolite speech, we need to become *more* aware, and work to ennoble what we say as well as what we do.

Kids and Porn

One category of film is particularly repugnant: child pornography, popularly called kiddy porn. Films like *The People vs. Larry Flynt*, while not aimed at children, glorify to the adult population the perpetration of child pornography. Larry Flynt's publication *Hustler* years ago famously featured a regular cartoon called *Chester the Molester*, whose artist, Dwaine Tinsley, was convicted of—guess what?—multiple counts of child molesting. *The People vs. Larry Flynt* was a mainstream film offered by the giant Sony Corporation, not some fringe group playing it in art houses. Its success on some level legitimized anything that stimulates, amuses, or feels good, no matter what the consequences to those who cannot defend themselves.

No moral person accepts children's performance in hard-core pornography, and in fact laws affirm that this type of "acting" is child abuse. Little needs to be said regarding the murder of innocence that occurs for the unfortunate young victims of this industry, which, sadly, continues despite its illegality.

Pornography starring children is horrendous, but also deplorable is that children sitting in their own living rooms fiddling with the remote control can unknowingly bring adult pornography into their lives. Under federal laws, cable systems must offer access channels open to anyone. Rejecting material for broadcast is nearly impossible for cable operators, who must carry all content unless it's prohibited under the orders of local franchising authorities, who seldom act. So *Philip Craft's Political Playhouse*, a nude discussion group on censorship that runs a string of vulgar words across the screen, and *Out Late with Ricky D*, another nude talk show with clips of erotic dancers, continue to air, ruled merely indecent rather than obscene. Efforts to require the scrambling of such material have met with legal resistance from the ACLU.

Family Night at the Movies

It's a difficult call whether to report the following under the impact of film or the contribution of parents themselves to the destruction of childhood. Parents no longer want to sit through a charming little cartoon such as *Thumbelina* or *Balto* with their children—they prefer that "custody Saturdays" and family Sundays entertain them, too. So filmmakers are finding they need to offer fare with more of an edge. As reported by Bernard Weinraub in the *New York Times*, "The traditional family film, once a lucrative staple of Hollywood's studio system, is quietly dying as the industry feeds an increasingly restless audience with bigger stars, more provocative themes and stories with an edge unheard of even a decade ago." He notes that the "appetite for more sophisticated and even violent movies has surprised even Hollywood," and quotes Walt Disney Pictures president David Vogel saying, "It's no longer an innocent period of time." Kids have been jaded by hip TV shows, the Internet, "and, perhaps most important," continues Weinraub, "the breakup of many traditional families and the accelerated childhood of boys and girls. These trends have led to a blurring of pop culture tastes among baby boomer parents and their children."

An example: Sony Pictures Entertainment president for marketing Robert Levin says of *My Best Friend's Wedding*, the 1997 Julia Roberts romantic comedy, "Among 10-year-old girls, even 8-year-old girls, this film keeps building." The heroine in the picture, a chain-smoking, hard-drinking independent journalist, tries to win back her old flame and fails, with the implied attitude of "Heck, he's copped out to those boring values of marriage so I'm better off anyway." A great role model for an eight-year-old.

In an article aptly named "Cut the Cute Stuff: Kids Flock to Adult Flicks," Bruce Orwall writes in the *Wall Street Journal* about the hardening of toddler tastes. "Just a couple of years ago, parents were fretting over whether some Disney animated movies were too scary for kids," he reflects. "Now, kids are successfully convincing parents to let them see heart-thumpers like Universal's 'The Lost World: Jurassic Park.'" Cases in point are Beverly Hills mother Cori Drasin's young daughters, who saw the film *Austin Powers: International Man of Mystery* seven times and adored *My Best Friend's Wedding*. Her six-year-old considered Warner Brothers' *Contact*—perhaps the most highbrow Hollywood film in the summer of 1997—a favorite and can even discuss the film's meaning: "You never saw [the aliens]. That's what the movie was all about." Ms. Drasin explains, "They're exposed to more mature things on TV, so when they go to the movies they expect to see the same things," demanding more than "the formulaic, happy-ending Disney stuff."

Worse yet, the new preparation model encourages parents to *intentionally* subject their offspring to fictional movie traumas—to ensure that their first exposure occurs when the parent can mop up the damage. In *Family Circle* magazine, director Oliver Stone remarks, "I wouldn't want either of my children [ages ten and three] to see an obscene or dangerous movie they might not understand unless I had the chance to explain it to them."

Films as Tough as the Kids

Most fascinating is that in throwing up their hands and abandoning the "family market," studio execs like Disney's Vogel use the same old excuses: "There isn't this innocence of childhood among many children," he opines, "what with broken homes and violence. We can't treat children as if they're all living in tract homes of the 1950s and everyone is happy. That is ridiculous."

Of course, some families do live sad and wrenching realities. But childhood has survived difficult times before. In the 1930s, when one-third of the workforce was unemployed, kids endured poverty and physical insecurity. In the 1940s, they watched their fathers march off to war and their mothers cope with a sparse wartime economy. Yet, in the 1930s and '40s, filmmakers for the most part didn't succumb to the woes of the world around them—producing instead mainly uplifting and diverting cinematic entertainment.

Writers at the time were quite conscious of the question, however, and even made a movie about whether or not to explore life's travails. In one of our favorite pictures of all time, *Sullivan's Travels* (1941, from writer/director Preston Sturges), a film director (Joel McCrea) tired of making comedies, and yearning to be taken seriously, decides to discover the seamy underside of life. He ends up on a southern chain gang with the dregs of humanity. One night the pitiful work crew earns a reward for their good behavior, and when the wardens announce what the treat will be, they erupt in cheers and whistles of excitement and appreciation. What brings such a reaction from a band of hardened criminals? The showing of a Mickey Mouse cartoon.

The guards tie a sheet to trees in a swamp for a screen, and as the reel turns, the gleeful and grateful inmates hoot, stamp, and release tears of laughter at the antics of the cheerful rodent. The film director character, moved by their enthusiasm, realizes that these men were restored by this few minutes' relief from their miserable plight. He concludes that the men would have despised a film that portrayed life on a chain gang, because what they needed and craved was escape.

Sullivan's Travels communicates a profound truth: people living through trials and torture seldom yearn for art or entertainment that reflects their suffering. More often, they need visions of hope and the promise of deliverance. The depression years produced what has become known as Hollywood's Golden Age, even though few films of that era dramatized soup kitchens, shantytowns, or apple sellers on street corners. Why should we suppose that a hungry, unemployed worker will feel most fulfilled or satisfied by viewing cinematic treatments of characters in similarly bleak situations? The box-office records of the 1930's suggest that hard-pressed Americans unequivocally preferred escapist fare (musicals, westerns, adventures, screwball comedies about the super rich) that allowed them to spend an hour and a half in the dark, forgetting about their problems.

For children, it's even more dubious to assume that they somehow benefit from seeing their own difficulties endlessly reflected on TV or at the movies. If you're a seven-year-old who is struggling to survive with an alcoholic and abusive father, why would you want to see a TV movie about another alcoholic and abusive father? A child who each day views the self-destructive behavior of a prostitute mother with a heroin habit hardly needs to watch such behavior dramatized by actors on screen. Michael and his three younger brothers lived through their parents' separation and divorce in the mid–1970s, and they can verify that while enduring that experience, the last films they chose to see were those that stressed the excruciating pain of marital breakup—even though such movies happened to be much the rage at the time.

One of the most illogical assumptions underlying the decisions of today's media moguls is the notion that the decline of the traditional nuclear family makes idealized visions of such domestic arrangements irrelevant and unpopular. On what basis do the princes of pop culture assume that children in pain will always tune out *Father Knows Best* or *Leave It to Beaver* or, for that matter, *The Cosby Show*? A child's insecurity and emotional distress won't necessarily kill the appetite for such reassuring and soothing diversions; in fact, personal pain may make them all the more appealing and important. By the same token, preserving innocence—and fostering a predictable pattern of life, a sense of wonder, and optimism toward the future—must not be a project restricted to privileged kids and their parents. Protecting and restoring this childhood birthright is even more essential for youngsters who have already endured shocks and suffering.

Innocence Lost in the Airwaves

Just before the advent of television, our nation's favorite means of mentally escaping hard times was the radio. During the depression years of the '30s, and the wartime of the '40s, serialized stories, comedians, and singers lifted families' spirits as they gathered around the radio for weekly broadcasts. In the early '50s, the new medium of television usurped radio's hold on the country, though music stations always provided the conduit for new musicians and rock groups' popularity.

In the last decade, however, we've witnessed the resurgence of radio as a purveyor of ideas. Entertainment now combines with news analysis and philosophy, drawing immense audiences for national commentators like Rush Limbaugh, Howard Stern, and Don Imus. Rush focuses on the unvarnished conservative evaluation of issues, reaching 20 million listeners each week. Howard Stern speaks his uncensored mind, using offensive language and outlandish images to provide a brand of "entertainment" that helped generate the term *shock jock*.

Radio shrinks like Dr. Laura Schlessinger attract listeners voyeuristically enjoying frank assessments of callers' very personal problems. And at the top of every hour, newscasts blare the most catchy headlines, spicing all this discussion with superficially explained snapshots of surrounding reality. None of this is conducive to children's innocence.

Michael, whose national radio show based in Seattle began in March 1998, strives diligently to cover news, history, philosophy, music, movies, and family issues with an eye toward providing information listeners could not receive elsewhere. He's grateful for the hundreds of written responses arriving daily, reminding him of the impact of his every word.

Though radio talk shows aim for adults, particularly those in the coveted age range of twenty-five to fifty-five, they inevitably indoctrinate young children as their parents chauffeur kids in daily carpools. Many parents have confessed to us that they've shushed their children's cheerful chatter in order to listen to some particularly meaty comment Michael was making on the air. And because parents can listen to the radio while accomplishing other tasks simultaneously—like cleaning out the garage, cooking, straightening the house, or working—they often don't realize the number of hours their children spend absorbing its messages.

Inevitably, news-driven talk shows, even those that, like Michael's, include ample lighthearted entertainment, touch upon topics inappropriate for children, such as abortion, capital punishment, sex scandals, and crime. Parents need to stay alert to issues as they're presented, to provide explanation or switch the channel if necessary. Most talk-show hosts don't follow Michael's practice of warning parents of upcoming sensitive items so that they can remove children from the scene or temporarily turn down the sound. Diane finds that carrying a lightweight portable radio with "ear buds" that she wears in only a single ear allows her to divide her attention between the kids and the riveting but sometimes touchy topics Michael covers.

Some Call it Music: Assault by Rock 'n' Roll

We never listen to contemporary rock stations on the radio; neither do we have MTV (or any TV), so you can imagine Diane's shock when our middle daughter, Shayna, eight, pointed to the photo in the newspaper Diane was reading. "I can tell you all their names," Shayna boasted, referring to the five young women in revealing clothes shown in the photo. "That one's Baby Spice, then Scary Spice, Ginger Spice, Posh Spice, and Sporty Spice," she recited.

"How do you know about the Spice Girls?" Diane asked, trying to sound casual. After all, this group doesn't shy away from sexy lyrics.

"That's what all the girls talk about in Girl Scouts," Shayna replied. The group ranges from eight to eleven years old.

Danny Goldberg, chief executive officer of Mercury Records, purveyor of the current rage Hanson, explained to the *New York Times* that the average age of the female audience for rock music has been declining. "Now the teenage years seem to start at 8 or 9, in terms of entertainment tastes," he noted. "The emotions are kicking in earlier. It's a huge audience." Could it be that "the emotions are kicking in" because recording execs cater to them? Is this "huge audience" perhaps a source of profit? Michael received a call on his radio show from a ten-year-old listener who phoned to gush adoration for the actor Leonardo DiCaprio, who she first saw when her parents took her to see the film *Titanic*. Romance and sexuality are enticingly grown-up, and nobody seems willing to slow down the trend.

When political types as diverse as Tipper Gore (*Raising PG Kids in an X-Rated Society*, 1987) and Phyllis Schlafly condemn today's rock music, you know it's bad for anyone's character. And when mainstream publications like *Time* magazine run cover stories on its descent, well, we have a problem here. "There's an acid tang in nearly every area of modern American pop culture," writes Richard Corliss. "Heavy-metal masters Mötley Crüe invoke images of Satanism and the Beastie Boys mime masturbation onstage. Rap poets like N.W.A. and 2 Live Crew call for the fire of war against police or the brimstone of explicit, sulfurous sex."

Few parents can monitor the lyrics floating around their home, and indeed they can never get inside those ubiquitous Walkman headphones. But without vigilance, how can you keep antisocial material on the airwaves and CDs from wising up and dumbing down your youngster? At what point is it even possible or desirable to intervene?

By now, everyone's heard examples of the degradation glorified on the rock scene, particularly in the genres of heavy metal and rap. There's no need to harp on the damage to *any* listeners' sensitivities when they hear and repeat the kind of angry, misogynist, violent, and disrespectful rhymes that pass for art. The impact on adults and older teens who want to listen to this type of sound is not our topic, though it puzzles us how anyone could choose Guns 'N Roses over Gershwin. More to the point are the many *indirect* ways today's music makes sneaky entries into the gentle mentalities of very young children.

Take the public discussion a few years back about the 2 Live Crew album *As Nasty as They Wanna Be*. Little kids were very unlikely to actually sit and listen to this album, since it's not their style, and also the news was alive with descriptions of its contents, alerting parents. Just to refresh your memory, Robert G. DeMoss, Jr., youth culture specialist for Colorado Springs–based Focus on the Family, reported that the album contained 87 descriptions of oral sex, 117 explicit descriptions of male and female genitalia, 226 f words, and 163 uses of the word *bitch* referring to women. Now, the album sold 1.4 million copies even before the hoopla—how could tots avoid at least snippits of it, overheard as older siblings blasted their musical selections at the usual teen listening volume?

But besides that, they could not escape *discussion of the contro-versy*, which unavoidably came within their earshot on the TV, on the car radio, and even in phone conversations between concerned parents.

Freedom to sing whatever lyrics one chooses is not the issue here—it's that once little children overhear vulgar expressions of sex and degradation, it's difficult to return unscathed to the world of kindly dinosaurs and leprechauns. Pop music and the club cul-ture glamorize drugs and rebellion, enemies of childhood. We need voluntary public standards—not to curtail anyone's personal free-dom, but to preserve the *choice* to offer children an emotional envi-ronment free from fear, violence, raw sex, physical and substance abuse, disrespect, and tales of unnatural death.

Here's another example of the way harsh messages in today's popular music reach down to slash innocence. Hip-hop is a cuter title for rap music, and now that sales of actual music CDs are lag-ging, record companies are looking for new ways to bring in cash. They're broadening their appeal to kids by making *clothes* that advertise their bands. No big deal, you say—groups have always marketed their T-shirts. But it's the scale of the new effort that is staggering and worrisome, because it makes hip-hop known and desirable even to the youngest consumer. Suddenly it's uncool for a kindergartener to listen to kids' song classics like "The Little White Duck."

To give you some idea: Tommy Boy records sports a clothing subsidiary, notes a *New York Times* business section piece from summer 1997. "Other hip-hop-oriented record companies and artists have recognized the music-clothing combination and have accordingly expanded their businesses. Nervous Records, Duck Down Records and Loud Records have their own clothing lines, and several rap artists have also entered the fray," explains the *Times*. "Groups like the Fugees, Wo-Tang Clan and Bone Thugs-N-Harmony have all started their own labels and clothing lines."

Role models are powerful, whether they're older brothers in hip-hop shirts or simply the images of the entertainers themselves. Entering the picture are "tot pop acts," as they were dubbed in a recent *Time* magazine article, comprised of kids as young as eleven. "People are coming back to music that's fun and upbeat, and younger artists are filling that gap," says MTV vice president of music and talent Patti Galluzzi. The kiddie rage of the moment is Hanson, three brothers ages eleven, thirteen, and sixteen. There's the pop-grunge group Radish with its fifteen-year-old lead singer. And sixteen-year-old Jonny Lang has sold more than 150,000 copies of his debut album, "an impressive total for almost any bluesman but even more so for one who is still just a blues boy," claims *Time*'s Christopher John Farley. Just one question: Is there really any reason for prosperous high school juniors raised in this privileged country to be *blue*?

Or to be tough? Remember the happy face, popular in the 1970s? Those were the days when colorful Hawaiian-print surf shirts ruled clothes racks, when that unsophisticated circle with its line-smile was everywhere, along with the salutation, "Have a nice day!" By contrast, what slogans dominate now: No Fear. Scowling Bad Boys. "Gangsta" clothing that hangs so baggy off kids' hips that they can barely waddle. This is the climate that has been fostered by rap music and its drone of complaint and rage. We were stunned to see a fashion-conscious suburban mother dress her two-year-old in a miniature "gangsta" outfit, with wide baggy pants and a stylishly torn T-shirt. The toddler's hair was cut and greased so that it shot up in short spikes from his pudgy preschool face. No, dressing up a child isn't major, but where does a two-year-old punk go from there?

Read All About It

Books—they're the primary focus of interest for our precious eleven-year-old, Sarah. She devours literature with such eagerness that we've pried many paperbacks from her hands after she's fallen asleep. She loves Mark Twain, L. M. Montgomery, even Shakespeare. She quickly completed all the activities necessary to earn her Books badge for Junior Girl Scouts. She's tried to lure her younger sister, Shayna, toward her book collection, recommending volumes she particularly enjoys, though Shayna, more social, prefers live to fictional friends.

So we were all delighted when we found Shayna engrossed in reading the newly arrived *Junior Girl Scout Handbook*. Diane is a big booster of Girl Scouts, having been a member through elementary school and junior high and a leader of Sarah and Shayna's Brownie troop in Los Angeles. We all appreciate the values and camaraderie fostered by scouting, and the girls wear their green uniforms to every meeting with pride. Perhaps Shayna would learn knot-tying, or find a badge or two she'd like to earn.

But after spending a few minutes reading the *Handbook*, Shayna put it down, announcing, "This is a bad book."

"What do you mean?" Diane asked.

"It has things inside that I shouldn't be reading," Shayna replied, starting to read aloud: "The first sign of menstruation is usually a small amount of blood, not a 'gushing' of blood. Menstrual pads (sanitary napkins) or tampons can be used to absorb the menstrual flow . . . "

"I don't think you need to read that right now," Diane said, nonchalantly snatching the book away. Shayna, though in fourth grade, was only eight years old. We hadn't given her that information yet, and we certainly did not want or expect the *Junior Girl Scout Handbook* to do it for us. We realized that even in our innocence-conscious home, we had not been conscious *enough*.

We still support and take pride in our daughters' Girl Scout activities, and consider the organization one of the finest vehicles for joining together girls in wholesome, educational pursuits. But even the Girl Scouts seem to have adopted the preparation model. Perusing other pages in Shayna's book (in private) we found a page on feelings: "Georgia's mother had been ill with AIDS for many months. She would probably die within days, the doctor said. Georgia reached out to hold her mother's hand." (This surely would have made Shayna cry—and for what purpose?) A page headed "What Is a Family?" sought to illustrate diversity in living situations by showing seven girls, only two of whom lived with both mother and father. We found sections on teenage pregnancy, drug and alcohol addiction, separation and divorce, along with plenty of useful information, including media awareness, communication skills, nutrition, science, and of course, earning Girl Scout badges. We, as parents, wanted to be the ones to introduce the topic of adolescent development to Shayna, and wish that we could have prevented her learning about it accidentally, with feelings of embarrassment, from the unlikely source of her *Junior Girl Scout Handbook.*

Print media of all sorts feed children what we used to consider mature themes, both in and, as we discovered, outside the context of school. The following example illustrates how the messages of a particular short novel affected one family.

Shortly after Michael lectured in Toronto on the assault on innocence, we received a book club edition of Judy Blume's book *Deenie*, with a letter describing the "troubling experience" a father had after purchasing it for his eleven-year-old daughter. While "thumbing through prior to giving it to her," the writer reports, he came upon passages he terms "a deliberate attempt to explain, encourage *and* demonstrate how a young girl can experience sexual arousal, that is masturbation." Exasperated, he hoped we could "use the book as an exhibit in alerting parents as to how literature is being misused."

The slim paperback contains the story of a seventh-grade girl who, due to the back condition scoliosis, must wear a body brace. The book seems harmless enough, given the endorsements printed on its back cover: "Deenie's conformity with adolescent real life interests will no doubt endear her to junior high girls."—*ALA Booklist.* "Ms. Blume has a keen awareness of the teenager. Her book is rich in dialogue and characterizations: it should be popular."—*Publishers Weekly.*

Though the book appears to be marketed to teenagers, the type is too large, the plot too short, and the main character is just twelve years old. Girls beyond sixth grade would probably consider Judy Blume beneath them, despite the opinions of *Publishers Weekly* and the *ALA Booklist.* However, younger kids love to read about older girls. Any bright seven-year-old could easily pick up *Deenie* and read it in an evening.

You may remember our disquieting experience with our daughter Sarah at age seven when our local librarian recommended another Judy Blume book containing references to menstruation. It could have been worse: *Deenie* describes sitting on the toilet and "getting my period," and her difficulties with donning her protection while wearing a brace. She masturbates and gets a sex-ed lecture in school telling her it's OK and normal. For older girls, this might reflect real life. But for seven, eight, nine, or even many ten- or eleven-year-olds, these topics are unnecessary.

Why is it that Sarah can delight in L. M. Montgomery books at any age but feels grossed out and baffled by the easy 140-page "real world" stories of Judy Blume? Answer: because Judy Blume gives her scary information that makes her uncomfortable; ideas *she* feels unready and unwilling to learn. But then, Sarah understands (because her parents are vocal on the subject) that her childhood is something precious that she—and we all—should safeguard.

What is distressing in *Deenie* are some of its underlying assumptions; for example, that masturbation is something every young girl does (where's the evidence?), and that twelve-year-olds treat menstruation so casually they're not embarrassed to call into the hallway for someone to bring them "stuff" (to the contrary, any sensitive girl is extremely private about such things). In giving this material to little girls, those who do *not* masturbate and who are *not* aware or comfortable with the details of menstruation forever lose their carefree ignorance, and their parents lose the opportunity to personally acquaint their daughters with this topic when most appropriate to the particular child and most conducive to parent-daughter closeness.

Most emphatically, we do *not* advocate any kind of censorship. In fact, we find it ludicrous that the Mark Twain classic *Huckleberry Finn* is being banned from Washington state libraries because it contains one racial slur unacceptable for young eyes. While the term is certainly offensive by today's standards, its incidental use in the historical context of Mark Twain probably does less damage to young readers' sensibilities than *Deenie* has. No parent can completely screen all the words that enter their children's minds, but they ought to be alert to the fact that seemingly safe sources can also injure innocence.

Poop-ular Culture

Smaller kids not yet able to read may get all giggly when a classmate picks his nose in public, startles his friends with a loud gas emission, or cracks a bathroom joke about defecation. But now adults have begun catering to such infantile excitements, lowering us to the level of animals by approvingly buying books about bodily functions. We certainly don't blame publishers Sandy Miller and Madeline Kane for importing and translating Japanese writers' brightly illustrated books about the universality of unpleasant regularities. Their *Everyone Poops* has sold 480,000 copies; *The Gas We Pass*, 380,000 copies; and *The Holes in Your Nose*, 70,000.

Most purchasers probably don't think about the implications of the attractively packaged stories. One of the differences between early childhood and maturity is that adults *control* their secretions and relegate them to private spaces with hygienic precautions. It is our job as parents to teach these manners to our children, thus raising them up beyond mere physicality to an understanding of the civilized versus the animalistic. We've seen *Everyone Poops* displayed at public libraries. We've seen it featured at the Pacific Science Center's store in Seattle. Now, try a thought experiment. Imagine reading a bowel movement book to *your* little ones. Are you embarrassed? Just a little? Do you consider that to be a "hang-up"? Or could your embarrassment be evidence that you've graduated from preschool?

A couple of years ago, Diane was instrumental in creating a Jewish elementary school for our local community, and heard this story while helping with teacher selection. In interviewing a wonderful candidate, the excellent principal, Mrs. Judith Aronson, asked the prospective teacher about the library of her own books—some six hundred volumes—that she'd offered to bring into her classroom.

"Tell me about some of the books," Mrs. Aronson inquired.

The teacher named several classics and a few new selections, all of which drew nods from the well-versed principal. Until the teacher rattled off the title *Everyone Poops*.

"Tell me a little more about that one," coaxed Mrs. Aronson.

"It's a colorful book that shows different animals making poop," the teacher replied. "You know, elephants, dogs, birds, all kinds of animals, and children, too. But it's tastefully done, they're all delightful drawings, nothing gross. The premise is that it's just a natural function, we're doing something just like all the animals."

"I think we'll pass on that one," Mrs. Aronson said gently.

Later, the teacher asked Diane why Mrs. Aronson had dismissed that particular title. The point that Diane made with her is that this message, that we are "just like all the animals," while certainly true in some respects, is not a lesson we wanted to teach our children. We want to *differentiate* ourselves from animals whenever possible, including during the function of elimination, by entering a special place, by closing the door, by wiping afterward, by flushing, then washing our hands, and, as observant Jews, by saying a special Hebrew blessing in recognition of the miracle of the body's smooth mechanics, once we've departed from the room. If defecation is discussed at all in school, it is only to emphasize that as human beings, we perform that act quite differently from animals, and by doing so, bring ourselves just a little closer to the nobility for which we strive.

Is this a big deal? Of course not—children hearing adults celebrate animal poop is not going to bring about the downfall of the empire. But that's just the point: all the subtle messages—the "little things"—destroy innocence by erosion. To maintain childhood's special place, parents need vigilance about the assumptions neatly tucked into seemingly innocuous fare.

Kids' Books: It's a Scary, Bloody Shock

Ever hear of R. L. Stine? How can you *not* know about this master of kiddy gore, America's best-selling author? This purveyor of bloody, eyeballs-popping, bodies-decomposing chills and thrills for children as young as eight years old (or five if they're good readers) has 180 million *Goosebumps* books in print, as of August 1997, according to his publisher, Scholastic Books of New York. Of course, now R. L. Stine has several ghostwriters (pardon us) who crank out the tales, marketed in various series to an eager, enthusiastic audience of literally millions of youngsters per week.

What could be wrong with that? Kids who otherwise might be watching TV are at least exercising their reading skills, right? Think again. The proliferation of R. L. Stine "literature" may be the most clear example of the insidiousness of the assault on innocence. Parents are sighing in relief to see their children's noses buried in a book, while their kids, visually ingesting a vocabulary of blood, are palpitating away their childlike sweetness. How? Not only are they immersed in a world where "normal life" moves from one frightening climax to another, but as they delight in descriptions from gross to disgusting, they are being desensitized to the pain and horror of victimhood, injury, and death.

Writer Diana West, in an excellent cover story in *The Weekly Standard*, goes even further, describing a hormonally driven "fight or flight" reaction as youngsters encounter each scary pinnacle in the action: "And so, reading becomes a crude tool of physical stimulation, wholly devoid of mental, emotional, or spiritual engagement," she summarizes. "Does that sound like a working definition of pornography?" Whoa. "This certainly is a disquieting thought. But after immersing myself in this murky genre (30 books in all), I could not help but perceive an unmistakable pornographic pattern of means and ends."

Ms. West describes the "puddles and pools" of blood, the impaling, convulsing, immolation, drowning, "hot tar, boiling grease and chunky vomit" that characterize Stine narratives, whose genre she defines as "shock fiction," and concludes, "Whether sexual, deviant or just plain violent, the aim of all shock fiction is the same: to set off a bodily response which debases the act of reading—and more important, the reader himself."

Is this how we want to introduce our youngest readers to the world of literature? Is this kind of titillation what we want them to view as the way to have fun? And is this the sort of content with which we want to fuel their imaginations? We give our children a resounding no.

Defining Perfect as Normal

While R. L. Stine presents "normal" life as one spurting scream after another, young girls who read teen magazines receive another type of distortion of the real world—one that inspires such unattainable aspirations that young ladies have killed themselves in pursuit of them.

The cover of *People* magazine (June 1996) lines up extremely lithe TV stars Courtney Cox, Pamela Lee, and Heather Locklear and contrasts them with an attractive teenager looking doubtful about her own shape. The yellow letters scream, "Too fat? Too thin? How media images of celebrities teach kids to hate their bodies."

"You see thinness so much you become conditioned to want it," says seventeen-year-old, ninety-seven-pound (at five feet even) Wendy Levey in a caption under her photo. "If no one looked, I'd be much happier. I'd probably eat what I want."

Mary Pipher, Ph.D., a therapist who has made a career of working with and understanding eating disorders like anorexia and bulimia in young girls, laments in her recent *Reviving Ophelia: Saving the Selves of Adolescent Girls* that young women "are coming of age in a more dangerous, sexualized and media-saturated culture" than their parents. "They face incredible pressures to be beautiful and sophisticated, which in junior high means using chemicals and being sexual. As they navigate a more dangerous world, girls are less protected."

The result? "Research shows that virtually all women are ashamed of their bodies," Dr. Pipher told *People*. "It used to be adult women, teenage girls, who were ashamed, but now you see the shame down to very young girls—10, 11 years old. Society's standard of beauty is an image that is literally just short of starvation for most women."

Such impossible standards have oppressed many young boys as well. "The National Association of Anorexia Nervosa and Associated Disorders estimates that 1 million males suffer from anorexia or bulimia," notes the *People* magazine story, and 31 percent of men are dissatisfied with their appearance. Fewer boys are comfortable taking showers in gym; many resort to using anabolic steroids to get the buff look they crave.

The June 30, 1997, death of twenty-two-year-old Boston Ballet dancer Heidi Guenther of heart failure linked to anorexia focused national attention on this problem. At the time of her death, according to one report, the five-foot-three-inch dancer weighed just ninety-three pounds. Found in her possession was "a stash of over-the-counter laxatives. She was also taking herbal pills, which she may have been using as a diet aid." While pressure to be excruciatingly thin is particularly intense in the world of young ballerinas (described movingly years ago by L. M. Vincent, M.D., in a book called *Competing with the Sylph*), most little girls identify with ballerinas as role models, and if you ask a handful of five-year-old girls, at least a few will say they aspire to be ballerinas when they grow up. Diane remembers hearing among preteen friends who considered ballet training that "to be a ballerina you have to be very thin." For that reason, many rhythmically minded peers chose modern dance, said to be more forgiving about dancers' forms.

How does an unrealistic redefining of what is a normal body destroy innocence in children? Imposing adult ideas of beauty, especially when they are distorted and emaciated images, is an external complication to a process—growth—that is already inherently challenging for any child.

Natural physical changes from infancy to maturity are overwhelming and unsettlingly unpredictable. Children naturally monitor their own development, their increasing capabilities, and how they compare with others. Physical maturation is of course overlaid with leaps in intellectual, emotional, and social development—requiring constant adaptation. These genetically programmed processes of childhood leave youngsters impressionable and in need of reassurance—and then the media slap them with an impossible standard, a goal not only of health, but of perfection and conformity. The perfectly formed heroines in magazines, movies, and television tell them that they fall woefully short of the ideal, at the one time of life when they need to feel they're OK.

Even fashion photographers have of late gotten a little annoyed with the airbrushed perfection in traditional layouts. Trouble is, they've gone too far in the opposite direction. Now the trend is to glamorize the hollow, gaunt look of drug addicts, set in grungy, seamy scenes. Sound appealing? Well, in the business, it's been dubbed "heroin chic." We were floored to see an article in the *New York Times Magazine* describing layouts where a "naked and pale" model "crawls on all fours in front of an electric space heater" and where another, G-string chafing her skin, is marked with a designer's name on her buttocks. We were not only flabbergasted by the new layouts but by the premise that "Gee, now we're only offering 'real life' as an alternative" to that plastic, liposuctioned svelteness that all agree is annoyingly false.

Nan Goldin, considered the leader of the "realistic" fashion photo school, "documented the lives of her friends—drug addicts, drag queens, transsexuals and myriad downtown celebrities" and now "says she doesn't mind being emulated, but she does resent being blamed for 'heroin chic' and the pictures that have made drugs glamorous." Why? *Her* photos were in real, not staged settings. This is considered superior to "idealization that comes about as a result of retouching ... now so commonplace that it has become our standard for what's 'normal.'" They don't get it: *anything* that's presented as chic and hip to young girls becomes desirable. So what's a worse image for impressionable preteens to copy: flawless toothpicks or drugged-out zombies?

Shoppers receiving the Victoria's Secret catalog and many others that flood mailboxes know well these impossible stereotypes. But many remain unaware that the buxom, pinched-waist ladies demonstrating the underwear and other garments peddled are really not as pictured. We're informed by someone who works in the catalog art business that images in such pages are computer-enhanced. That's right—busts are made more voluptuous, waists whittled, and thighs chiseled. Lithographic liposuction, narrowing the bounds of what we allow ourselves to be.

Magazines read by teenagers, whether aimed at them or not, such as *Glamour*, *Mademoiselle*, and *Cosmopolitan*, have over the past twenty years radically changed their editorial view of the natural progression of an American woman's life. It used to be that feature articles would show young women attending high school, then college, dating chastely all the while, then finding the man of their dreams, falling in love, throwing a lavish wedding, and then beginning a family, with its problems of how to keep him interested, how to keep the passion alive, how to balance the kids and the marriage. Then along came the women's movement and the sexual revolution, and by the late 1970s, content adjusted. Revised magazine editorial policies endorsed women working, achieving in careers, putting off marriage. Soon the natural progression for the typical reader's life, as reflected in commissioned articles, ran as follows: high school, college, loss of virginity, dating and having sex with several guys, going with someone, living together, breaking up, finding a new guy in the dating scene, living together, and this time getting married, maybe.

Or maybe not: it could be that along the way our typical American young woman discovers she's a lesbian, in which case she finds a "roommate" and they live together while she pursues her career and reads her own poetry in coffee houses. Or, it could be that she is heterosexual, she breaks up with her live-in boyfriend and finds a new one, or she stays with him permanently and works on her career and they never have children. Or, if she tires of waiting for the old commitment-phobe, she gets pregnant and raises her daughter in a single-parent family. Or, her marriage doesn't work out, she gets a divorce, hits the dating scene, finds her own true love, and remarries. Stepkids! Or, after her divorce, she remarries and has kids—blended family. They're all equally desirable, certainly equally worth discussing in articles.

Preteenage girls often sit and pour over these magazines for hours. And what do they learn? They learn that *there's no ideal anymore.* Who needs marriage, when you can live together to "try out" a relationship before taking the leap? And don't tolerate insults, disagreements, or boredom. If you don't get what you want out of a relationship, get out or you're a sucker, or worse, a doormat.

Perhaps the most troubling lesson for young girls reading such magazines is that they are not to trust anyone, or anything, including the security of their own homes. When magazines present "a diversity of lifestyles" as normal, girls must begin to question their realities. Are their ostensibly happy parents living a lie—and will they suddenly shift gears to ... another daddy? A late-in-life sibling? A new career that takes away all the attention? The new editorial ideal is politically liberal, religiously uninvolved, and ethically challenged. Even if you agree that children need to feel good about whatever arrangement they happen to find themselves in, and we do—those living in insecure or less than ideal circumstances should know that all situations are *not* equally desirable, and that they can aspire to live their lives differently.

Advertising an Attitude

Print media assault innocence with more than simply the stories they carry. Advertising is usually centered on eye-catching pictures, each of which we know is worth a thousand words. Often ad agencies sell through positive associations rather than by touting the strengths of their products. We won't be seeing Joe Camel or the Marlboro Man anymore, but the reason they drew such outcry was not that they praised cigarettes but that they gave smoking an *image:* hip, grown-up, sophisticated, macho.

After talking to dozens of teenagers, we don't think that a billboard of a cartoon camel shooting pool, unlit cigarette dangling from his mouth, single-handedly addicted youngsters to smoking. It's true that the National Institute of Drug Abuse recently released the results of a survey showing that smoking among teens is up—with a shocking 30 percent increase since 1991 among eighth graders. But *peer bonding* and *rebellion* are the most potent reasons, not billboards or print advertising.

New York Times writer Richard Klein reports the way films reflect smoking's newfound favor as a mode of rebellion. He cites a study from the University of California at San Francisco, showing that "Half the movies released between 1990 and 1995 featured a major character who chose to light up on screen, a significant increase compared with 29 percent in the 1970's." These are most often the down-and-dirty characters, undeniably appealing but hardly respectable. Klein dismisses Hillary Rodham Clinton's campaign to blame an increase in teenage smoking on films, a rise that comes in the face of a concentrated effort by educators in the past few years to warn teens of smoking's perils.

"As the preaching becomes more intense," he adds, "tobacco use is eroticized and surrounded by the odor of what is reckless and tabooed, intensifying pleasure.... As in a dream, our Granny Government echoes the piety of anti-smoking voices at the turn of the last century, who raised the cry, 'Tobacco is a filthy weed, and from the Devil doth proceed.'" Klein concludes, "Our leaders also sound like temperance crusaders denouncing the 'demon rum.' Hearing this, one doesn't need to be 16 to have some sympathy for the Devil."

Some detractors of Joe Camel snickered that the way his face was drawn gave him phallic features to lure hormone-driven teenagers. But driving down the street and glancing up to the dumb dromedary on the billboard, one is hard-pressed to see the resemblance. Still, it's a crude assault on innocence when little kids see sleazy-looking cartoon characters drooling cigarettes in pool halls as they toddle their way to school. It doesn't jibe with *Bunny Rabbit's Picnic*.

Our poor daughters, at only seven and nine, as well as little Danny, then just three, received just such a jolt to their innocence every day on the way to their religious Jewish school in our neighborhood in southern California. Across the street from the school, hovering over a small shopping strip, was a billboard touting a frequently unemployed actress. This lady's stock-in-trade are her frontal protuberances, and these were displayed with the greatest possible cleavage in a bikini pose that left no peroxided follicle or cellulite-vacuumed crevice unexposed. She presented it all with a pout and her one-word name in large letters above her reclining form. Every day, as Mommy Diane drove the children to and from school, this lady's almost-nude body stole away a little more of our children's sensitivity about modesty and propriety.

The Snare of the World Wide Web

One of President Clinton's highest educational priorities was to put a computer in every classroom. And certainly there are some wonderful uses for them. Writing term papers and books is a breeze with a word processor. E-mail gives children and adults means to keep instantly in touch with loved ones and friends around the world. All this electronic mail could even raise the quality of writing and once again elevate written correspondence to favor. Computers offer ease in organizing, obtaining information, disseminating ideas. All of these activities can benefit those who engage in them by promoting connection and understanding of disparate philosophies around the globe.

But just as guns can be used for good or evil, for defense or assault, computers can enhance or harm. Elaborate screens and blocks have been developed to keep children from Internet access to pornography and degeneracy. Net Nanny (http://www.net-nanny.com), Surfwatch (http://www.surfwatch.com), and Cyber-Patrol (http://microsys.com) are three that can be downloaded from the Internet. Bess, the Internet Retriever, is a blocking system from the Internet service provider N2H2. Yahooligans (http://www.

yahooligans.com) is offered by the company Yahoo, a search company—and many other providers offer their own brands of protection.

The popularity of these devices proves the presence of much material from which children need defense. The problem, as many distressed parents report, is that these restraints do not work.

The antipornography group Enough Is Enough, based in Fairfax, Virginia, reports that the American Library Association's list of "50 Great Sites for Kids" provides unsupervised children in libraries with sites equipped with "hot links" only six clicks away from Internet pornography. Enough Is Enough introduced in fall 1997 an Internet Safety Kit, "a powerful resource to help parents understand the Internet, to enable them to protect their children at home and to work for responsible school and library policies. . . ." So far, libraries have resisted any Internet screening as an invasion of children's right to privacy. Are we the only ones crazy enough to think that children's right to privacy does not extend to all activities—that perhaps there might be areas where children need supervision?

Without such supervision, "An innocent on-line search for 'toys' can reveal graphic images of 'horny housewives and their boy toys,'" according to *USA Today* op-ed writer Donna Rice Hughes in early 1997. "Even the most diligent parental supervision and the best content-filtering software at home will not protect children from Internet porn." She notes that many sites "post free teaser images as lurid as those found in alt.sex.snuff.cannibalism. . . . "

OK, let's say you're a responsible parent and have taught your children their boundaries on the Internet. That's not to say you can control what their friends find, or what they come across when using computers at the library or school. But for the sake of argument, let's just say they stay off the Internet and simply use their computers for entertainment. You know, video games.

"Too many games on the market this holiday season are more violent, more antisocial and generally more disgusting than ever," said Senator Joseph Lieberman (D-Connecticut) at Christmastime 1996. The proliferation of video games that feature not only quick death but Satanic images was enough of a phenomenon to spark a major article about it in the *Seattle Times:* "Darkplay: Why So Many

Computer Games Have Violence and Devil Imagery." According to writer Steven L. Kent, "There's no doubt that games like 'Doom,' 'WarCraft II' and 'Quake' have a larger quantity of violence than motion pictures or television. If such ultra-violent motion pictures as 'Natural Born Killers' and 'Reservoir Dogs' had half as many killings per second as 'Duke Nukem 3D,' audiences would become bored, numb or nauseated."

The creator of the wildly popular Doom, John Romero, explains in the article that buyers see the Satanic references as enhancing their emotional involvement in his game. "When you can invoke fear in people, whether it's through satanic imagery or dark passageways with monsters growling," he adds, "that's better feedback for the player."

While it's true that parents can't hover over their children's shoulders every second, at school or at their friends', they can have policies in their own homes that will set solid boundaries and convey to the kids a strong position. It may sound radical, but we don't think it's necessary for children to have direct access to the Internet *at all*. E-mail is provided by a number of free services such as Juno without connecting to the Internet, and there are few legitimate occasions when a child younger than college age would need much beyond that. Any child can use—yes, actual printed books to get information for school papers, available easily and conveniently at school libraries. Children should still learn computer skills—software chosen by the parent is abundantly accessible, and with that there is at least direct parental control.

Of course, most families have only one computer, and the adults who use it may want Internet access. So you make rules. It is *not* a given that children will break rules; that there is no such thing anymore as the honor system. Families that foster frank, open discussion with children about problem material on the Internet can communicate that pornography demeans both women and men, cheapens a precious relationship, and lowers their aspirations and character. Writing out a set of rules for using the family computer would clarify the limits for your children further. And there's no need to have a modem plugged into the phone line when children use the PC, except perhaps for the few moments it takes to connect with an e-mail service.

Whenever we speak on popular culture's hazards to childhood, we receive questions about the relative perils of the personal computer over television. Because children can control the images and programs, the computer has a major advantage. And computer use beats TV in the amount of attention and brain activity kids expend. As a medium that involves the child, and in particular promotes communication and use of the child's creativity, the computer is better than a medium that places the child in a passive near-stupor.

Having said that, we feel that parents should severely limit both television *and* use of the computer because they pull children away from face-to-face interactions with their families and friends and substitute a phony world on a screen. Fun and even communication on the computer may tug urgently, but they are far less important and rewarding in the ultimate sense than experiencing sensations like wind, kisses, running in a field, and the emotions resulting from performing kindnesses for others. Experiencing the physical world—the changes of the seasons, the blooming of flowers, the colors in the sunset—offers us a true appreciation of living, and a spirituality that simply cannot be expressed or enhanced by hours sitting alone indoors cultivating carpal tunnel syndrome. Even a child who is simply shooting baskets in the driveway is acting, moving, *doing* in the real world—and working out emotions in a physical way that time in front of a fourteen-inch screen does not allow.

Media and Imagination

"Television requires images as opposed to thought . . . the starker, the bolder, the more sensational . . . the more negative [the image or] the charge, the more likely somebody is going to remember it."

—Bill Bradley, former U.S. senator from New Jersey

This was a boldface pull-quote from the final article in a candid and impressively researched series in the *Los Angeles Times*, "Critics of Media Cynicism Point a Finger at Television," which went so far as to implicate its own editors in pressing journalists to inject "attitude," "edge," and "bite" into their stories. It's a fierce competition among the media for audience, so editors "create a pressure that is most easily satisfied by a dash of flip cynicism . . . what I call 'cheap edge,'" says the *Times* Washington bureau chief Doyle McManus.

"Attitude," "bite," and "edge" fit with the tattooed, nose-ringed, slouchy-clothed youth you often see in public places. But they're concepts at odds with the childhood we want for our children. We don't want them ignorant of current history; neither do we want them limited by it. And the only unencumbered time they'll have to invent their own images, to explore their own fantasies, to create their own possibilities, is the few precious years before puberty.

"The modern experience of childhood," writes professor of English Mitchell Kalpakgian in the *New Oxford Review*, "is often an impoverishment of the spirit and imagination, a drab, joyless world where there is 'nothing to do' or everything is 'boring.' Why? . . . [Children] do not learn to look within or discover the power of imagination, but depend upon the external stimulation of video games, movies, television, radio, and such. With no inner life or imaginative spirit, the realm of the soul remains undiscovered and one's sense of reality is reduced to the material, the physical, and the ephemeral." This is the tragic cost of modern life: amidst the noise and the giddiness and the furious diversions, with all our wealth and bewildering choices, our children feel impoverished. We no longer search our inner resources for answers, or even for the questions. There's plenty of time in adulthood to confront all the external challenges. But if children require outside stimulation at all times, imagine the panic if the power goes out, and they find themselves truly alone.

4

The Assault on Innocence by Schools

Schools are no longer childhood-friendly institutions.

- Most American parents have never used or discussed a rubber dental dam. But if their children attended big-city public schools a couple of years ago, they may have heard far more than they needed to know about this handy appliance. Until recently, youngsters learned, as part of an HIV-AIDS prevention curriculum, that holding the piece of thin rubber against female genitals during oral sex prevents transmission of the deadly virus. More recently, diminutive latex dams have been eclipsed in AIDS prevention circles as the protection of choice—by generous sheets of plastic wrap: "Tear off a big piece so you can cover all the necessary parts. . . ."

- A kindergarten friend of our Danny's, visiting our home to play with our son, observed the bag of outgrown clothes we'd set by the front door to give to a local charity. On top of the heap were two sweaters and a parka. "I know why you're giving those away," Danny's little friend offered. "We learned in school that the earth is getting warmer, so you won't need them anymore."

- In sixth grade, Peter Johnson of Boulder, Colorado, "became obsessed with death" as a result of "death education," a program in which students faced disturbing life-or-death exercises under the rubric "situational ethics." The boy was most distressed by "the lifeboat scenario where somebody has to be sacrificed, and they kill off the old people," Peter's mother explained.

- First graders at the Runkle School in Brookline, Massachusetts, underwent classroom "counseling" about the pending sex-change operation of one child's mother, soon to be his father, reported the *Boston Globe*. The only parent notified of the session was the transsexual, who, as part of the process, "spent a great deal of time in the classroom."

These are just four examples of ways schools chop short children's innocence, and in so doing defy the values—and the rights— of parents.

Lurking in the Shadows

Schools are scaring kids by inserting frightening and often unproven lessons into a wide range of subjects. Childhood should be a time of confidence, but in school, kids receive terrifying warnings about the environment, the intentions of relatives, the traps set to entice them into evils like smoking. Schools teach them to distrust parents and to fear friends. They teach that lurking in the shadows are gang recruiters, evil vendors of addictive substances, and perverts looking for victims. In history, children learn that our country acts shamefully. In science, they learn that the air is becoming poison and the earth is dying.

Under the guise of promoting self-esteem and tolerance of others' values, schools deny children guidance and concrete rules of behavior, forcing them into a role of authority, as if they were adults. For example, lessons encourage youngsters to discern which family members are likely to molest them. Environmental curricula suggest that students must personally help clean up the world. Civics class eggs them on to correct corrupt politicians. In social situations, teachers, reluctant to discipline, force pupils to trust their unformed consciences to decide what's right, with the caveat "We must tolerate any perspective lest we injure someone's self-esteem."

Childhood cannot survive relentless fear and premature responsibility. It's that simple. And that dire.

Why the Assault: The New Preparation

Preparation. We've changed the definition radically. We used to prepare our kids for the working world and for home life with concrete skills necessary every day. You know, learning how to read a map. How to sew a gym bag. How to saw wood. How to find a destination from a bus schedule. How to make change for purchases.

People once needed schools to teach them these skills, but with ubiquitous machines and technology, educators admit that many basic abilities are obsolete, and others should be left to specialists. Planning a driving trip? Punch out computerized driving directions from the Internet. Need a tote? Buy a gym bag with a stylish label. Adding on to the house? Leave sawing to licensed contractors with sophisticated cutting equipment. If you're one of the dwindling few without a car, then phone the rapid transit operator for help with your route. No need to ever present proper change for a purchase—the bar-code-reading cash register tells the clerk what coins to hand you.

Children now use calculators for arithmetic, with the accurate assumption that in their automated futures they won't need to scratch a few numbers on a pad. They learn reading, but only to peruse R. L. Stine or laconic menus on the computer screen. They master typing instead of writing with a pencil.

As technology increasingly covers basics, schools shift their preparation away from concrete 2 + 2 academics and toward more *amorphous* preparation—like promoting interpersonal skills, self-esteem, and cautiousness toward sexuality, substance abuse, and other threats. These are the kinds of lessons that schools never used to touch—in part because there was little need for it. But more and more, schools are becoming full-service institutions, "caring for the whole child" in a way once left to parents, as well documented by Eric Buehrer in *The Public Orphanage: How Public Schools Are Making Parents Irrelevant*. He terms this situation "educational co-dependence" and it works like this: parents can't or won't teach values, but kids still need to acquire them. Schools, therefore, willingly fill the need—so thoroughly that they make parents feel like unwelcome interlopers.

Educators think they have a duty to prepare kids for today's grim reality, and they can't help it if innocence suffers when they offer facts kids "need" to know. Suspicion becomes a basic survival skill, based on the assumption that the world is and will be perilous. At the same time, students need to learn caution lest they offend anyone's fragile sensitivities regarding race, gender, or sexual orientation. The effect is to end carefree childhood comfort, replacing it with paranoia, worry, and hypersensitivity.

In today's context, the words of the old standard "School Days" take on new meaning.

School days, school days, good old Golden Rule days

Uh-oh. Gotta change this lyric. We can't have "Golden Rule days" when children may no longer presume to do anything unto others—especially when the very phrase carries unconstitutional biblical associations. Students now learn to refrain from making any judgments about others' preferences out of sensitivity to multicultural differences.

Readin' and writin' and 'rithmetic, taught to the tune of a hickory stick

Swats with a hickory stick have been outlawed in some states and qualify as physical abuse. And school personnel wielding weapons with which to intimidate students violate zero-tolerance rules.

You were my queen in calico

Be careful with terminology. *Queen* could be considered homophobic or, if in calico, could refer to the transgendered community.

I was your bashful barefoot beau

Child Protective Services might want to know about a student without footwear. The school psychologist might wish to institute assertiveness training for a reticence disorder.

You wrote on my slate, "I love you Joe" when we were a couple of kids

A likely case of sexual harassment: unsolicited intrusion on Joe's slate and personal space (even if warranted for possibly contaminating air in the workplace with his naked feet).

Fish Gotta Swim, Teachers Gotta Teach

Though the new preparation model holds that educators can fight social problems by warning children about them at ever-earlier ages, a look at the research proves that the approach is wrong. Programs disseminating information about sexuality, pregnancy, or the temptations of drugs have backfired, only exacerbating the dilemmas they seek to solve.

But educators can't help it; teaching more knowledge is the only thing they know how to do. They organize information into manageable blocks, give it over, and mark milestones of completion. Schools have not been designed or equipped to cater to individual sensitivities and are certainly not set up to guard children against the burden of knowing too much. For teachers, ignorance is always the enemy, so you can *never* know too much. Educators are more comfortable passing on information rather than withholding it to preserve childhood. Guarding innocence means that teachers have to restrain themselves from doing what they exist to do.

Understandably, educators place a huge value on their mission. Diane is often amused at the deference she earns when introduced in schools and colleges as *Dr.* Medved rather than *Mrs.* Medved.

Because being educated is so highly regarded, years spent tenaciously jumping through hoops in postgraduate academia earn survivors disproportionate awe. It's really no wonder that when educators see a problem in society, they conclude that the only way to fight it is to arm kids with all the gruesome facts they can find.

No More Broken Homes—They're Just "Alternatives"

How did schools slip away from their original charge to teach fundamentals and good work habits? Parents and schools worked far more in sync until the disastrous experiment in forced bussing helped to destroy family involvement and local control. Some civil rights leaders derided the entire concept of "neighborhood schools" as merely an excuse for racism, but parents who lived close to the site of their children's education could certainly feel a greater sense of participation—and partnership—than parents who lived on the other side of town. No one who was alive then can forget the havoc sweeping court orders wreaked on the stability of schools. Some campuses closed, others found their local populations replaced by non-neighborhood children who lived hours away by bus.

Other trends dovetailed. In the '70s, baby boomers' New Age, antiestablishment philosophies made selfishness trendy, escalating divorce rates and presenting teachers with weird permutations of the family. Given the new range of students' backgrounds, school personnel revised their terminology to reflect nonjudgmental acceptance of anyone and any living arrangement. No more "broken homes," "illegitimate children," "immoral" alliances. Now there were just "alternatives."

Diane remembers earning her California teaching credentials in the early 1970s, in the midst of this change, by student-teaching at the newly founded Santa Monica Alternative School. There, first through fourth graders decided when and with whom they would learn reading. Sixth and seventh graders sat on the shady campus most of the day receiving school credits for "expressing their emotions." Teachers taught math to a few students sitting on top of desks—if and when students chose to show their interest.

The nation seemed to revel in its uninhibited and exploratory mood. And social problems like drug use, promiscuity, unwed parenthood, and widespread divorce mushroomed. Parents threw up their hands at these challenges, claiming that they were too busy in the workplace simply making ends meet to do much about them anyway. In order to fight the social malaise of drugs and violence threatening their very campuses, educators adopted the preparation model and took on the job of values inculcation—a job formerly left to parents.

The values which schools began to promote essentially embraced the license of the decade. They lowered standards, dropped dress codes, eliminated requirements in history, English, and foreign languages. The result? Most families with the interest and wherewithal to pay for private schools (including, years later, the Clintons for daughter Chelsea) abandoned the public schools. Hoards of parents, especially those with strong religious convictions, preferred to place their children in schools with stricter standards, less violence, and more traditional values.

Though many districts have lately corrected many of these slippages, the '70s shift irreparably damaged public schools. Recent studies show that even *public school teachers* send their children to private schools in hugely disproportionate numbers—in Boston, 52.1 percent of white teachers do; in Los Angeles, 30.1 percent of all teachers do; in Minneapolis, 29.6 percent of black teachers do. This is a whopping difference from U.S. parents as a whole, only 12.1 percent of whom enroll their children in private schools.

With such wholesale defection, public schools have often become merely government schools (rather than parent-driven or sometimes even parent-*respecting* institutions), and private schools have become the refuge of those who want to more fully assert their values. In other words, exposing kids early to all possible threats is the official, government-approved educational method, and those who would rather protect their children's innocence have, where possible, pulled away.

Still, we root for the public schools. Many dedicated teachers and many thousands of concerned parents of public school students (and we're among them) lament this direction and seek to restore childhood for public school children by reestablishing schools' respect for the family. Many other parents haven't raised their voices simply because they don't yet realize what's going on.

Play It Where It Lays

One justification for the assault on innocence in schools is that educators have to work with the students who come to them. To use a golf analogy, they "play it where it lays," accepting the situation realistically and deciding, based on their kids, how to respond most beneficially. They see that children come to school in varying degrees already conscious of the harsh realities of life. For example, no child escaped the impact of the press' allegations about President Clinton's behavior. Children learned about sex acts and terms previously considered strictly adult and had to confront questions about values as played out in the highest office in the land.

Unfortunately, many kids also know too much about other serious problems. Many are suffering from their parents' divorces. If they lived through the O. J. Simpson trials of 1995 and 1996, they know about spousal abuse. Or, sadly, they may know of abuse from first-hand experience. In 1994, there were 2.9 million cases of reported child abuse and neglect nationally, a vast change from 1977's 838,000 cases. In 1996, 13 million Americans used an illegal drug *at least once a month*—and 9 percent of youngsters from twelve through seventeen reported having used an illegal drug that year. Any child with a TV at home hears about abortion, sexual harassment, the character flaws of our nation's leaders, car-jackings, and assaults.

How can we suggest that these children are innocent? And why should we ask our teachers, who by default must "mop up" after some of these tragedies, to act as if they are unusual?

We *don't* assume that only children with a fairy-tale childhood qualify for the designation "innocent." All children, no matter how pathetic their situation, yearn for escape, seek eagerly the placid space and time that are their "entitlement" as children. Some children enjoy this opportunity in large measure; others to a smaller degree. But no matter what the background of the student, educators can enhance and preserve—or at least be conscious of—the special qualities that allow children to be just that.

How Schools Assault Kids: No Such Thing as Right or Wrong

We've just discussed *why* schools lead the assault on childhood. Now let's look at *how* they do it. The first method is through honoring self-esteem over objective standards for learning.

Schools face a difficult job in their mission of preparing children for the future. And it's much more difficult now that advocating a single morality is passé and teachers must not only condone but highly regard the plurality of rights and wrongs that has emerged in our nonjudgmental culture. Now, no feelings are better than others—they're all legitimate and valid once expressed. With this philosophy, teachers can't give kids guidance about behavior that's appropriate, or even *more* appropriate, in specific circumstances. Lack of standards cracks innocence with a double-whammy:

1. Backing off from morals forces children to be adult, in that they must establish for themselves a moral and ethical belief system which teachers are expected to respect rather than shape.

2. Tiptoeing around students' self-esteem distracts schools from the task of promoting excellence in "hard" academics like English and math and shifts the task to one involving intangible, subjective feelings. "Esteemism" has shifted the focus from subject matter to the temporal emotional state of the individual.

Worshiping Self-Esteem

Yes, self-esteem *is* unequivocally important, but mountains of data show that by the time children get to school, their self-esteem is pretty much unshakably established.

Joseph Adelson, professor of psychology at the University of Michigan, surveyed the research data and, in "Exaggerated Esteem:

How the 'Self-Esteem' Fad Undermines Educational Achievement," summarized his findings: "Self-esteem, then, is very deeply rooted, and once in place it is hard—not impossible but hard—to dislodge or overcome. I put this so strongly precisely because the self-esteem literature, particularly in the field of education, does not. . . . In this literature, self-esteem is not inherent but circumstantial, and can be raised or lowered by a teacher's behavior. It is also extraordinarily delicate, and easily bruised."

Schools *could* teach traditionally revered character traits and at the same time maintain students' (subjective) self-esteem; there's no either/or. But that balance of focus has in recent decades moved decidedly toward self-esteem. William Damon, in his excellent book *Greater Expectations: Overcoming the Culture of Indulgence in America's Homes and Schools*, discloses how education has tipped toward "child-centered," in a queer distortion of child development expert Jean Piaget's ideas that children learn by doing. The outcome is that anything kids do and feel gains more attention and glory than non-kid-generated content, like facts and courtesy.

Parents do think the schools should teach values. Damon cites a 1993 Gallup poll indicating that 90 percent of parents agree that public schools should teach the Golden Rule, moral courage, caring, ethnic tolerance, and honesty. Our point is that with the idea that children are their own ultimate teachers, schools rank the virtues they teach *upside down*. The way schools stack it, self-esteem takes precedence over every other moral or ethical value—even over *honesty*, which 97 percent of parents want reinforced in schools.

Consider the implications. Even students who consistently get the wrong answer in math are great students; they just need to try again. In fact, report cards have replaced the word *fail* with the euphemism *needs to improve*, lest the truth hurt children's feelings. The result is that *failure* has become a dirty word instead of an honest, honorable evaluation of status. When kids got real grades, if you failed in math it was bad, but at least you had a frank statement about your performance in math. Now children never hear that they can be poor at anything, so later, if they ever get fired, if they are rejected from a college, or even if they can't get some consumer item they've bought to function—it's the other guy's fault.

Without frank assessments of their daily work at school, they come to expect praise and approval in every context, and can't cope with many normal difficulties of growing up. Because educators twisted the term, *failure* no longer describes your performance; now, panicky kids believe it evaluates *you*.

"One of Those Forgotten Kids": Self-Esteem vs. Right and Wrong

"The principal causes of our adolescents' difficulty are the presence of conflicting standards and the belief that every individual should make his or her own choices, coupled with the feeling that choice is an important matter."

—MARGARET MEAD, *COMING OF AGE IN SAMOA*, 1928

Teachers afraid of bruising their charges' self-esteem weirdly try to apply the old argument that morality is relative in the practical, down-and-dirty elementary classroom. So kids in school get away with behavior that would have brought immediate discipline in years past—profanity, slovenly dressing, and disrespect toward elders, especially teachers. Teachers' eagerness to enhance self-esteem allows the level of crudeness and snottiness to slide to lower and lower levels. Walking down the halls of local public schools, we have been shocked by the rudeness of children toward teachers and the willingness of teachers to shrug and even laugh it off.

The reason is that without strict standards of right and wrong, acceptable behavior flows and bends with available excuses.

What behaviors *do* educators accept from children? Well, it depends.

It depends often on the student's *background*—if he comes from a home that used to be called broken but is now a "single-parent" family, then we must all understand if he steals out of the teacher's pocketbook it's because he's just "acting out" and needs counseling. Fourteen-year-old Barry Loukaitis of Moses Lake, Washington, entered his algebra class and fatally shot two fellow students and the teacher, wounding another student, with a .30-.30 rifle. At his trial in September 1997, two years later, a second teacher who had walked in on the shooting-in-progress testified that he'd told the police Loukaitis was "one of those forgotten kids. Quite frankly, it didn't surprise me he snapped."

What to do in a given situation depends on situational factors as well, such as the *time of day*. The child who gets in a fight right before lunch might be excused as hypoglycemic or suffering from fatigue (perhaps because, respecting the child's self-esteem, his parents enforce no bedtime).

In other words, if we can find any external cause to blame for poor performance or bad behavior, then we must tolerate it—moreover, we must show compassion and rush to provide the support and assistance the student needs to cope.

Right and wrong can depend on one's *viewpoint* at the moment as well. From the viewpoint of the boy who hit his fellow student on the playground, he was merely defending himself (read, protecting his self-esteem) because the other chap called him an insulting name. OK then, go ahead and take a swipe. We understand.

The other day, after witnessing such an incident between two five-year-old boys, Diane overheard the adult in attendance respond with that sickly sweetness one reserves for condescending to children: "Now Joey, we use our words, we don't use our fists." Joey kept hitting his playmate, in fact, with increased viciousness. The adult continued with her melodious plea, this time a little louder, as Joey kept swinging. "We use our words, not our fists." Joey never did have to use his words because finally the other kid socked him a good one in the stomach.

We want to teach our kids that anger is something *not* to be expressed. If you feel it, OK, then immediately think about a *constructive* way to take care of the source of the anger. It's a Jewish principle that "anger is always self-destructive," and a Christian teaching to "get rid of all bitterness, rage, and anger," and the goal is to hone your reactions so that, ideally, you avoid anger all together.

But in schools, anger is just part of the legitimate array of emotions teachers encourage kids to express. You're angry? The accepted answer is to say, OK, go jab a punching bag, scream at the person who makes you mad, write a letter letting out all your rage. It's true that no one encourages physical aggression—though sometimes it's excused—but still, no one says definitively that even *feeling* angry is wrong or even out of place. Instead, teachers say anger is real; your feelings are *good*. You just have to use your words.

Kids raised with the idea that their feelings are always right, and that feelings excuse behavior, end up selfish, arrogant, and rude. And such policies in schools sharply undermine what goes on in the classroom. Instead of sending a belligerent or even violent child to the corner with a dunce cap, teachers kneel down to kid level and try to reason with them. "Now Johnnie," the teacher might say, "why did you hit little Susie?" Then Johnnie tries to con his way out of the situation, and the teacher replies, "But when you hit Susie, it hurt her. How would you feel if another child hit you?" And the discussion goes on, and the kid concludes that when he slugs Susie, he'll enjoy a discussion of how it feels.

When Boston College professor of education William Kilpatrick studied the nonjudgmental approach, he found some disastrous results:

- Classroom "bull sessions" of many opinions but no conclusions, often with no topics taboo

- An undermining of the need for adults to set a good example

- "A generation of moral illiterates: students who know their own feelings but don't know their culture"

and, most importantly,

- "An educational system with a de facto policy of withholding from children the greatest incentive to moral behavior—namely the conviction that life makes sense . . . "

Once students with this perspective graduate from the educational system, we may all be in trouble. Two pieces in the *Chronicle of Higher Education* showed that a fear of criticizing anyone else lets students condone the Holocaust ("Who's to say the Nazis were morally wrong?") and human sacrifice ("The Aztecs practiced it") and leads kids to consider animal rights on a par with, if not more noble than, human life. Leaving the burden of right and wrong to children produces confusion rather than clarity's peace of mind.

No Wrong Answers, Just Good Tries

Afraid to rumple the edges of any student's precious self-esteem, educators "dumb down" academic subjects. That's the premise of Charles J. Sykes' *Dumbing Down Our Kids,* which is jammed with amazing illustrations of how educators have abandoned standards of excellence. Just a few tidbits:

- A "reading report card" finds that 25 percent of high school seniors can barely read their diplomas.

- A third of Americans think humans and dinosaurs walked the earth at the same time.

- A significant group of educators urge teachers not to correct students' spelling lest they interfere with a new fad of "invented spelling," which deems incomprehensible words the laudable work of "independent spellers," who, advocates say, will eventually "get around in their own way and their own time to spelling words correctly."

No wonder Springfield, Massachusetts, canceled its local spelling bee in May 1997 "on the grounds it had become too stressful for children."

Educators in Middletown, California, were embarrassed when national attention focused on a group of eighth graders' letters to the local newspaper. The children addressed vandals who had ransacked their school, but when the paper decided to run their letters as written, the strongest message was about the students' illiteracy: "Dear Vandales," wrote one student, "I really think that you were stuped to mess our classrooms. Our teachers our upseat and so are the students." Another: "Dear Vanduls, I hope your happy now that you just cost us thosands of dollars and ruind are new computers . . . ."

Two Plus Two Equals Whatever You Want

"There were four birds in a nest and one flew away. How do you think the flying bird felt?"

—A MATHEMATICS PROBLEM IN THE NORWIN,
PENNSYLVANIA, SCHOOL DISTRICT

It's bad enough when schoolkids have to "discover" proper spelling. But now a new curriculum assumes kids are better off when they spend precious school time groping around for the most satisfying answers to *mathematical equations.*

Parents across the country are aghast at a program dubbed "whole math," after a failing though popular nonphonic reading method called "whole language." Lynne V. Cheney, former head of the National Endowment for the Humanities, writing in *The Weekly Standard*, describes this astounding innovation: "Also known as fuzzy math or new-new math, whole math is an instructional scheme based on the idea that knowledge is only meaningful when we construct it for ourselves." Using physical objects like pieces of paper or tiny tiles, elevated to higher status by their new moniker, *manipulatives*, students take phenomenal lengths of time to figure out principles *we* all learned by instruction and practice. Its designers determined that "Instead, from kindergarten on, there would be a calculator in every hand so that young minds would be free of irksome chores like addition and multiplication and thus be able to take on higher-order tasks—such as inventing their own personal methods of long division. No more teacher as 'sage on the stage,' instructing a class of students; a teacher would serve instead as 'guide on the side,' offering non-judgmental questions and comments to groups of students working out their own mathematical meanings."

Teachers embrace this approach for a good reason: they're taught to respect it in graduate school. A 1997 poll by Public Agenda of nine hundred U.S. education professors found that 86 percent said it was most important that "kids struggle with the process of trying to find the right answers." Contrast this with the paltry 12 percent who said it was more important that "kids end up knowing the right answer to the questions or problems." And 92 percent said that "teachers should see themselves as facilitators of learning who enable their students to learn on their own," while just 7 percent said that teachers should be "conveyors of knowledge who enlighten their students with what they know."

In the course of blithely reinventing the wheel, children can debate even the sum of two plus two. Enjoying the advantage of others' progress—to avoid having to repeat trial and error—is the basis of civilization. What a burden for a child to flounder searching for an answer that everyone *else* knows is correct—especially when no one will even tell you how close you are. Placing this burden on children forces them to take a certain unnecessary responsibility, and helps to erode childhood.

Too Much Respect

The underlying problem here is that telling children that they're capable of teaching themselves gives them too much respect. When we give authority over mathematics and showing appropriate feelings to a little girl, she's placed in the position of an adult who should know much, when in fact she knows little. Talk about a "level playing field"!

Children only learn the most productive ways to feel, as well as to behave, when we *teach* these to them, explicitly and repeatedly, as they face emotion-producing events. As Miss Manners says in her etiquette book, the most effective method for impressing rules of civility on children is to "nag, nag, nag." By providing only understanding and support, teachers take away childhood by *not* giving feedback about whether or not children's feelings are useful. Childhood, we believe, is that unique time set aside for *guided* (and therefore *sheltered*) development.

We as a society give children latitude on their behavior, determined by their ages. When you see a three-year-old wipe chocolate ice-cream-slathered hands on the front of his shirt, you may think "yuk," but little more. If you see a fifteen-year-old do the same thing, you think it bizarre. Similarly, if you hear a toddler commenting on a nearby adult who passes gas, you chortle; if you hear a college student making the same remark, you think him crude and rude.

To preserve childhood, we shouldn't drop these distinctions by giving kids respect for their immature feelings until they are worthy of it. At the same time, we want them to know that we don't *expect* them always to know what's appropriate, and so, as the authorities, we take it as our primary job to instruct them, correct them, and offer them ample opportunity to practice proper behavior. All with great love, kindness, and reinforcement.

Just as it's rude to correct an adult, it's cruel *not* to correct children when they have wrong answers, or show poor manners or judgment. Even the vast number of behaviors that fall in the gray area, not *clearly* bad manners, or *necessarily* counterproductive, call out for instruction in a positive and upbeat way: "This might come out even better if you try . . . "

Glorifying kids' self-esteem above their achievement not only produces needless burdens for children, but also creates painful distortions when they're adults. Children who expect praise for every notion that originates with them are arrogant. Diane, in her psychology practice, sees grown-up spouses who carry with them the marriage-busting trait, learned in childhood, of denying they can be wrong and finger-pointing to the other in every bad situation. "If everything I do is good, and I'm always right, then everything that's bad is *your* fault," goes the reasoning. Wouldn't you love to be around some brat—or spouse—like that? And forget them trying to change—they're perfect, remember, and they've got no motivation to improve unless they can recognize their own share of failure.

Afraid to Face the World

At the same time that teachers work to make students feel good about themselves, they teach content that makes kids feel bad about the world around them. Authors of curricula seamlessly integrate into their social studies and literature materials countless messages that *the past was disgraceful, the present is dangerous, and the future is grim, horrific, and dismal.*

At the beginning of this chapter, we mentioned sixth grader Peter Johnson of Boulder, Colorado, who "became obsessed with death" as a result of "death education." Author Dana Mack describes one father's distress over his third grader's "depressing" public school curriculum: "In six weeks they studied the Holocaust, the civil rights movement and migrant farm workers. I'm thinking, here you are only eight years old. . . . You're going to feel impotent to go out and . . . face the world at such a young age."

What an unnerving discovery for a child—to find out in school that your ancestors are either evil or victims. Once children identify themselves as victims, they suddenly have a great excuse for lack of achievement. And they have great motivation to play up their victim role, earning them not only general status but admittance to a strangely elite club. We've known bright children of black doctors and lawyers, for example, who speak in black dialect not because of poor language skills but because being part of an oppressed minority is "cool." But there's a cost to all this. Children sophisticated enough to emphasize their victimhood can't be naive. They've lost the hopeful belief in the essential goodness of the world. Believing yourself a victim destroys the optimism of childhood.

Culture-bashing curricula present complex issues simplistically—or with a slant. For example, by middle school most students have read in their history textbooks that the "white man" gave smallpox-infected blankets to Native American populations, who died in great numbers as a result. But along with ahistorical discussions of this "genocidal" crime there is no mention that the Europeans *also* brought the preliterate, technically stone-age culture of Native Americans such aids as horses, the wheel, and writing. Children will learn that the old world infected the New World with measles, but they will get no hint that the Western Hemisphere introduced syphillis to Europe.

"The National Standards for United States History," paid for with $2.2 million in federal funds and issued by the National Center for History in the Schools at UCLA in October 1994, caused a national uproar by its flagrant determination to show our history in a bad light. Developed to specify the content of history programs in districts across the country, the standards went out of their way to promote minorities and diversity at the expense of history's main events. Lynne V. Cheney, director of the National Endowment for the Humanities, an organization that partially footed the bill, called the standards "a travesty," adding "I think they're not only likely to bring an end to the standards movement but will cause a final erosion in people's faith in public education." One member of the sponsoring National Council for History Standards told *Insight Magazine* that their work presents "a history of protest, a history of groups," and poses "many tendentious, leading, biased questions that set up a false dichotomy between aggrieved groups and an oppressive majority or society."

What were the critics incensed about? The "Standards" specifying what kids should cover featured the Ku Klux Klan in seventeen citations, while such luminaries as Paul Revere, Alexander Graham Bell, the Wright brothers, and Thomas Edison failed to receive even a single footnote. George Washington warranted a brief nod without mention that he was our first president. Neil Armstrong's "one giant leap for mankind" was out; "the 'Standards' do, however, herald the former Soviet Union's 'advances' in space exploration," noted former Vice President Dan Quayle. Their slant overall is toward the worst aspects of our culture rather than the best. Fortunately, they were not widely embraced, so the academics went back to work—spending more tax money to revise them.

A survey of adults by James Davison Hunter (University of Virginia) and Carl Bowman (Bridgewater College) shows the reverberations of this negativism. More than 80 percent of respondents agreed that "ours has been a history of war and aggression," and though citizens support our country's founding principles, the professors found "pervasive pessimism about the actual state of our nation's institutions and America as a whole."

"No Thanks" to Thanksgiving

Schools manage to spoil kids' visions of even the festive highlights of the year. Thanksgiving, always a joyous celebration of our land and the sustenance God has allowed us, is in thousands of schools now a secular apology to the Indians. This would have floored

George Washington: "It is the duty of all nations to acknowledge the providence of Almighty God, to obey his will, to be grateful for his benefits, and humbly to implore his protection and favor," he declared in his 1789 Thanksgiving Day proclamation. When Abraham Lincoln established Thanksgiving as a national holiday in 1863, he specified its purpose: to thank God for the year's blessings.

Now children often receive an opposing message. Author Eric Buehrer reports that a Pasadena, California, preschool program director even sent parents the following: "To many Native American peoples today, Thanksgiving is a day of mourning because it is a reminder that in return for their help, knowledge and tolerance of original European settlers, they were 'repaid' with the theft of their land and the genocide of their people."

Christmas, formerly the season for songs about Santa's journey and the reading of Dickens' *A Christmas Carol*, has become merely another opportunity to teach serious multiculturalism. In this spirit of equality, religious and secular celebrations mingle into an amorphous lesson in tolerance—Hanukkah gets elevated from a minor to a major holiday and receives equal billing with Kwanzaa, the African-American separatist holiday invented in 1966 by Dr. Maulana Ron Karenga, conveniently allowing another discussion of slavery and African roots. The Anti-Bias Curriculum, issued by the National Association for the Education of Young Children, officially suggests that teachers blend December holidays into one nonreligious celebration or ignore Christmas altogether.

Scared by a Tainted World

Revised history and holidays are only part of schools' insistence that ours is a ruined world. Social studies texts terrify children with lessons about the planet they are destined to inherit. They maintain, for example that:

- Humanity is destroying the ozone layer, precipitating a global warming that could mean our demise.

- We're covering our country with trash that we wastefully refuse to recycle.

- Greedy developers and businessmen are despoiling the rain forests and causing myriads of precious creatures to become extinct.

Environmentalist curriculum writers squeeze in their messages everywhere they can. The Addison-Wesley text *Secondary Math: An Integrated Approach: Focus on Algebra*, according to the *Washington Times*, "is sprinkled with comments and photos of children named Taktuk, Esteban and Minh, includes the United Nations Universal Declaration of Human Rights in three languages, lectures on endangered species, offers a discussion of air pollution, the Dogon people of West Africa, chili recipes and the role zoos should play in today's society."

Facts Not Fear: A Parent's Guide to Teaching Children About the Environment by Michael Sanera and Jane S. Shaw provides a balance to the alarmist theories public schools typically feed children. Not only do the authors reveal the hidden agenda of environmentalists—to bring as much land as possible to the custodianship of the government for its return to a "natural" state free from the "cancer" of human beings—but they show how the infusion of scare tactics into kids' classrooms fills them with false information and fuels a depressing pessimism about their futures.

Some specifics gleaned from actual texts by Sanera and Shaw, and the reality of each situation:

Kids hear that the polar ice caps will melt from global warming, and soon "only the tops of very tall buildings will be above the water" in New York City. That's what, a thousand feet of water? The scary image doesn't jibe with even the most liberal estimates of polar melt-off—ranging from six to forty *inches*.

Out-of-date information keeps recycling in environmentalist texts to reinforce a grim view of the world. In 1992, two years after chlorofluorocarbons were eliminated from Styrofoam cups, plates, and fast-food containers, *The Weekly Reader* still warned kids that these substances "go directly to the ozone layer and destroy it," encouraging remorse with each Big Mac and milkshake.

Textbooks plant fears that the earth cannot support its population, making children feel guilty for even *existing*. "We in the United States account for about 5 percent of all the people in the world, but we use a quarter of the planet's energy and goods," admonishes *The Kids' Environment Book*. "Think about that the next time you hop in the car to go to the store." Truth is, the United States also produces a quarter of the world's output; "Without U.S. technology," write Sanera and Shaw, "the poor nations of the world would be poorer still."

Michael Sanera reviewed more than 140 science textbooks and more than 170 environmental books written for children, and concludes, "School children across America are being scared green by environmental education." That's because children never hear the bountiful countervailing information that is at least as scientifically sound as the data used to support the frightening position. Information such as:

- A drop in the world population growth rate

- Price declines in natural resources such as copper and oil, which indicate their abundance

- Information that recycling can actually drain resources, and paper and plastic disintegrate at about the same rate in landfills

More good news from other sources: toxic wastes entering the environment are declining sharply every year, reports the Environmental Protection Agency. For example, between 1994 and 1995, releases into the air fell 7 percent, into the water 10 percent, and onto land 6 percent. *A Moment on the Earth* by *Newsweek* writer Craig Easterbrook notes reassuringly that industry cleaned up emissions by 43 percent over a seven-year period; forests are more plentiful than they've been for seventy-five years, and smog has decreased by 40 percent in twenty-five years—but children continue to be besieged by only alarmist news.

"When you look at what is happening in environmental education, it sets any reasonable person reeling at the abuses," Dr. Senera told the *New York Times*. "What the kids tend to get is the catastrophic, doomsday version of environmental problems."

In his evaluation of Wisconsin texts, he concludes, "With few exceptions, I found that textbook treatment of environmental issues is influenced by an ideological view that presents human beings as evil, and blames the United States in particular and Western industrial societies in general for every environmental ill."

Both Sides of the Controversy

Contrary to what children learn in school, the topics of global warming and loss of rain forests—and other hot-button environmental issues—are *controversial.* While many scientists see gloom and doom on the horizon, just as many others come to quite opposite conclusions. We think that schools should frame any action in the positive—it's good to recycle because it's good to be thrifty. Thrift and avoiding waste are virtues. Of course, teachers can acknowledge negative information children may bring up, but when issues are controversial, they need to acknowledge *that* as well, and offer both sides of the argument, with equal respect.

But the best tactic of all is for educators to stick to the basic subject. A review of school science textbooks by a panel from the George C. Marshall Institute in Washington, D.C., found that they "contain too little science," and that instead of facts, "some advocate political positions." "The field should place its emphasis on building environmental knowledge, not on promoting a particular kind of behavior," concludes the panel.

As an aside, Senate Bill 1873, the National Environmental Education Amendments Act of 1996, was proposed to require the Environmental Protection Agency to back "balanced and scientifically sound programs." The legislation passed the Senate but by October 1997 was relegated to committee by the House for further study, and may remain there until melting polar ice caps flood Manhattan.

Mommy and Daddy as Enemies

Perhaps the most devastating message a child could receive from school is that *your own parents* can't be trusted and that school offers your only safe haven.

Both Michael and Diane attended public schools all the way from kindergarten through high school. And when our parents sent off their little darlings in the morning, they felt a fair sense of confidence that the values they wanted to implant in us—and their own authority—would be supported and echoed by the entire school establishment.

Parents today no longer enjoy that confidence. Teachers, principals, and other public educators have in many ways defined themselves in an adversarial position to parents. They imply that they will *rescue* children from the benighted, old-fashioned, restrictive, and prejudicial values that parents want to impose on them. In so doing, they teach that school is a source of enlightenment and concern, with its counselors and health programs and contraception freely available. By contrast, home is dangerous, it's a place where kids can't trust even Daddy's embrace, where relatives might proffer "uncomfortable touches," and where drugs like beer and aspirin and killers like cigarettes tempt unsuspecting offspring.

Charles J. Sykes, in *Dumbing Down Our Kids*, tells about "protective behaviors" curricula that "are distinctive . . . in encouraging children to be concerned about problems that had probably never before occurred to them" like Daddy's tickle, Grandpa's hug, or sitting on Uncle's lap ("Now pretend that Barbara doesn't like sitting on her Uncle's lap because he squeezes her too tight and puts his hand near her private parts."). Dr. Sykes wonders, "The next time a relative asks them to sit on their lap, or a parent tickles a child, or a grandparent hugs a child tightly, how will that child react? What doubts and fears will be kindled? And in the process what will have been lost in the innocent joy a child feels when touched by a loved one?"

Programs set up to teach children how to avoid sexual or physical abuse can cause problems that are far greater than the actual risk of abuse warrants. "If a child is taught that he or she is 'empowered' to do something about a problem, that sets up a situation of complicity, of responsibility," says Joan Duffell, director of community education for the Committee for Children in Seattle. "It means that if something bad does happen to the child, they feel doubly bad because they've been led to believe that they could have prevented it."

Richard A. Gardner, professor of child psychiatry at Columbia and author of two books on the subject, sees other risks of such instruction. Because programs teach that even the flimsiest situations are "abuse," children become unsettled by *any* encounter. And malicious kids can twist the most innocent of situations into ammunition for "sticking it" to teachers or any other adults they don't like.

In fact, Washington Education Association lawyer Jerry Painter advised Seattle teachers to "hug from the side" and told them "the elbow and the middle of the back are the safest places to touch to avoid the appearance of impropriety," according to an Associated Press story.

Dr. Gardner would dump all the abuse-prevention programs: "I've never seen one person whom it helped," he insists, "but I've seen dozens of cases where a prevention program was a big contributor to hysteria."

Dana Mack, in her book *The Assault on Parenthood*, admits, "I personally know that to have a child in the public schools is to combat anxieties about home life brought home from school. My own child worries that her parents drink wine with dinner, that our marital spats will lead to divorce, and that we haven't the wherewithal to handle an emergency properly. For that eventuality, she has memorized a slew of 800 numbers given to her over the course of the years by her teachers."

Schools *teach* children to worry, via exercises they complete as part of antidrug, health, and family life curricula. Mary Breed, of Fairfax, Virginia, pulled her children out of public schools because of antifamily instruction: "My third-grade daughter was told to write in a journal five things she couldn't tell her mother," she laments. In the Here's Looking at You curriculum, sold to districts nationally, an assignment requires primary-grade children to write secret notes to their teachers reporting "problems at home." The program uses appealing animals to lead kids toward suspicion of their parents. "The underlying concept here," author Dana Mack told us, "is that children are learning substance abuse in their families. For example, the implication is that if a parent asks the child to bring a beer from the refrigerator, they're involving that child in drug abuse." With kids clandestinely revealing family problems to teachers, we shudder—it feels too close to Stalinist policies that used to encourage children to inform on their parents.

Taking Over Parents' Role

So watch out—educators now think they know more than parents do about communicating with their kids. And that seems especially true regarding traditionally delicate subjects. Children, meanwhile, must pit a powerful institution against the two people they most love, forcing them into an anxiety-provoking conflict.

For example, religious Christian and Jewish families, choosing to look to the Bible for their values, would like schools at least to allow their children to maintain their scripture-based beliefs. In other words, these parents want the schools to keep hands-off their religion. In practice, however, the official policies of schools become antireligious. Schools refuse to allow anything biblical near the classroom. For example, a teacher who dared to post the Ten Commandments in his classroom was forced to remove them, and schools have disciplined teachers who chose to place their private copies of the Bible on taxpayer-supported shelves.

But in discussing two extremely sensitive topics—premarital sex and homosexuality—schools refuse to acknowledge any religious diversity among students in the classroom. Most public schools blithely overrule religious parents' wishes—insisting on feeding their youngsters values contrary to the Bible that remains sacred to the vast majority of Americans.

"At the Silver Lake High School in Kingston [Massachusetts], the ninth-grade health text *The New Teenage Body Book*—taught sexuality as a matter of trial-and-error and personal choice," writes Jeff Jacoby in the *Boston Globe*. By "personal choice," the book means "anything you want to try," not the choice to refrain. Here's an excerpt from the text: "to give pleasure to another person may be less threatening in the early teens with people of your own sex." Yes, that's a schoolbook *recommending* homosexuality—for "early teens"! It goes on, dashing any tender reader's pang of conscience: "You may come to the conclusion that growing up means rejecting the values of your parents." No wonder the "students were told to keep the book in their lockers and not take it home."

The result of such instruction is that children who might not yet have physically matured feel they need to proclaim sexual choices. Gina De Vries at age twelve announced to parents and friends that she was lesbian, and at age fourteen declared herself "a queer youth activist," which *Time* magazine says is "an identification she uses effortlessly, as though she were saying 'ninth grader' or 'aspiring poet,' other terms that describe her." Her efforts earned her an appointment on the lesbian and gay advisory committee of San Francisco's Human Rights Commission. The *Time* article, "Out, Proud and Very Young" quotes Columbia University researcher Joyce Hunter, who says "3 percent to 10 percent of U.S. teens now tell pollsters they are gay, lesbian, bisexual or 'questioning.'" She adds "the change has been enormous" since she began study in the field in the early 1970s.

Gay activists claim the change reflects the "liberation" of a climate that allows children to demonstrate publicly their sexual preferences. We certainly would support the right of children or anyone to represent themselves in any way they choose. But why should deciding sexual orientation come up in a school curriculum at all? Before kids heard ongoing discussions in school elevating "sexual diversity" to an exalted status, most youngsters never even *thought* about their sexual preferences until faced with choosing someone to date. Almost everyone assumed that he or she would just grow up, get married to one of the opposite sex, and raise a family. By raising the issue over and over, schools *cause* otherwise unpressured kids to question their sexual identity.

Jeff Jacoby, in his *Boston Globe* article, cites more amazing infringements on Massachusetts parents' relationships with their children:

After "Homophobia Week" at Beverly High School, the father of one thirteen-year-old found out about his daughter's program when she "came home and announced: 'Dad, I learned that you're a homophobe.'"

Skip this one if you're sensitive:

A seventh-grade true-false exam in East Bridgewater included such items as "Bigger penises give a woman more pleasure during sexual intercourse" and "Some women can have a wet orgasm just the way men do."

Pardon us for reporting these instances. If you're shocked, we're sorry. Anyone concerned with guarding innocence knows that parents, not the schools, should be the ones to discuss such topics—and children should not have to confront such issues until a more mature age.

The following is an astounding example of the brazen way some school districts push their own values without parents' approval—and in this case, they're proud of it. "We're on a trailblazing path," said Provincetown, Massachusetts, school board member Susan Fleming of their August 1997 decision to teach *preschoolers* and up about homosexual issues. In discussions and by bringing the group known as Parents, Families and Friends of Lesbians and Gays into kindergarten classes, the district plans "to end the 'dominance' of teaching from the point of view of 'white Europeans . . . who are also very heterosexual, very Christian, very male.'"

Schools also disregard parents' values in the books they offer to students. While we do not endorse censorship, we were shocked at the insensitivity to pleading parents shown by letting first graders read the prohomosexual *Heather Has Two Mommies* and *Daddy's Roommate*, both included in a raft of gay-education books purchased for the Seattle public schools under a 1997 grant from Seattle Councilwoman Tina Podlowski.

The books have been around awhile—since 1989 and 1990, respectively—and they're clearly designed for little children. *Daddy's Roommate*, written and illustrated by Michael Willhoite, has full pages of brilliantly colored drawings and few words. A young boy narrates a description of his family, beginning with his matter-of-fact announcement that "My Mommy and Daddy got a divorce last year." Daddy and his new roommate, Frank, do everything together, including sleep in the same bed, but it takes Mommy to explain emotionlessly, stirring a pot on the stove, that Daddy's gay, and "Being gay is just one more kind of love." It's a book that might be explanatory for a given child who finds himself in such a position. But it would most likely puzzle and frighten children from conventional homes, planting in their minds the possibility that *their* daddy might divorce *their* mommy and go live with a man.

Similarly, *Heather Has Two Mommies*, by Leslea Newman, illustrated by Diana Souza, is an effort at an explanation for a slightly older child to whom these circumstances apply. But as a title available to primary grades on school library shelves, this more detailed book blasts innocence by giving children too close a look at processes they would not understand and have no need to know about.

Here, Mama Kate and Mama Jane decide to have a baby: "Kate and Jane went to see a special doctor together. After the doctor examined Jane to make sure that she was healthy, she put some sperm into Jane's vagina. The sperm swam up into Jane's womb. If there was an egg waiting there, the sperm and the egg would meet, and the baby would start to grow."

Puzzled children might naturally assume that all babies are similarly created through visits to a "special doctor" and that poor old dad has no role in the process whatsoever. Readers follow along as Mama Jane confirms her pregnancy. Little baby Heather is born with the help of a midwife, and soon she is old enough for day care. There, she is at first sad to discover that she has no daddy—but luckily, all the children in her play group—except Juan, whose father is a doctor—come from nontraditional families. One has a mom and a sister, another has two daddies, a third lives in a family where all the children are adopted (and one is in a wheelchair). The caregiver concludes, "It doesn't matter how many mommies or how many daddies your family has. . . . The most important thing about a family is that all the people in it love each other."

Parents are not shy about reacting. "They should stick to teaching these babies that 1 plus 1 equals 2, instead of what daddy and his boyfriend are doing in the bedroom," shouted Neil Lodato outside his five-year-old daughter's school, P.S. 13 in Queens, New York. A program that includes *Heather* and *Daddy's Roommate* designed to teach "respect for homosexuals" beginning in first grade caused former school board chairwoman Mary Cummins to reply, "Why single [gays] out for respect? Tomorrow it will be skinheads."

Does such passion alone mean that the irate parents are right? Not necessarily on every issue—but any point on which so *many* parents have such strong feelings should be respected to *at least* the degree that schools respect the feelings of the tiny minority, gay parents.

Schools also can usurp parents' closeness with and protection of their children in the guise of counseling them. Parents rallied to prevent the Virginia Board of Education from installing counselors in elementary schools, worried that they would approach personal subjects, from death to child abuse, in a way inconsistent with their values. The protestors argued that the money would be better spent on reading specialists and classroom equipment, and that parents should be the ones to approach sensitive subjects with their offspring.

Schools have gone so far as to order examination of the genitals of eleven-year-olds, as in the case of Susie Tucker and fifty-seven other sixth graders in the East Stroudsberg Area School District in Pennsylvania in March 1996—without asking or even notifying parents first. At the exam, Susie and other classmates cried, but they were refused permission to call their parents and barred from leaving.

Nationally syndicated columnist Don Feder writes that the real message schools *wish* they could convey to parents is "Look, you're morons. Most families are dysfunctional. We're not going to let you pass your superstitions and prejudices on to the next generation. ... We will determine their values." You'll notice that one important commonality across all these school-parent clashes is that parents are the ones who want to protect their children's innocence, and schools are the parties seeking to "prepare" children by, earlier and earlier, revealing details that used to be reserved for adults. Actually, parents are angry on *two* counts: that their parental role in determining the values accompanying sensitive material has been taken over by the schools, and that their children are exposed to this material, often without their permission.

The Failure of Sex and Drug Education

It would be bad enough if schools spoiled children's innocence for a good reason. But in the case of sex and drug education, they frighten children and confront them with grim, seamy, and unnecessary facts to no avail. After years of implementation in thousands of public school districts, the evidence is in: neither sex nor antidrug education work.

Sex education in our schools has failed in its goal to reduce irresponsible teenage sexual activity. It's failed in its goal to reduce teen pregnancy. It's failed again in its goal to reduce sexually transmitted diseases.

Similarly, antidrug programs that teach children about an array of "addictive substances" haven't proved effective in keeping our youth away from them. A comprehensive study by the California Department of Education in October 1995 found that "more than 40 percent of students polled in a random sample told researchers their decision whether or not to use intoxicants was influenced 'not at all' by programs teaching drugs' harmful effects and strategies for preventing use." What's worse, the 5,000-student, 240-school study found that 90 percent of high school students had a negative or neutral attitude toward drug prevention programs.

A study tracking 10,000 fifth- and sixth-grade students in nineteen North Carolina school districts for four years questioned the effectiveness of DARE (Drug Abuse Resistence Education), used in 70 percent of that state's schools, finding better results at campuses with other programs. The data showed that 18 percent of eighth graders and 24 percent of ninth graders reported drinking alcohol more than ten times or being drunk at least once in the previous thirty days, while 18 percent of eighth and ninth graders had used marijuana in the previous month, with 5 percent acknowledging heavy use. And in the face of a strong antismoking media blitz, 26 percent of the older students had smoked cigarettes in the previous thirty days.

Using drugs is actually *gaining* in popularity. A national study by the Washington, D.C.–based policy organization Drug Strategies reported that 26 percent of fourth through sixth graders *across the country* (40 percent in Los Angeles County!) "believe everyone tries drugs." Furthermore, 82 percent of Los Angeles County thirteen- through eighteen-year-olds believe that "most teenagers will try marijuana," and 86 percent of this group say "marijuana is everywhere."

Recent studies show even more disturbing trends. "More children ages 9–12 are experimenting with drugs, and fewer of them believe drugs are harmful," says *USA Today* in its report on a Partnership for Drug-Free America study released in March 1997. The study showed dramatic increases in drug use since 1993, with 8 percent of sixth-grade, 23 percent of seventh-grade, and 33 percent of eighth-grade students saying they had tried marijuana. Imagine: one-third of thirteen-year-olds have smoked what has become known as "bud."

The study found that "children consider parents a reliable source of drug information," and yet only 29 percent of these sixth, seventh, and eighth graders—just eleven through thirteen years old—would even tell their parents if someone offered them drugs! That's down significantly from the 36 percent of two years ago. This is distressing; the evidence suggests that students exposed to antidrug programs since kindergarten are becoming *more estranged* from their parents rather than more open to discussion of the topic.

Richard D. Bonnette, president of Partnership for a Drug-Free America, said of the results, "This is particularly significant because these children—most of whom don't use drugs now—are seeing fewer risks in drugs just as they're about to move from elementary school to junior high or middle school, where according to the data, drug experimentation rates skyrocket."

High school–age students' drug experiences are even more worrisome. A September 1997 national study commissioned by the National Center on Addiction and Substance Abuse at Columbia University found that 41 percent of high school students said they had actually seen drugs sold at their *school*—while only 25 percent said they'd seen drugs sold in their *neighborhood*.

Perhaps the most relevant finding in this survey is that only 8 percent of seventeen-year-olds say their teachers have a strong influence over their drug use. Unfortunately, 49 percent of these seniors also say they've never had a serious discussion with their parents about drugs.

What do these studies suggest? That parents should take a more active role in staunchly defining proper behavior regarding drugs, and that schools could save millions of dollars if they cut the special programs and urged kids to begin talking to Mom and Dad again.

Primed for Sex

Yes, schools are indeed preparing students for drugs. They also prepare them for sex.

We have amassed such a stack of research on the failure of sex education in the schools that it's difficult to decide which evidence to cite first. Perhaps we'll let the author of a comprehensive article on the subject (*Atlantic Monthly*, October 1994) say it for us: "None of the technocratic assumptions of comprehensive sex education hold up under scrutiny," writes Barbara DaFoe Whitehead after carefully analyzing the data. "Research does not support the idea that early sex education will lead to more responsible sexual behavior in adolescence. Nor is there reason to believe that franker communication will reduce the risks of early-teenage sex. Nor does instruction about feelings or decision-making seem to have any measurable impact on sexual conduct." An evaluation by the Carnegie Corporation of one program, I Have A Future (IHAF), written by unsuccessful candidate for Surgeon General Dr. Henry Foster, "found that not only did IHAF fail to reduce the number of pregnancies, but that those in the program were *more likely* to engage in frequent sex than those in a control group."

Professor Jacqueline R. Kasun also studied the effectiveness of sex ed and found that the seven programs she reviewed produced no decrease in teen pregnancy, though almost predictably, six of the seven did show *increases* in sexual activity. She notes that Planned Parenthood's Guttmacher Institute, the National Education Association, and researchers for Northwestern University and the Department of Health and Human Services all conclude from their research that data are lacking to show that sex ed cuts illegitimacy or sexual activity.

There's more: Educators erroneously push condoms as the magic preventative for everything from pregnancy to HIV. Reports of school staff routinely offering prophylactics, often set out in huge wicker baskets, are so ubiquitous as to sound passé. Glen C. Griffin, M.D., visited the "Wellness Clinic" at Little Rock (Arkansas) Central High, "where last year 10,000 condoms were dispensed as part of a 'male responsibility' program for the school's 2,000 students." While waiting, the doctor picked up a pamphlet that jauntily suggested "safer sex is having fun without taking risks." Silly us. We thought high school "fun" meant cheering at football games and trying on nail polish.

Writing in *Postgraduate Medicine*, Dr. Griffin cites former Deputy Secretary of Health and Human Services William R. Archer, III, M.D.: "Condom education has been touted as the great cure-all for AIDS and pregnancy among teens. It is not. One out of three sexually active teenagers will acquire an STD [sexually transmitted disease] before graduating from high school. And in most cases, a condom would have done little to stop it."

We've seen lots of recent hoopla in the press about the helpfulness of schools' free distribution programs in promoting condom use among sexually active teens, supposedly without increasing teen sex rates. In fact, in September 1997 the *New York Times* ran a front-page story with a three-tier headline: "Condoms in School Said Not to Affect Teen-Age Sex Rate; New York Schools Study; Researchers Call Easy Condom Access 'Harmless' Weapon in Fight Against AIDS." The article described a study headed by Sally Guttmacher (daughter of the namesake of Planned Parenthood's Alan Guttmacher Institute) of New York and Chicago high school students' condom use. But when you look beyond the headlines about this well-publicized study, several questions arise.

According to the *New York Times*, the study compared 7,000 students in twelve randomly selected New York City high schools, where condom distribution began in 1991, with 6,000 students from "10 demographically similar schools in Chicago" without a condom program during the 1994–95 academic year. The researchers found that 59.7 percent of New York students and 60.1 percent of Chicago students were sexually active. Of these, "60.8 percent of New Yorkers used a condom during last intercourse, versus 55.5 percent of the Chicagoans."

Because the media gave this study such prominent coverage, scholars in the field looked carefully at its results. Among them was David Murray, Ph.D., director of research at Statistical Assessment and Testing in Washington, D.C. He considers this study, supposedly heralding the success of condom programs, worthless, because of its plethora of methodological flaws, especially myriad factors confounding each other. For example, both

the New York and Chicago students received years of sex education, varied widely in age (from fourteen to eighteen), had differing
contexts for their self-reports, and differed greatly by ethnicity—
and none of these factors was taken into account in the results.

Yet one variable received enormous play: condoms in the New
York schools. Dr. Murray notes that whether schools offer condoms or students walk around the corner to purchase them is
merely another variable, certainly one that is far less significant
than the implicitly condoning messages about sexuality gleaned
over a period of years and simply reinforced by the campus basket
of prophylactics. A scientifically valid study testing the effect of
condom programs would need a control group—that is, a comparison group of students who did not receive sex education or condoms distributed at school.

And we don't think that a self-reported 5 percent difference in
condom use in last intercourse is such a clear-cut triumph for condom distribution programs. After all, if you believe these results,
and self-reports about sexuality are notorious for unreliability,
these students seem to be engaging in sexual activity at alarmingly
high rates. Is the price to parental communication and teens' modesty worth it when, as this study finds, just a fifth of students
offered condoms even bothered to take them?

Dr. Murray suggests that the Guttmacher study does offer one bit
of interesting data, however, and that is the difference in sexual
activity between ethnic groups. For example, why is it that 69 percent of African-American students in Chicago high schools report
sexual activity, and just 29.6 percent of Asian-American students
do? Why is it that 58.7 percent of "new" African-American students
(though we don't know whether they, too, received sex education
in another school) say they're sexually active, compared with just
8.5 percent of "new" Asian-American students? Something very fundamental about the values of these students, caused by out-of-
school factors, whether religious or social, must be affecting these
students' behavior. Educators and researchers who really seek to
enable high schoolers to resist their hormonal urges should find
out how these Asian-American students remain chaste in decidedly
unfettered milieus rather than touting condom programs among
discouragingly sexually active teenagers.

The big news of the study was, of course, that with or without free condoms, despite ethnic differences, the students in both urban populations reported very similar rates of sexual activity. The researchers interpreted these nearly identical rates to suggest that all these free condoms floating around the school supposedly didn't cause "harm." In other words, their availability didn't push teens who wouldn't have otherwise indulged into becoming sexually active.

That's important in order to justify distributing condoms and to quiet parents who oppose condom giveaways. Armed with these results, condom boosters can say "See, your tax dollars *are* well spent! Offering condoms free to kids in schools doesn't bring the promiscuity you fear—and may actually save kids' lives!"

We wonder the extent to which the rate of teenage sexual activity, comparable between the districts studied, may have been more influenced by the populations' similarity in one crucial factor than by the relatively minor difference of condom availability. That crucial similarity is that *both New York and Chicago students had received years of AIDS and sex education*. Could it be that being fed information about sex, disease, contraception, and condoms over several grades has at least as much impact on sexual activity as a basket of prophylactics left out on the school nurse's counter?

Could it be that both urban groups are more sexually active than a cohort who never received sex instruction? Since sex ed is so prevalent in urban schools, we may never know the answer, but contrast the 60 percent sexual activity rate of Chicago students, all of whom received HIV/AIDS and sex education, with the 53 percent of high schoolers nationally who had had intercourse as of spring 1993, according to the Centers for Disease Control. Though the New York–Chicago study heralds "success" for the free condom program, it doesn't even touch upon whether having the devices available encourages *increased* levels of activity among those *already* lumped in the "sexually active" category. Bottom line: researchers eager to justify condom giveaways *interpret* ambiguous results in line with their philosophies, and the press popularizes it. That prospect alone troubles anyone hoping to slow down kids' jump into adult behaviors.

It's not the condoms per se that parents find objectionable; the assault on innocence comes from the entire milieu and official attitude, in which schools consider teenage sexuality a given, and prepare students for this "fact" from an early age.

Sliding into Sexuality

When Barbara DaFoe Whitehead conducted her research, she went to great lengths, including attending a teacher-training conference of the Network for Family Life Education in New Jersey. The session opened with instructions to "Turn to the person next to you. Make eye contact. Say 'Hello, penis.' Shake hands and return the greeting: 'Hello, vulva.'"

Are you embarrassed to be chuckling at that? Desensitizing both adults and children to sexual language is part of the innocence-destroying process. In the earliest grades, teachers ease children into this subject by first discussing their *emotions*. "In early sex education feelings talk and sex talk are closely related for good reason: little schoolchildren do not have the capacity to understand big adult issues directly," Dr. Whitehead explains. "But many are now exposed to big adult issues at an early age, and so it is necessary to find routes to understanding. Early sex education thus turns to affective pathways and to a therapeutic pedagogy."

If gently sliding children unknowingly into sexuality sounds frightening to you, imagine what it does to the children, in both the short and the long term. "The unifying core of comprehensive sex education is not intellectual but ideological," Dr. Whitehead cautions. "*Its mission is to defend and extend the freedoms of the sexual revolution* [italics added], and its architects are called forth from a variety of pursuits to advance this cause."

"In New York, second-graders stand before their classes to name and point to their genitals. In California, children model genital organs in clay and fit condoms on cucumbers," notes Professor Jacqueline R. Kasun in *Policy Review*.

Wait! We don't want our Sarah, Shayna, or Danny indulging in "the freedoms of the sexual revolution"! We don't want them "comfortable" with sexual language, or nonchalant about models of genitals. We've taught them the Jewish concept of *sniut* (modesty) that is directly at odds with sex ed programs.

If sex education fails, what works to retard promiscuity and reduce teen pregnancy? Fear (of AIDS) and "directive abstinence" (resistance skills) work for boys, according to a major study by Leighton Ku, Freyn Sonenstein, and Joseph Pleck. Abstinence programs do work, and the evidence is mounting, including a study in Planned Parenthood's *Family Planning Perspectives.* Dr. Whitehead reports that teens with moderately strict parents have least sex; those with permissive parents have most. Religious teens refrain from early liaisons; conversely, premarital intercourse is highest among those with no religious affiliation. Girls from single-parent families are more likely to engage in early sex than those raised in two-parent homes. But it seems clear that postponing sexuality—or promoting traditional families—is not the aim of public school sexual education. Instead, under the mistaken premise that "all knowledge is empowering," these programs crush the essence of childhood.

Letting Kids Be Kids

We'd hope that schools would help parents refine and uplift their children, but instead, policies imposed in those hallowed halls dull, lofty aspirations and thwart the natural exuberance of childhood. Aggressive campaigns to root out sources of violence and sexual harassment in the schools turn the innocent actions of little kids into sinister threats. Lexington, North Carolina, first grader Johnathan Prevett got in deep trouble when he dared to plant a kiss on the cheek of a classmate. When our five-year-old Danny returned from kindergarten admitting that he had also so honored a flattered classmate, we launched into a warning that he could earn suspension for that kind of "sexual harassment." No longer is a kiss just a kiss or a sigh just a sigh—even if you're seven years old.

Kids get nailed when they unthinkingly bring "weapons" to school under strict zero-tolerance policies designed to increase safety in the halls. "Principals have no prerogative," said District Superintendent Don Henderson of Hopkins, South Carolina. "When a weapon is found, the police have to be called." Except that in this case the suspect was eleven-year-old Charlotte Kirk, a sixth-grade honor student who was suspended for a week—for carrying a knife in her lunch box to cut her chicken. "Mom was busy and dad had gone to work" that morning of October 18, 1996, so Charlotte packed her own lunch, including a smooth-edged knife for the leftover chicken.

Charlotte's misfortune came within weeks of five-year-old Ryan Hudson's suspension for carrying a beeper to Kiln Creek Elementary School in Newport News, Virginia; the ten-day expulsion of a fifteen-year-old Indianapolis girl who brought a Swiss Army knife to school to scrape resin from her violin strings; and the suspension of a thirteen-year-old Ohio girl for daring to carry Midol onto school property. A year later, Colin Dunlap, a student at DuPont Junior High School in Belle, West Virginia, earned suspension for giving a fellow student a cough drop. And how about the November 1997 case of first grader Seamus Morris, who dared give a classmate a *lemon candy*? His teacher at Colorado Springs' Taylor Elementary School called the fire department because she spied the "unknown substance," and the six-year-old suffered a suspension.

Then there's the amazing case of the teacher-enabler. In October 1997, thirteen-year-old honors student Justin Hodges and his friend Matt Merritt were suspended from Bailey Bridge Middle School in Richmond, Virginia, because they possessed a single Alka Seltzer tablet—which was given to Justin that morning in school *by his science teacher* for use in an experiment! The tab was an extra, and Justin stuck it in his pocket and forgot about it until reaching for his lunch money, when he took it out and began playing with it with his friend. Beyond a ten-day suspension, the boys' punishment for "possession of a non-prescription drug on school grounds" included a drug intervention class.

In each of these cases, educators banished common sense and good judgment based on the particulars of a case, and instead generated hysteria. Perhaps the most noteworthy illustration of zero tolerance is that of ten-year-old Jeffrey Parks, who was expelled from John Rogers Elementary School in Seattle because, while fishing for lunch money in his pockets, he found a gun. That is, a *one-inch-long* green plastic molded replica that belonged to his GI Joe doll.

Why can't we let kids be kids? Because once we eliminate child-hood and treat children as adults by introducing sexuality and knowledge of drugs in kindergarten, all kids can be viewed as potential harassers. Now that they're sophisticated and hard-edged, all kids, in the most harmless of circumstances, can be suspected of perpetrating violence. Seattle School District spokeswoman Dorothy Dubia defended the expulsion of gun-totin' Jeffrey Parks, saying that the policy was very clear: a sign on the front door of the school reads "Weapons of any kind are prohibited." A kiss is not a kiss, and an inch-long plastic gun is *not* a toy.

Teachers with the purest of motives now feel afraid to touch even hug-needy children in their classes lest they face accusations of molestation. We have mentioned the case of the elderly Kansas crossing guard who was fired in spring 1997 for hugging one of his little charges. A dad in Bristol, Connecticut, was banned after a flawless ten years of volunteer Little League coaching when he gave one boy a congratulatory pat on the backside in May 1997. Teacher Roderick Crochiere of Hartford, Connecticut, was fired and suffered a nervous breakdown after a student came forward and accused him of fondling her during a music lesson six years earlier. No charges were pressed, but Crochiere's case went to the State Supreme Court before his teaching license was reinstated. Richard A. Gardner, author of *Child Abuse Hysteria*, told *Insight Magazine* in 1994 that it's "only in the last ten years that I've started to see obviously false accusations. I used to see a handful of such cases, every once in a while. Now, there are thousands of cases, all over the country."

In the suspicious, paranoid mind-set of public school administra-tors today, kids can't be kids and teachers can't be caring. Saving childhood requires returning to a time when adult authority figures are not only allowed but expected to provide encouragement that lets children feel secure and appreciated. Schools are failing in their mission if they can't teach children prudence and common sense without causing them to flinch in fear with each embrace.

5

The Assault on Innocence by Peers

"Back then, we were young cocky punks, plain and simple."

—MIKE WEBER, TWENTY, FORMER
GANG MEMBER

Such a cavalier attitude. Just three years before, his gang had earned headlines for their drunken troublemaking, aggression with weapons, and particularly for assaulting and raping high school girls in a competition to earn points for sex with the greatest number of conquests. By age twenty, he'd spent time in jail for assault with a deadly weapon; shortly after his release he got in a fight, falling with a stab wound that required sixty-five stitches to close.

During the gang's heyday, after several teenage girls came forward with complaints, the police made a sweep and arrested a handful of the alleged offenders. All but "a 16-year-old charged with lewd and lascivious behavior with a child of 10" were let go after only a few days' custody. After their release, the boys returned to their high school as heroes, welcomed back by their cronies with cheers, hugs, and slogans on T-shirts. They appeared on national TV morning shows, bragging that their parents bought them condoms by the boxload and boasting of their achievements: one youth claimed to have earned sixty-six points for his assaults.

135

"The girls turned on me because it made it easier. It was easier to blame me, to think, 'She must have done something to have something so horrible happen to her.'"

—GINA DAY, RAPED BY A MEMBER OF THE
GANG WHILE A SOPHOMORE IN HIGH SCHOOL

Before, she had been a cheerleader and honors student. Then one day, one of the gang members called her out of a meeting at a Catholic church "to talk," and instead raped her. For telling the authorities, Gina's friends ostracized her, even girlfriends she'd known since kindergarten. She eventually dropped out of school to study at home, demoralized and frightened by gang members who would "take swings" at her in the halls and call her a bitch, a whore, and a slut. Gina appealed to school authorities for help, and repeatedly named the perpetrators on the forms they gave her, but administrators took no action to stop the abuse.

It's sordid stuff. Boys out of control, basking in their own power to intimidate with violence, force, and bravado. All eighteen or younger, they victimized girls and terrorized classmates.

In the three years after their 1993 arrests, one of the gang's leaders was gunned down in a fatal Fourth of July fray. A second one went to prison, sentenced to ten years in the California Men's Colony for thirteen fraud and burglary convictions. A third, who claimed feeling "stressed out and depressed," fathered two children but remained unmarried and had difficulty holding a job. In those three years, key gang members fathered at least seven children out of wedlock.

You may be mouthing the cliché "It's a tough life on the mean streets of the inner city, surrounded by drugs, poverty, and crime."

But you'd be wrong to apply it here. These kids were the Spur Posse, a collection of affluent, achieving athletes who attended Lakewood High, in a stable Los Angeles suburb of 76,000 residents. The arrogant gang members willingly lapped up the attention of the press with swagger and self-congratulation. Even the parents of the young thugs felt powerless in the face of the influence of their offsprings' cohort.

"Nothing my boy did was anything any red-blooded American boy wouldn't do at his age."

—DONALD BELMAN, FATHER OF GANG KINGPIN
DANA BELMAN

"The kids' friends become their family. They watch TV and want more and more. They aren't content with just living. They drink too much. They think everything is supposed to be fun."

—DOTTIE BELMAN, MOTHER OF DANA
BELMAN, EX-WIFE OF DONALD BELMAN

The Spur Posse shows the strength of peers to pull even kids with everything going for them down to depravity. When news accounts flooded the media, parents of preteens and adolescents shuddered in fear that their children, for all appearances doing fine, were really as corrupt and perverted as these likable-looking jocks.

And for all their tragedies, the Spur Posse influence continues to afflict its members. "They haven't changed," says gang founder Dana Belman's mother, Dottie. "All the kids are still out doing what they got their names in the paper for. It's been shocking and terrible."

Teenage boys have always found nefarious ways to express the sudden surges of their testosterone-powered manhood. But never before have they taken so lightly behavior that is serious, danger-ous, and even deadly. The stylishness of "pushing the envelope" is a draw for girls as well, as formerly taboo behavior becomes chill-ingly trendy.

The assault on childhood by peers advances on five fronts: drugs, sex, criminality, self-mutilation, and rudeness.

"I Smoked but I Didn't Inhale"

When William Jefferson Clinton uttered those immortal words in the campaign of 1992, he not only brought chuckles to constituents but delivered a potent message about the power of peers to push kids toward drugs. Even though the Rhodes scholar was no slave to the demon weed, in a situation where a marijuana cigarette passed from lip to lip, he felt too embarrassed to just say no. If you believe his account, young Bill took the only socially acceptable course—he faked it, putting the roach to his mouth nonchalantly—and holding his breath.

"The Centers for Disease Control talks about drug fads being in five-year cycles. Everybody was into crystal meth. . . . Now they're doing what they call 'chiva,' which is heroin. . . . They do what they call 'drips.' They put it in a little nasal dropper and stick it in their noses. It goes right to the brain. All my high-school age kids are doing it."

—KATE PAVICH, SUBSTANCE ABUSE
COUNSELOR FOR THE ORANGE COUNTY,
CALIFORNIA, HEALTH CARE AGENCY,
JULY 1996

Yes, fads among eagerly conforming teenagers still frustrate parents. Nike athletic shoes. Baggy pants. Irregularly shaped haircuts. These kinds of startling fashion statements are nothing new. But popular fads have seldom played so destructive a role as they do today. In the month before the survey, drug use for eighth graders—kids just thirteen years old—nearly tripled in only six years, from 5.7 percent in 1991 to 14.6 percent in 1996. In 1991, 36 percent of high school seniors had tried marijuana at least once, but by 1996, 45 percent reported at least one exposure. *This* fad's a lot more dangerous and unlawful than hula hoops.

Teens overwhelmingly condone breaking the law with drugs. A 1997 national study by Columbia University asked kids whether they would report someone using drugs at school, and only 22 percent of seniors said they would. What's worse, just 26 percent would report someone *selling* illegal drugs at school. They all want to be cool.

"Just say no" sounds good to adults, but even in the tightest spots, kids *want* to say yes. They want to rebel, and one of the easiest ways to do it is to ignore anything an adult tells them to do. Remember, 40 percent of kids polled from 240 schools say drug classes like DARE influence them "not at all." Research now shows that the only antidrug programs that work skip the adults and engage kids only with each other, in discussion and role-playing.

Teen Magazine told three "true stories" in the first person about girls' experiences with drugs and alcohol. Listen to Karen, who came from an intact family that she found "boring":

> Everyone was drinking and smoking. One guy handed me a plastic cup filled with some liquid. He told me to drink it. I took a sip. It was the most awful-tasting stuff I had ever tasted. But I pretended that I enjoyed it and took another sip. Melissa came over to me and whispered in my ear that if I drank the whole thing at once it wouldn't taste so bad. I took a deep breath and swallowed all of it. . . . Another guy came up and offered me another drink which I gulped down. Melissa came over to me and offered me a "joint."

Talk about uncritical conformity. Whatever these guys told poor naive Karen to do, she was going to do because she desperately wanted to impress them. Doesn't matter that the paper cup a stranger hands her has "the most awful-tasting stuff I had ever tasted." He told her to drink it, and hey, he's a guy. Reminds us of the film *Young Frankenstein*: "Walk this way" says the bent Igor, and the visitor to the Transylvania castle follows the hunchback with the same crippled gait. In the same way, kids don't evaluate the merit of requests or dares or even facial expressions of friends. They do whatever it takes to be accepted—be cool first, think later.

I Just Wanta Be Loved

Schools may think they can control teenage sexuality with logic and scary stories, but no—statistics show that many teens as young as twelve become sexually active. Parents, studies indicate, have a better shot than schools at helping youth avoid teen sex, but it takes an entire upbringing of old-fashioned values and an ongoing close relationship (not a village), both too rare and precious in our fast-track society.

All the blocks set carefully atop each other tumble, though, when a teenager thinks she's "in love."

A whopping 83 percent of girls between twelve and nineteen surveyed by Mark Clements Research, for *Parade* magazine said that girls engage in sex because boys pressure them, or for fear their boyfriends will drop them if they don't. In addition, 86 percent of the girls thought boys pressured each other to have sex, and 70 percent said that girls pressure other girls. As one fifteen-year-old respondent put it: "Many girls 'do it' to be popular and to feel loved and wanted." Added a sixteen-year-old virgin, "It is very hard to abstain when it seems like everyone but you is having sex."

In a sexual context, the peers who count are not school chums, but that one guy who's got you parked in his car, or that one voluptuous girl who's dressed to kill. Gaining guys' approval means playing the seductress. "Girls Just Want to Fit In, But the Dresses Many Are Donning Aren't Very Fitting" heads a *Milwaukee Journal Sentinel* story describing the outward sexualization of girls who in the old days would have worn puff sleeves and dotted Swiss: "'Limo wear' has devolved from frothy ball gowns and ballerina pumps to slinky slipdresses and killer stilettos, from Sandra Dee to Tori Spelling, from sweet to tart. Today, many junior-sized girls are pouring themselves into $150 gowns so provocatively styled, so fearlessly slit and drenchingly sequined that the adjectives range from 'sophisticated' to 'sexy' to 'slutty.'" It's clear they're a come-on: "These clothes are just like a label saying, 'I'm ready.' It's like the girl is saying, 'I want to have sex,'" notes Cleveland psychiatry professor Sylvia Rimm.

"The peer group is the most powerful component of the young adolescent's audience, and this is why young adolescents are so bent on conformity in dress, behavior, and language," writes David Elkind in the *Boston Globe Magazine*. It's the behavior angle that propels them into early sex: "If all my friends have boyfriends, I don't want to be left out," said a fourteen-year-old we asked. And the standard in many circles is that a boyfriend expects sex by the third date. From there it's a short hop to unwed pregnancy: 80 percent of teenage girls under age twenty who have had sex at least once get pregnant. That's 40 percent of *all* teenage girls.

So the pressure to have sex at a young age comes from two

sources—for boys, the passion of the moment; for girls, a desire to be loved. And from friends. These are powers nearly impossible to combat with admonitions from institutions, especially since officials only begin their warnings at puberty. By then it's too late. Parents need to start teaching underlying values about self-discipline and self-respect at infancy. Once kids enter the world of sexuality, they lose their innocence forever.

Crime and Innocence

As the public grows more fearful, and more outraged at horrific murders by children, states increasingly pass laws to allow sixteen- and seventeen-year-olds to be tried as adults. When thirteen-year-old Barry Loukaitis, who opened fire on his math class in Moses Lake, Washington, killing three, was sentenced in October 1997, he received two consecutive life terms *plus* 205 years, without the possibility of parole.

"This generation is the young and the ruthless," muses James Alan Fox, criminal justice professor at Northeastern University in Boston, commenting on the Justice Department's 1995 comprehensive report on juvenile crime. It's a report that showed that the murder rate for youngsters fourteen through seventeen increased 165 percent from 1985 to 1995. The same study highlighted a stunningly widespread prevalence of firearms—22 percent of kids in inner-city high schools said they owned a gun, and 10 percent said it is "OK to shoot a person if that is what it takes to get something you want."

And kid criminals are not just a small band of inner-city thugs. We've dropped the age of responsibility because an astonishing number of youngsters have early-on lost all trappings of childhood. In 1995, according to the *Sourcebook of Criminal Justice Statistics*, 16.4 percent of murders were committed by children under eighteen—that's almost *double* the 1977 figure of 8.5 percent.

One of the most shocking illustrations of peer influence was the October 1997 murder spree of Luke Woodham, a sixteen-year-old sophomore at Pearl High School, in a suburb of Jackson, Mississippi. Police maintain he was part of a conspiracy to kill those disliked by a band of seven teenagers, who allegedly called themselves the "Kroth." Entering school with a .30-.30 hunting rifle concealed beneath a baggy overcoat, according to witnesses, Woodham calmly and methodically killed Christina Menefee, sixteen, who had shown the pudgy, studious teenager kindness in the past, and Linda Dew, a seventeen-year-old who, classmates say, like Woodham, endured other students' teasing. But it was leader Grant Boyette, who authorities claim dabbled in Satanism, admired Hitler, and used Woodham as his puppet, who propelled the murderous fury and allegedly told Woodham to "just kill her [Christina Menefee] and be done with her so he'd never have to see her again." Police investigators say it appears that Boyette also coached Woodham through the torture and bludgeoning of his "beloved" family dog, Sparkle.

After the school's assistant principal cornered Woodham in his car, holding him at gunpoint until his apprehension, police found the boy's mother in the family home, dead from repeated stab wounds. A "manifesto" one of the accused accomplices brought to police revealed the names of other students targeted for extermination and said that the deadly group had been meeting for more than nine months to plan activities ranging from napalming the school to making their escape through Mexico to Cuba.

Gangs of various sorts have commonly bonded young boys for generations, but their acts have never been as vicious and heartless as they are today. Diane interviewed Tony De La Rosa, a Mexican-American native of East Los Angeles, for her book *The American Family: Discovering the Values That Make Us Strong*, coauthored with Dan Quayle. Now in his late sixties, Mr. De La Rosa recalls his youth roaming the streets with his older brothers when they formed the notorious White Fence Gang. At the time, he recollects, "It was just a neighborhood gang, for friendship." There was certainly an edge of violence, and his brother even "got shot once," but he assured Diane that the gang was more of a bonding experience than a means of rebellion or flaunting the law.

Now, the purpose of many gangs is both: bonding *and* crime.

"In Chicago, a 14-year-old girl is shot to death by an 11-year-old gang member who is in turn found dead a few days later, two bullets in the back of his head; his suspected killers are 14 and 16."

Nancy, sixteen, tattoos around her eyes proving her gang-member status, reminisces about her life of crime and decadence from California's Camp Scott, where she is incarcerated for possessing an opium pipe and threatening a police officer: "When I went to school, I saw certain things—I loved it! The gangs, I loved them. The people in them were always laughing. . . . So I did all these things, just to do them. Every bad thing, I did it good. . . . My life has just stopped since I been here. But when I get out, it's going to be just the same." The lure of laughter with friends has potent consequences.

Dan Korem studied gangs internationally for his book *Suburban Gangs*, and found that the most prevalent type is formed for the express purpose of committing crimes: "The lure of delinquent gangs is typically financial, physical or sexual assaults, and thrills—the rush of doing something on the edge that gets the adrenaline going." He talks about "pre-gang groups" of twelve- and thirteen-year-olds, many of whom enter through skateboarding, where "the anarchy symbol, skulls, upside-down pentagrams," and other markings identify riders' boards. And he cites one 1992 gang in Lancaster, Pennsylvania, made up of kids just ten to fourteen, caught "threatening youths, assaulting others and shoplifting" before law enforcement officers broke up the group.

Kids eager for acceptance and faced with the group mentality take risks they'd never consider alone. Writing in the *Los Angeles Times*, Bettijane Levine describes local crimes over just a few weeks' time:

- Four fifteen- and sixteen-year-olds "looking for someone to scare" in Lake Tahoe were charged with blasting four bullets into a fifty-nine-year-old man out for a stroll.

- A trio of youths, one of whom was twelve, were charged with kidnapping and shooting to death a fifty-seven-year-old Pomona man as he pleaded for his life while they took his Toyota for a joyride.

- A fourteen-year-old boy was murdered in Tustin, California, for trying to reclaim a stereo his grandfather had given him. Charged were five fifteen- to seventeen-year-olds.

- A pair of girls, ages thirteen and fifteen, were charged with beating a thirty-two-year-old woman to the ground and attempting to steal her purse and her car in West Hollywood.

In each of these cases, the barely pubescent accused did not act alone. Two, three, four, or five consciences were not better than one; to the contrary, the effect of others was to goad rather than guard. And with youth now steeped in self-esteem–elevating curricula, as well as "values education" that refuses to say one course is superior to another, children trying to impress each other have few brakes to apply to their passions.

"If you ask why I get in trouble, I'd have to say it's from hanging around with the wrong people, at the wrong time. . . . The only way I fit in when I'm with them is if I do something bad. In order to earn respect, you got to do it too."

Speaking is "Tamara," fourteen, interviewed in the *Los Angeles Times*. She has bright blue fingernails, black lipstick, and a stud through her nose. She's been expelled from school for beating up "some girl who was yapping in my face." She has been arrested repeatedly, for a variety of crimes including grand theft auto and petty theft. Her first arrest was at age twelve when she left home in her mother's car after "pulling two kitchen knives on her."

Though peers tend to drag down a borderline kid, in Tamara's case, they might have saved her life:

"My friends, they won't let me get my hand on a gun. They say I'm trigger-happy. I had a gun once. I saw one of my enemies . . . I would see her and think 'Oh man, she just says stupid things. She's like a little rat.'. . . I was like really seriously about to shoot her. My friends, they were like, 'It's not worth 25 to life.' . . . My friends, they talked me out of it. Then later I thought, if I had done her, she wouldn't be here to bother me."

Hormone-driven boys have always been society's major trouble-makers, though now the ages at which boys participate are younger. Unlike earlier times, however, a significant number of young girls like Tamara are becoming involved, giving up Barbies and picking up Barettas. In 1965, 37.4 per thousand eighteen-year-old girls arrested were apprehended for violent crimes. By 1988, the figure had skyrocketed almost fourfold, to 133.4 per thousand. The jump is even more shocking regarding drug offenses; in 1965, 25.2 per thousand eighteen-year-old girls arrested were taken in for drug violations; by 1988, the rate had ballooned to 364.

"Some girls are living out a troubling interpretation of feminism that contends . . . that girls can do anything boys can do, and just as well. Including breaking the law," writes Elizabeth Mehren. It's a permutation of the new nonsexist, nonracist, nonethnic stance taken in schools and media: we used to protect women and children, assuming their more tender natures. Now we consider it discrimination to assume *anything*, and differences once guarded we intentionally erase. Both childhood and femininity suffer.

Piercing, Tattooing, and Branding: "There Is a Definite Brotherhood"

Just a fad: as a true baby boomer, Diane once wore flowered bell-bottom pants, love beads, and peace symbols. Diane remembers more than one occasion when her dad told her to go back inside and put on a decent-length skirt. Then there was the hair-and-beard issue—Michael once annoyed his parents with unkempt facial growth, and the author's photo in his first best-seller, *What Really Happened to the Class of '65?* (1976), shows a head haloed by four-inch-long curls. Leave aside the fact that clothes styles are comin' 'round again; decorative fads in the past may have seemed radical, but at least they were temporary. You could always cut your hair or put on a longer skirt, as many of Diane's cohorts were forced to do when they failed the kneel-on-the-chair test at school.

Even in those days, peer-group identification was based on externals. Membership in "the Woodstock generation" was largely a matter of age and wardrobe. Countercultural boomers even developed a special handshake, providing instant bonding at peace marches and Dylan concerts.

Differentiation from the older generation has always been the major task of adolescence. Unfortunately, now that task begins far earlier than before, and its visuals carry far more malevolent messages: they prove wearers' stoic acceptance of pain and, because skin damage is permanent, a flagrant disdain for the future. Childhood is clearly wounded when the latest fad for any kid allowed to crawl a mall is scars that were once the trademark of seedy sailors.

In July 1996, Diane appeared as a guest expert on *Town Meeting*, a highly rated Seattle TV program that tackles a different issue each week. The topic was "Tattooing, Piercing and Branding," and she was pitted against the owner of a piercing parlor and an audience filled only with his clients. As he spoke, the stud through his tongue glinted in the floodlights; the rings lining his eyebrows and the tops of his earlobes quivered with each nod. Diane, dressed in a skirt suit, was an easy target for the strident audience: "Why is piercing our navels different from piercing your ears?" challenged one multiholed teenage girl. When Diane revealed never-punctured lobes, the girl was unfazed: "How is it different from your wearing nylons then?" Her point: we both wear what we wear to fit in. Albeit with different crowds.

Perhaps the popularity of tattooing, piercing, and branding was inflamed by TV, sports, and rock stars, but children have adopted them as major symbols of their camaraderie. If peers didn't approve, there would be no market for the burgeoning number of tattoo parlors, now estimated at 4,000 nationwide—up from just a few hundred in 1960. In 1996 alone, the number of such establishments rose 19 percent. "In the last five years, there has been a significant rise in tattooing," said San Francisco dermatology professor Dr. Michael J. Franzblau. A three-day convention in Detroit in February 1997 drew thousands of paying participants, some of whom competed for most elaborate tattoo artistry and most amazing display. Of the fifty-one Miss USA Pageant contestants in 1998, twelve had body tattoos and five had navel rings. In past years no contestant had sported either.

Maria Michieli, eighteen, of Sterling, Colorado, reports that tattooing "swept through her high school class last year," and that "many of her classmates wanted to fit in with the cool look."

John Durante, twenty, says of his friend tattoo artist Richard Siburt, who designed the dragon formed of a series of small brands on his back, "Now that we have both been through the experience we are closer together; there is a definite brotherhood between us now."

Tattoos, particularly on the face, are characteristic gang identifiers, but have also been adopted by other groups to express their connection to their tribes. Photographer Marina Vainshtein, twenty-two, was aware that she violated Jewish law when she had scenes of the Holocaust and Hebrew words emblazoned on her entire back, shoulders, and arms, but she also considers her multiple piercings and spiked purple Mohawk hairdo a means of identifying with her people. Johns Hopkins grad student Marguerite Chabbath Adams pierced her nose "to honor my North African heritage—Berber women wear nose rings—and to support the new tribal movement" of belief in a great goddess.

Though mainly high school–age youngsters indulge in the piercing and tattooing rage, many junior high kids have embraced the fad, too. When smaller children merely *observe* this trend among older siblings, their innocence diminishes as they're confused about the desirability of pain and misled about the seriousness of permanent scars that now mark adolescence.

An upbeat *New York Times Magazine* story about the new college cohort profiled the achievers at the elite University of Wisconsin, Madison, as refreshingly "smart, ambitious, and uncomplaining." They don't care about politics, don't get along with their parents, and, oh yes, they celebrate their independence at Tiger Rose Tattoo, located "just off campus." These are the role models their younger sibs admire.

The Lure of the New Primitivism

This admiration simultaneously reflects and reinforces the currently fashionable fascination with primitive practices and aboriginal societies. Political correctness often glorifies such neolithic cultures as more authentic alternatives to the phony refinements of Western civilization. One of the messages of multiculturalism is that we have much to learn from the primal wisdom of indigenous peoples who purportedly lived "in harmony with nature," communing with the spirit world, developing some mystical higher consciousness in various rain forests and jungles around the world. Anthropologists tell us that all of these primitive cultures featured some form of scarification, tattooing, or mutilation—displaying standards of bodily decoration that the pierced-eyebrow, tattooed-cheek, purple-haired server behind the counter of your local coffee shop might readily understand. American teenagers who eagerly disfigure themselves may not consciously imitate brutal tribal practices of the Amazon, central Africa, Tonga, or Borneo, but in their contemptuous rejection of "civilized" standards of superficial respectability they inevitably emphasize an earlier, more elemental form of human expression.

The lure of "the new barbarism" has proven a powerful element of contemporary adolescent culture, and a distinguishing characteristic for many of those mall-based tribes formed by lonely, disconnected kids. Beyond the rage for painful and permanent body decoration, consider some of the reigning fads in pop music and the culture surrounding them. Ethnomusicologists explain that one of the common features of all primitive musical expression is the emphasis of primal, pounding rhythm over elaborate melodic or harmonic structures. This characterizes the chants of ancient Hawaiians, Yoruba tribesmen in West Africa, or traditional Navajo medicine men—as well as contemporary hits in the world of hip-hop. It's no accident that when Igor Stravinsky wanted to evoke the cruel, sacrificial fertility festivals of ancient Scythians in his groundbreaking 1913 ballet *The Rites of Spring*, he gave similar primacy to the driving, brutal beat over catchy tunes.

Considering the tribal practices of the youth culture at the moment, some of the dancing as well as the music demonstrates the ongoing emphasis on primitivism. Look at the kids, some as young as nine and ten, twisting and spinning at any recent rock concert, or consider the athletic, energetic expression at your local high school prom. These motions (and emotions?) surely show more in common with the gyrations of prehistoric hunters gathered around some forest campfire, ecstatically dancing before their gods, than they do with the subtly controlled, semi-formalized movements of Astaire and Rogers or, for that matter, a Viennese waltz.

In his celebrated 1954 novel *Lord of the Flies*, Nobel Prize–winner William Golding stressed the bloody, implacable appeal of unfettered barbarism to a group of adolescent males removed from the constraints of civilized society. Stranded on a desert island after a plane crash with no adult supervision, even the privileged boys from an elite boarding school soon revert to the standards of prehistoric hunter-gatherers—complete with pagan rituals, fierce initiation rites, ritualized chanting, blood lust, body marking, and, ultimately, murder. Too many groups of unsupervised teenagers in today's society have achieved similar transformations—even without a plane crash. Primitivism is not innocence—and for our offspring the two principals stand in fateful opposition.

Practical Dangers, Cultural Degradation

The bodily disfigurement that represents the most visible indicators of that primitivism involves practical dangers as well as cultural and emotional degradation. Nevertheless, a majority of states have no laws regulating who may be pierced or tattooed (only nineteen states require parental permission; two outlaw tattooing altogether), so the market for this disfigurement knows no age bounds. Crowding in phone booths and swallowing goldfish were silly pursuits; tattoos and brands, on the other hand, scar youth for life and require expensive laser surgery or other detailed removal techniques to return skin to normal.

But some may not return to normal at all. Piercings in particular carry serious risks, as described in a 1995 *Los Angeles Times* story. The parlor proprietor with the tongue stud should tell his patrons that "teeth can be broken from biting down on jewelry in or around the mouth," according to dentist Dr. Eric Z. Shapira. "A stud can become impacted and have to be surgically removed, and you could have an airway obstruction if you aspirate [jewelry] and it goes to the lung." More complications include speech impediments, excessive drooling—and with any piercings, nerve damage, blood clots, and the development of large raised scars called keloids.

With flea markets and portable vending carts becoming major sources of piercing, the danger of infection via piercing guns and needles escalates. The herpes simplex virus, HIV, and hepatitis can be spread even by guns that don't touch the skin, if a fine spray of blood hits the instrument. Piercing needles reused and not cleaned properly are probably the foremost cause of infection. Punctures mistakenly made in cartilage, especially in the nose and upper ear, can mean scarring that distorts the shape of the features, requiring difficult and delicate surgery to repair. The risks of skin-puncturing decoration led the American Medical Association to issue a statement in 1996 urging state regulation of tattooing.

Tattooing, piercing, and branding, then, represent far more than simply artistic expression. They show the descent of peer identification, from symbols that are temporary and superficial to those that are permanent and problematic. They reflect a culturewide devaluing of the body, from a God-given temple for the soul, perfect in its creation, to a living sketch pad or a billboard for personal, often countercultural, messages. Kids who succumb to the trend not only rebel against their parents but marginalize themselves in society at large, narrowing their chances for mainstream employment and increasing discrimination against them everywhere they go, even if that prejudice remains subconscious. A tattoo or brand is a permanent statement that innocence is over—you are deliberately marked forever.

A few years ago, we temporarily tried a baby-sitter for our kids at the recommendation of a close friend. Eighteen-year-old Rebecca had faxed us her résumé, which showed her well experienced in child care. We interviewed her on the phone, and she was charming, respectful, and offered terrific ideas for entertaining our children. She lived only a few blocks away, and since she was taking a few college courses part-time, could adapt her schedule to ours. We asked her to start that weekend.

Rebecca bicycled over to our house, arriving on time, and greeted us with a smile. She had flowing, curly brown hair and wore no makeup. She was clean and neatly dressed. She carried a bag full of goodies and games for the children. So why did we have a problem relating to her? We just couldn't keep our eyes off the silver ring through her left nostril.

We tried to ignore it and stare into her lovely light brown eyes when we spoke to her, but inevitably our own eyes wandered down to her nose because, as she spoke, the ring moved with her facial expressions. We introduced her to the children: "This is Rebecca," we told our middle daughter, Shayna, who was five at the time. "What's that thing in your nose?" were the only words she could utter. Rebecca handled their queries graciously, explaining that her unconventional jewelry was merely an adornment. And she was smart enough to admit that it was an affectation of her young years, something she wanted to try because it was "in," and a fad she might later regret and allow to close and heal.

It didn't matter; our young kids, aged seven, five, and two, could only relate to Rebecca as the girl with the nose ring. They enjoyed playing with her, and then told their friends about their sitter with, ooh! a hole right through her nose. "How do you breathe?" "Isn't it awful when you get a cold?" "How do you blow your nose?" "Didn't it hurt?" Our children were fascinated, and we hope undamaged, but the fact that we had this young lady in our home desensitized them, perhaps in a subtle way but nevertheless irretrievably, to "the new barbarism" and treating one's body with disrespect.

Gothic Cults Snare Teens

News of the grisly multiple murders rocked the peaceful Woodridge neighborhood of Bellevue, Washington, in January 1997. Alex Kevin Baranyi, seventeen, a recent dropout of the community's public Alternative School, stood accused of strangling acquaintance Kimberly Wilson, twenty, and bludgeoning and stabbing her sister, Julia, seventeen, and their parents, William, fifty-two, and Rose, forty-six. Baranyi and a seventeen-year-old accomplice "were part of a 'gothic' clique whose members wore dark clothes and re-enacted mythical personas," according to a *Seattle Times* account. The paper also noted that Baranyi enjoyed "sword-and-sorcery adventure films," particularly "'Highlander,' a movie series and later a television show about immortals." He had "thought about killing someone for about a year because he was 'in a rut,'" according to documents filed in King County Superior Court.

Adolescents' attraction to mystic cults is nothing new, and a small group of occultists lingers on the outskirts of every high school's social system. Ouija boards, New Age meditations, and even séances pique the curiosity of youngsters whose bodies seem to magically transform themselves and whose hormones sometimes drive their emotions beyond logic.

Mark Edmundson's *Nightmare on Main Street: Angels, Sadomasochism, and the Culture of Gothic* suggests that America, in the shadow of the millennium, turns to a Gothic mentality as a means of explaining "transgressor blacks" (e.g., O.J. Simpson) and "enraged women" (e.g., Lorena Bobbitt and Tonya Harding) in the news, and as a substitute for declining conventional faith: "With the Gothic, we can tell ourselves that we live in the worst and most barbaric of times, that all is broken never to be mended, that things are bad and fated to be, that significant hope is a sorry joke, the prerogative of suckers."

While certainly mainstream America sees Gothic culture as a curious academic interest, a minority of teenagers searching for the most shocking means of rebellion find it arresting. Dan Korem in *Suburban Gangs: The Affluent Rebels* classifies occultic gangs as one of the three types of gang affiliations (the others being delinquent and ideological gangs) attracting middle- and upper-class youth and stirring "more exaggeration, hysteria, and controversy than the other two types of gangs combined." Gothic, a catchphrase for just about any pursuit that emphasizes "the dark side," has become a fad, enticing teens eager for peer acceptance toward its dangerous behavior.

Voted "Biggest Suck Up": The Epidemic of Rudeness

American parents are giving new lip service to the idea of "character education," while their children are giving new lip. Book buyers purchased millions of copies of William Bennett's *The Book of Virtues*, keeping the title hovering near the top of best-seller lists for months and attesting to widespread interest in old-fashioned values and principles.

But you could ask what percentage of those volumes sat on coffee tables unread. Four years after the former education secretary's book topped the charts, schools continue their emphasis on self-esteem and nonjudgmentalism over right and wrong, parents divorce in droves, and NBA Rookie of the Year Allen Iverson gets a forty-million-dollar contract to advertise signature Reebok athletic shoes while facing trial for marijuana possession and carrying a concealed weapon. "I know there are a lot of kids who look up to me," Iverson told the press. And plenty others who look down on the six-foot basketball champ.

We've slid to a lower standard in so many ways, but especially discouraging to refined minds is kids' uncritical acceptance and emulation of scofflaw media stars who disrespect elders and casually use crass language.

When was the last time you saw a child rise when an older person entered the room? When was the last time you saw children wait to be served food until the grown-ups got their share? When, indeed, have you run across kids who address adults they meet as Mr. or Mrs.? More likely, when parents introduce a business associate, kids grunt; when riding on a bus, they sit right where they are and look away when a senior citizen hobbles aboard. Generally, kids think nothing of criticizing their parents to their friends, or peppering their speech with expletives.

Timothy Jay wrote *What to Do When Your Students Talk Dirty*, and offers workshops for educators on the proliferation of cursing on campus. "Almost all the people who come to the workshops agree students are swearing a lot more in the 90s," he says. "It's worse than it has been before." According to an article in *USA Today*, a recent poll of high school principals showed that 89 percent deal with profane language and provocative insults toward teachers or other students on a regular basis. And pupils don't even consider *hell* or *damn* swearing anymore—instead they favor scatological terms, most commonly "the f word." Jay says kids often swear to identify with their peers—friends consider them prudish or nerdy if they don't.

High school junior Tighe Herren of Louisville admits he curses frequently "for emphasis." He says *everyone* in middle school and high school talks that way, so it becomes a habit. And mouthy students don't find instructors objecting. "Most teachers are accustomed to hearing it," so it's no big deal, Herren adds. He offers a typical teen sentence: "I'm so f— pi— off. I can't believe I have to do this f— assignment." The gross insensitivity of teens to verbal baseness is a strong indicator of how far they've traveled from naïveté.

Disgusted with the disrespectful behavior he's seen in kids over the years, former pro football star Mike Singletary of the Chicago Bears and his wife, Kim, resolved that their seven children will behave with dignity. In his insightful *Daddy's Home at Last*, he describes movingly the deterioration in respect among youngsters and offers inspiring means to counteract this disturbing trend.

High school yearbooks have degenerated from stiff group photos and dignified declarations of life goals to embarrassingly accurate representations of students' rude observations. "Oh yes, yearbooks are still very hip here, very hip," says Mary White, faculty advisor at Seattle's Cleveland High School. They annually feature such senior class distinctions as Owner of the Ugliest Car, Most Likely to Borrow Money, Most Dazed and Confused, and Biggest Suck-Up. "Senior Quotes," according to a *Seattle Post-Intelligencer* article, have "become a compendium of nearly indecipherable comments that accompany every senior's final school photo." Mercer Island, Washington, yearbook advisor Neil Lind says the goal of his upperclassmen was "to slip as much past us as you could, the key thing probably being where you did your drinking, or worse, and certainly what you didn't want your parents to know, much of it outlandishly dirty."

One father in the Ballard district of Seattle was so nervous about the impact of words printed with his son's senior picture that he had the school principal recall the entire school's yearbooks after they were already distributed. "Many" copies were returned. The sentence allegedly written by the student read, "I don't care about anything besides getting a good grade, and I'm willing to cheat to make that possible."

Perhaps youngsters "don't care about anything" because their elders implanted the "kids know best" mentality from the start. Children need and crave boundaries of their power—and to understand their place in the world vis-à-vis adults—but with childhood discarded, we've stopped offering them this reassuring structure. Diane was disturbed last year when Danny enrolled in our neighborhood Jewish preschool and was told to call his teacher, a woman over sixty, by her first name, Pat. Diane insisted that Danny acknowledge her authority with the Hebrew word for teacher, making her title *Morah* Pat. Of course, with fourteen other tykes calling the teacher simply Pat, Danny ended up saying Morah Pat only when describing his daily activities *to his parents*.

What does this do? It gives even toddlers the idea that they are somehow equal to adults; that they needn't differentiate subordinate from authority. The blur confers on *them* the burdens of adulthood, contributing to arrogance in some kids, insecurity in others—or in many, a snotty *facade* of rudeness that masks internal uncertainty.

Why the Assault from Peers: Disintegration of the Nuclear Family

For a period of almost a century, people came to America to forge a new identity for themselves, to improve their lot, and importantly, to offer the hope of a better future for their children. This ability to transform oneself into something new is almost a direct product of our unique geographical circumstances. To get here people had to cross an ocean at one time or another. That necessary voyage has always represented a defining experience: you left your old world behind and came to a new world—escaping all former bonds and bounds into unlimited possibility.

An extreme example was the founding of the state of Georgia— home of Scarlett O'Hara and the sweeping grounds of Tara. Georgia began as a *penal colony*—a new land settled by James Oglethorpe with former prisoners. But those prisoners left behind their shackles and emerged on our shores as new people, in time shifting from the dregs of society to successful land and plantation owners and even aristocrats.

This was the lure for all subsequent immigrants as well. In our own family, Michael's grandfather, whose name was Medvyed in the Ukraine, came to America with his brother. Just because they were in different lines at Ellis Island, his brother became Kaufman because, famously, the immigration clerk couldn't pronounce Medvyed or didn't want to write it down. Still, both men emerged renewed, with fresh opportunities for the future.

Without their original cultures, their childhood neighborhoods, or their wise elders, immigrants in America looked toward the future—investing all their energies in their families, and particularly in their children. Those newcomers may have soon realized that even *with* all their energies, their own lot would not dramatically improve, but that didn't matter—a better life for their *offspring* was enough to spur them on.

And so we have a tremendous emphasis on nuclear family in this country. In fact, many sociologists suggest that America essentially invented the idea of the nuclear family to replace the old idea of the extended family. It's precisely because so many people came here and left extended families behind—or people moved to the frontier, far removed from most relatives—that this little constellation of mother and father and children became enormously important.

But over the last thirty years, four developments have disrupted the nuclear family—and caused peers to step in to fill the breach: two-career couples, skyrocketing divorce rates, increased mobility with consequent lack of attachment to neighborhoods, and lack of parental control over their children's friendships.

Kids have *always* been a strong influence on each other. But when the nuclear family flourished, peers couldn't pull kids so far down, so fast. You'd never expect to see the array of serious problems we now confront unless some fundamental control had gone awry. The four factors above have led to huge increases in the extent and seriousness of peers' impact.

Before the 1970s, kids with "bad reputations" might "get in trouble." Recently, the out-of-wedlock birth rate reached 70 percent for blacks and 25 percent for whites, with a million teens pregnant, half aborting, annually. Before, every high school would have a small drug-prone fringe; now, one in four nine- to twelve-year-olds has been offered drugs, and the percentage of twelve-year-olds who say they know a friend or classmate who has used illegal drugs like acid, cocaine, or heroin jumped by 122 percent in just a year, from 1996 to 1997. In "the old days," violence in schools would consist of an occasional fistfight; now stabbings and shootings have teachers trembling, and *zero tolerance* is a term every student understands. The extreme has become the mean.

Let's look at the reasons:

A huge increase in *two-career families* has meant that no one's home to supervise, to banter about what happened that day, to chauffeur kids to activities and then stay to oversee them. Nobody's home: the idea of "latchkey kids" developed over the last two or three decades as moms entered the workforce, handing their children a key on a chain and free run of the house. These kids are forced to grow up and take responsibility for themselves; kids as young as seven, younger if there's an older sibling around, who in the past would never stay home without a baby-sitter. Their parents aren't there, but nearby are a lot of other kids in the same situation—so they form a bond even closer than their connection to absent parents. One of the strongest links with friends is that commonality of absent adults—and their mutual feelings of abandonment and resentment of their parents. The effect is polarizing—it's kids against those selfish, uncaring grown-ups, an "us against them" that intensifies as years pass.

Don't Need You Anymore

You can observe the change in a historical context: when kids were useful in subsistence farming or running the family business, like miniature adults, *parents needed them.* Then came the mid-twentieth century, childhood's heyday, when postwar parents, flush with possibility, lavished their attention on children. At that point, parents viewed their little ones as innocent babes requiring protection. Children *needed their parents.*

Now, both adults and children tend to live out crowded agendas in isolation from each other. So *no one needs anyone else:* adults no longer need children—and children no longer need their parents. While both Mom and Dad work, go to the gym, and shop, Jennifer and Justin shuttle between "full-service" schools, counselors, after-school sports, and Internet homework. Parents and children barely pass in the kitchen, eating their yogurt leaning over the kitchen sink. So the peers who accompany their children through hour after hour of scheduling become ever more important and influential.

When peers replace absent parents, the result can be devastating—not only to childhood, but to the youngster's long-term future. A few examples: girls who have little contact with Dad may seek out replacement love from boyfriends, succumbing to sexuality when all they wanted was attention. A survey by Mark Clements Research for *Parade* magazine found that 66 percent of the teenage girls they polled said "having parents who didn't give enough love or attention, or having parents who didn't teach morals, increased the likelihood of teen pregnancy." Dan Korem, in his book *Suburban Gangs*, says kids join up because of what he calls "the missing protector factor," a need to feel safe that used to be filled by family. The top two reasons why high school kids disengage from their studies, according to research on 20,000 students in California and Wisconsin, are parents who are not involved in school, and peers who devalue school achievement.

Marital breakdown has a peer-bonding effect, too, even if *your* marriage is fine. With so many families that look secure from the outside cracking up, kids have less trust in their *own* families. So children listen more warily to Mom and Dad, which diminishes their authority, and the peers who survive and rise above all that grown-up fickleness take on new importance: At least you can trust your friends to be there.

Bands in Moving Vans: The New Tribalism

Our *rootless, roleless society* is another factor increasing peer influence. At first glance, this seems counterintuitive—you'd think kids might cling more to their families in a new environment. But it's the opposite: when families move a lot, children feel an increased need to fit in wherever they go; they work harder and act more quickly to acclimate to the norms of their new circle. If they're uprooted repeatedly, many children become desperate to be accepted, and they'll go to even greater lengths to show they're worthy of inclusion.

And since mobility is such a common facet of American life, bands in vans have created portable subcultures. It's the "new tribalism" encouraging roving forms of identification. For example, fans of the Foo Fighters or Public Enemy share an instant bond; they've got lyrics and rhythm, concerts and clothes to connect them and assure them of a place in the group. These tribes are synthetic communities that cross geographic boundaries, offering members an immediate source of belonging.

Kids' attraction to this new tribalism comes as the family has, in the last thirty years, opted out of a major function it's served historically around the world—*providing its members with an identity and a role.*

Everyone craves a sense of place in the scheme of things, and one's family association, observable from birth, used to provide that. Birth status, since it's out of an individual's control, offers a sense of *placement* as well as place; consider, for example, the Hindu caste system. Royalty builds on this—kings, because subjects believe they're divinely selected, receive their power by birth alone. Biblically, clan, tribal, and national affiliation determined responsibilities and status, including the priesthood. Family associated people with a piece of land for farming or a trade, and the family business was often a legacy passed from father to son.

One's "station" by birth was once his destiny. Inheritance customs for millennia set out what offspring could eventually expect—but now people draw up wills leaving fortunes to pets or charities and sometimes omitting next-of-kin just out of spite as a financial last word. In the "old days" if Daddy was rich, you could count on your identity as a person of leisure; now the old guy might bypass his spoiled offspring and direct his fortunes to his second, much younger wife and their new babies.

Now, stable homesteads seem a passé curiosity, and very few people are born into their occupations or careers. No one assumes that a bride will leave her parents' home to live with her groom's tribe (or vice versa). Surnames shuffle as women retain their birth names and children take on hyphenates. You can't tell much about a person based solely on his name anymore, except perhaps his national or ethnic origin, and even then only on one side, unreliably. We still favor the father's surname, but with no assumptions. Our daughter Sarah went to school with two little tykes who each carried around a mouth-crowding hyphenated name. The big giggle among the first graders was "First comes love, then comes marriage, then comes

Zweiberg-Schmidt Rosenberg-Siegel sitting in a baby carriage!"

Americans now gain their identities by *choice* rather than birth. By choosing a career, by choosing a mate, by choosing a name—and for kids, by choosing their friends.

Of course, the real identity-defining choices come when the child *separates* from his birth family. The caption under a photo of a young woman in jeans waving to others under the bittersweet gaze of her father in September 1997 was "Hand in hand with her parents—and with a new stuffed frog—Chelsea bid goodbye to childhood and the White House yesterday." Good-bye childhood, hello identity.

What do all these societal changes mean? Confusion. Young people have so many options, they look to peer tribes for a set of concrete expectations. For example, in a society tolerant of all sorts of unusual behavior, what's expected of, say, a young man? Should he be tough and macho? Or a caring, "feel your pain" kinda guy? Before the 1970s, young people had latitude regarding their personalities, but they had one ideal for their futures—the standard of marriage and babies. You could be an artist or a high-stakes stockbroker, but you knew that you'd eventually "settle down and raise a family."

But now we see talk shows posing the profound question: How did my son grow up to be a skinhead? Well, the answer is that as a skinhead, he has a clear purpose and a rigid set of expectations. Sigh—he's found his niche.

In Defense of Discrimination

Discrimination. Sounds like a dirty word. Conjures up all sorts of nasty prejudice, racism, unjust condemnation.

Most sensitive people fear appearing racist, sexist, or unsympathetic to any religion or ethnic group. Discriminating against a person—saying he's inferior or no good—is about as politically incorrect as one can get. Our history of racism in this country gave the whole notion of discrimination odious associations.

And because of these associations, parents may stop short of discriminating between healthy and harmful friendships for their children. And because they're afraid to forbid friendships that are clearly deleterious, they allow their children to succumb to temptations by any low-life associate who cross their paths. This post-'70s "wisdom" is designed to prevent alienating their youngsters from them, but it's backfired miserably, facilitating kids' rebellion through the free reign they have in their social lives.

A reasonable parent doesn't worry about her child playing with black or Catholic or immigrant or retarded kids. She's worried about her child playing with *bad* kids.

Here's a hypothetical case: imagine that two children become friends. They go to the same church, their parents have harmonious values, they share the same rituals and interests. In that circumstance, would any parent care if the friend had skin of a different shade?

But change the scene so that the friend who's identical physically and ethnically has destructive values—smokes, cuts school, carries a gun—in that case discrimination is completely appropriate. But parents are so conscious of the surface that they neglect to investigate the underlying values and behaviors of their children's friends.

The Bible story of Abraham in the book of Genesis (Genesis 21:9–12) emphasizes the importance of associations. Abraham's wife Sarah, finally a mother at age ninety, receives her husband's approval to send away his secondary wife Hagar and their son Ishmael. Why? Ishmael was a bad influence on Sarah's son, Isaac.

Well-meaning psychologists and school counselors generally advise adults not to insist that their progeny cut off a budding friendship, even with a notoriously bad classmate. Their rationale is that the child will simply find ways to sneak around the edict, further dividing parent and child. Instead, worried parents learn they should express their concerns to their children and recommend that the child take the initiative to sever the relationship.

And when that doesn't work, then what? Just hum nervously as you watch your youngster head off to destroy his character and his future? That seems to be the case too often, as children take advantage of their power to make final decisions. Parents shrug, and kids head for the most antiestablishment testing-ground for their aspiring autonomy.

The problem is that in our present culture, parents are often too busy or too laid back to assert themselves. In the next chapter, we'll explore how this deprives children of a precious phase of their lives. But it also works to make peers more prominent. Without parents enforcing rules based on health, consideration, and ethics, kids go the other way, in the natural self-centered direction of immaturity. The underlying reason why society insists that children attend school is not just to teach them academic subjects but to teach them the self-discipline and self-control that will allow them to *study* their academic subjects, abilities they'll need for any worthwhile pursuit. The point is that *we have to teach them.* These virtues don't come naturally, and in fact go *against* every child's inclination to pursue immediate pleasure no matter what the consequences.

We have to teach them. And the way to do this is not to wait until your sixteen-year-old daughter brings home a handsome but sex-crazed dopehead and then lecture her on making poor choices. Just as we assign first-grade homework to teach time management, parents need to discuss and evaluate their children's choices in friends from the earliest ages.

With our daughters, and now with five-year-old Danny, we push the issue: "Do you think Bernard is someone who is polite and well-behaved?" we might ask. Usually Danny replies with brutal honesty, but sometimes he plays into an unruly friend's mischief. In that case, we explain why Bernard won't be invited over to play again. Danny doesn't protest—much—because he knows that each visit from a friend, no matter who, brings a "postmortem" where we evaluate behavior, including his own. And he overhears when we assess adult visits as well, so he sees that we hold ourselves to the same standard.

In fact, as we write this chapter, we take our sweet eleven-year-old Sarah aside. "We're writing about parents interfering with their children's friends, and we're thinking about someday, when you want to go somewhere with someone we don't like . . . "

Sarah interrupts.

"Oh Mommy, you know I'm very picky about my friends and I'd never want to go somewhere with someone you didn't like." Sometimes they come up with the perfect answers. We've spoken so often about the importance of associations that sometimes we think she's overly selective about potential playmates. Still, better to be picky—and surround herself with people she respects—than to play with just anyone because it's convenient. The old adage "proximity breeds familiarity" has a basis in truth—and we'd like our children to become familiar with people they can admire as well as enjoy.

6

The Assault on Innocence by Parents

All parents love their kids. And most of them trust that their kids will be OK—even if they don't know exactly what their children are doing all the time.

- Mom and Dad are still at work when Sammy, ten, and Megan, twelve, get home from school. They're old enough to take care of themselves, and they help themselves to a snack. Megan gets on the phone to her girlfriend, and Sammy settles down to surf the Internet. He's particularly interested in a new fantasy game where buddies on the web use Satanic formulas to "get what they want," including the demise of particular teachers and the gruesome ritual killings of animals.

- On this typical Tuesday after school, the crowd hangs out at the mall, where the girls shop for dresses for the junior prom—sleek strapless numbers slit to their panties, with push-up "miracle" bras, worn with stiletto heels. "Some people lay the issue at the feet of paymaster parents perceived as too weak or too indulgent to withstand pressure from a teen who wants to make a megawatt entrance," notes a news story on the phenomenon.

- The kindly officer from the DARE program holds up Study Print 9 to the class of first graders. It's a picture of a man standing at his front door, smiling and waving to a girl on the sidewalk—who looks worried and upset. The officer asks the children why the girl looks worried—and explains that the girl is properly wary of strangers—defined as "anyone you don't know well."

Nothing special, happens every day. And that's the problem.

How can parents just sit by while media, schools, and peers separate their children from childhood? Don't parents know what's going on? Don't they care?

What's worse is that parents *themselves* contribute—often unwittingly and with only the best intentions—to the destruction of their own little ones' innocence. This chapter has two parts: the first describes what parents do to erode the innocence of their children, and the second describes why.

Follow Your Passions: Kids Know Best

One way parents damage their children is through the philosophy that kids know best: kids are hip, kids are "natural." Kids know what they want, and parents shouldn't inhibit or restrict them from getting it. Former 1960s and '70s hippies aren't the only parents who offer their kids adult choices from the earliest ages. But they may be the group of parents most vocal about it.

Steve Strauss, author of a book on rock 'n' roll and a former UC Berkeley student asserts, "One thing I learned, with the drugs, war resistance, and music of that era, is that although people may criticize you, and you may be misunderstood, you should follow your passions." And so, he never criticizes his own kids, even when he can't stand their music.

Lisa Hathaway, mother of Jessica Dubroff, the seven-year-old aviator who crashed attempting a cross-country flying record, described her free-spirited child-rearing methods in an interview on the *Today Show*. "She didn't do 'worry,'" said the mother about her daughter in fittingly hip terms. A minute later she added, "I did everything so this child could have freedom of choice. . . . Liberty comes from being in that space of just living your life. . . . I couldn't bear to have my children in any other position."

"Go with it." Many parents live and profess that allowing others, including children, to act on their feelings is a sign of respect for their individuality. But if childhood isn't the time to learn rules and limits, when is? And what kind of childhood is it when parents treat you as if your wisdom is greater than theirs? Pretty soon roles reverse, and kids make such adult choices as where to live, where and when to vacation, what to eat, what clothes to buy, and what time, if any, is bedtime. We're talking discipline, morals, superior versus inferior. We're talking parents' duties over children's rights.

A *Los Angeles Times* article recounts the sad tale of a couple who didn't have the heart to say no to their son. It started when the kid negotiated for three cookies instead of two. He soon cajoled his mother into doing his homework. The problem escalated in just a couple of years to demands for a four-hundred-and-fifty-dollar bike; when his mother asked for a Christmas gift list, the cost of his requests totaled six thousand dollars. What did the mother say to that? "Yes, love," because he got angry "when thwarted." By junior high, the parents had lost all control, and in high school, the boy ran away and ended up in a group home.

And what becomes of the *rest* of such free-range children? Most likely they're the ones who feel constantly frustrated because the world doesn't conform to their wishes. They're loud and snotty because they expect compliance from everyone around them. They may never marry because they can't bend to mesh with any potential partners. Or, if they do pair up, they're the "control freaks" or the ones who ultimately find distracting affairs because, after all, they've just got to follow their passions.

Recently we were appalled when visiting the home of a family where—pardon the analogy—the kids rule the roost. In fact, it looked as if the henpecked mother was about to lay an egg. Her nine-year-old son literally climbed the walls, shimmying up a door-jamb by putting his feet on either side of the frame. His six-year-old sibling practiced karate—on an eight-year-old brother, both of whom yelled and chased about the house, knocking over furniture. The little girl of the family, four and clearly a tomboy, screamed at her mother that she would not, ever, wear a dress, even though the family was late for church. The mom made a lame command to the doorway climber: "Brian, I wish you wouldn't do that," which was ignored. She tried to reason with her daughter: "But Grandma got you this beautiful dress," to which the girl stamped her feet, turned around, and sulked away. The two ninja wannabes kept on kickin', never stopping, even when they narrowly missed one of their parents' adult guests.

What's wrong with this picture? One: no father on the scene. OK, we can excuse that one; in most homes, Mom has to take care of discipline while Dad is working or away. But in many functional homes an overwrought mom can at least depend on the dad's enforcement when he arrives, which helps her keep control in the meantime. Two: the mother is *asking* her kids to behave, as a favor to her, rather than asserting that she is boss and they are children. Every home has a pecking order; here, the ranks go the wrong way.

Many aging baby boomers implement through their kids the principles that pitted them against their own parental figures such as:

- Only *they* knew how to really live (psychedelically, slovenly, selfishly).

- Only children could lead adults out of the mess oldsters had made of the world (mainly by being compassionate with other people's money).

- The younger generation knew best because it could see and act beyond the confining social conventions and restrictions that had made their parents into the uptight, benighted, and pathetic wimps they were.

Just Say Yes

Never mind that many of those once-righteous boomers are now themselves the uptight, fast-lane materialists they eschewed. And never mind that the reality of parenthood puts them in an awkward conflict between convention and their "liberated" philosophies. When it comes down to it, parents may actively abet their children's ruination in the hallowed name of free expression, but their subconscious motivation actually involves the obvious fact that their laissez-faire approach is less difficult to enforce than strict rules. "Yes, follow your passions" sounds good, but truth is, it's a lot easier to attend to your own self-centered agenda when the kids are off "doing their thing."

Rock music symbolizes to many middle-agers the generational divide they once carved, so they're especially determined to go easy on music-related restrictions. Columnist Cal Thomas reports on parents who bring their too-young-to-drive children to a Marilyn Manson concert—you know, the group wearing T-shirts reading "Kill Your Parents" and who make obscene gestures while chanting "We love hate! We hate love!" The group's leader "pulled an American flag between his legs to simulate toilet paper" and played hymns while tearing up a Bible to warm up the audience. "My husband thinks we're somewhere else," confided Kit, who sat in the "quiet room" while her daughter absorbed the event. The dad forbade her attendance when he heard the band's lyrics on oral sex. Cal Thomas adds, "Kit, in true baby-boomer fashion, didn't want to see a pouty expression on her daughter's face, so she lied to her husband." The mom's rationale for making this trying trip? Why, it's principle: "I don't want her lying. I don't want her going behind my back," Kit insisted.

Defending the King

Parents extend support of their kids' passions beyond their own families and into the community. Consider the June 1997 story about the Camden, New Jersey, parents who thought their kids' high school punished them too much. The school suspended forty seniors on an out-of-state bus trip who smoked, drank alcohol, violated curfew, invited opposite-sex classmates into their rooms—and then disobeyed the chaperones who caught them—and said they had to forfeit attending their prom. That was too much for the parents to take. After their protests failed, they organized their *own* prom—drawing so much thumb-your-nose response that the school was forced to cancel the official event.

Columnist Maggie Gallagher muses, "I can't help but wonder whether it might make our kids happier to know that the larger world into which they are being launched is one . . . populated by adults and not by aging adolescent rebels. A world in which continually satisfying our desires is not nearly as important as doing the right thing." Problem is, Maggie, these parents think fulfilling their kids' whims *is* the right thing.

These parents crown their kids rulers and take on the role of soldiers defending their inviolate king or queen. "Your majesty, you can do anything you want, as long as you're happy," they grovel. They define their success as parents by the amount of time their kids are pleased. And they define their failure by the count of moments their children whimper or frown.

"Kids know best," even on the most basic of questions, like their genders. Just ask Elias Farajaje-Jones, forty-four, a divinity professor at Howard University. A couple of years ago *Newsweek* magazine interviewed this father of then-two-month-old Issa-Ajmu. The doting dad, a bisexual, was determined not to impose on the baby's options regarding the child's, or his or her parents' sex. He "breastfed" his child via a fillable strap-on tube, pierced both the newborn's ears, and when asked if the infant was a boy or a girl responded, "Ask the baby." "We are taught we have to be one thing," he noted. "Now people are finding they don't have to choose."

Lily-Livered Love

While many parents elevate children's desires because they believe in it, others end up simply giving in. Even the most well-meaning parents can slip into a please-the-child mode because they're just too tired to fight the battle for authority. While researching this book, Diane recognized a minor manifestation of this syndrome in our own household and Xeroxed a copy of two pages of William Damon's *Greater Expectations* for our two daughters. In the morning, as the girls, eight and ten, tried to shirk making their beds and hanging up their clothes (from the night before), Diane followed them, reading this excerpt, until they could take it no more:

> Many families in modern society . . . not only . . . relieve children of the expectation to serve others, they alleviate them of

responsibilities for their own personal care. Busy parents get children dressed long after the children are able to dress themselves, because the parents believe that it is quicker and easier that way.

Are you listening, Sarah?

Parents make their children's beds, clean up after them, make them sandwiches and snacks, drive them distances that could be easily and safely walked or biked—all out of a sense that asking such things of children would be either too much trouble for the parent or straining the capacities of the child . . .

Shayna, are you paying attention?

The child quickly acquires the belief that the bed is too hard to make, the distance too far to be walked. I cannot imagine a set of beliefs that could be more crippling for a child's developmental prospects.

Either their mother's tenacity or the prospect of crippled development cowed our girls into submission. Whatever the reason, the girls stopped demanding help getting dressed, made their own beds, and brushed their teeth. OK, the improvement lasted three days. But when they start to slip, reciting that paragraph—over and over—snaps them right back. That plus the threat of publishing their reactions in this book.

Parents Abdicate Teaching Morals

Passive parents just throw up their hands and leave their job to other institutions—schools mainly—but the following story illustrates an appalling tendency to abandon discipline to the court system. As reported by Associated Press writer Seth Hettena in December 1997, the parents of two ten-year-old school classmates in Mount Clemens, Michigan, confronted one another—in court. What horrific violence had led these two families to find themselves before Circuit Judge Michael Schwartz? Their kids' feud.

The judge warned fifth graders Kytan Schultz and Cassandra Reibel, "No more harassment, no more threats, no more obscenities or vulgar names, no more pulling hair, no more threats to the family, no more threatening calls to each other or relatives. If one of you causes problems to the other, I'm going to put you in the juvenile hold." It was the second time the law was brought into the dispute: Kytan's mother had obtained a personal protection order two weeks before, specifying that the girls could not inhabit the same piece of property—which kept Cassandra home from school for an entire week.

The case earned national outrage over wasting a circuit court judge's time on squabbles between ten-year-olds. Educators bemoaned the case because they thought it undermined public trust in their ability to keep order. But we missed mention of the *real* travesty of the case—the parents' own juvenile behavior. Imagine: two couples who'd rather go to court than work together to discipline and control their daughters. "When your children are hurting, isn't it the parent's responsibility to see to the protection?" mom Debbie Schultz asked. No, Mrs. Schultz, this isn't protection, it's abandonment of your duties. What kind of example do you set when you involve law enforcement and the court system in a pre-pubescent row? Who here is acting prepubescent?

Americans know there's something wrong with the values of today's kids. And they're not afraid to say it. A national survey released in June 1997 showed that 93 percent of adults responding believed that parents have failed to teach children honesty, respect, and responsibility. "Adults are not confused and they're not ambivalent," said the executive director of the research group, Public Agenda, which conducted the study. "Instead, they're virtually riveted by the need to teach kids integrity, ethical behavior, respect, civility, compassion, all those characteristics without which these children will never become responsible adults. . . ." Great. Don't just talk about it—*live* it.

An October 1996 poll by Elway Research of Seattle for the *Seattle Times* and others found that 85 percent of respondents agreed or agreed strongly that "Parents today are not taking enough responsibility for teaching their children values and morals."

A January 1995 *Newsweek* poll found that "almost half the American people believe that we have grown lax about enforcing moral standards."

Parents can assault their children by *refraining* from action. And that's exactly what many do by remaining mum on morals. They'll tell pollsters about the shortcomings of children in general but won't speak to their own offspring when it could actually make a difference. William Kilpatrick, in *Why Johnny Can't Tell Right from Wrong*, describes five reasons for the widespread reluctance to confront children with clear behavioral guidelines:

1. The appeal of lovable brats he calls the "good bad boy"

2. The idea that children are *naturally* good (so they don't need parental interference)

3. Parents' deferring to "experts" on how to raise their kids

4. The trend describing moral deficiencies as "psychological problems" requiring compassionate therapy rather than instruction

5. The myth that parents have no right to instill values since children should come upon them on their own

These are all excuses for parental laziness. Teaching children morals is tough, unpleasant work. Kids need to learn when to feel pride and when to feel shame, from parents who explain, correct, and enforce consistently. It means getting up from that one quiet moment of coffee and newspaper to separate your fighting children and castigate the aggressors. It means endlessly repeating the same messages. Perhaps most daunting of all, it means modeling the behavior you want your child to emulate.

Guilt is still an unpopular term, but *shame* is gaining new respect as the key to moral behavior. "A child who does not acquire a sense of shame and understanding of what's shameful has been deprived of the most important learning a human being can acquire," declares Boston University Dean Edwin J. Delattre. Both guilt and shame are essential to *conscience*, the internal device that tells us when we're going astray. As Jiminy Cricket sings in Walt Disney's movie *Pinocchio*, "Just let your conscience be your guide."

Children *need* morals, for modifying their own feelings—as well as their parents'. William Kilpatrick makes the solid point that "it's easier to love children who are lovable. And all things considered, better-behaved children are more lovable than badly behaved children." He acknowledges, "Of course we still love our children when they are nasty, whiny, disobedient, disrespectful, and selfish. But if that becomes their habitual behavior, the love of even the best parents begins to wear thin. By contrast, children who are obedient, respectful, and considerate have our love not only because it is our duty to love them, but because it is a delight."

We'd take it even farther than that: children who are nasty, whiny, disobedient, disrespectful, and selfish have *lost their childhood*, because expressing all those negatives requires a hard edge, a foul mouth, and a harsh cynicism that places them in the tough world of adults rather than in the exploratory, excitedly awed period of discovery, and optimism that is childhood. Moreover, a house full of contention from wiseacre children and exasperated parents is hardly conducive to a period of low stress that allows children to ease into the larger world.

The ramifications of parents' abdicating responsibility for teaching morals penetrate through layers of daily interactions and spiral through years of life. Katherine Dowling, a family physician at the University of Southern California School of Medicine, claims that parents' hands-off attitude fosters teen promiscuity. "A parent may feed and clothe his child, give her pricey toys, lessons in everything, but if he fails to pass on a sense of right and wrong, he is guilty of spiritual neglect," she writes in the *Los Angeles Times*. "A generation that cared for its children would instill morality from the earliest years and would not shirk from being unpopular with its teenagers by demanding certain ethical standards from them. But the current generation of parents just doesn't collectively seem to be interested enough to go to all the trouble of teaching honorable behavior. It's so much easier to throw up one's hands and just give kids prophylactics. After all, teaching chastity takes time, and who has time these days?"

A *New York Times* story about parents' reluctance to teach values quotes Kevin Ryan, director of the Center for the Advancement of Ethics and Character at Boston University: "Psychologists, educators ... have corrupted parents with 'happy think' philosophies, saying that all it takes are appeals to a child's better side, and that if the child always feels good there won't ever be any need to behave badly." But he acknowledges what we all know: "It doesn't work."

What *does* work? Inescapably, talk returns to the discipline tactic parents fear: spanking. Experts are now reevaluating their former stance that spanking is excessive, even abusive, notes a *New York Times* story. The 1996 Seattle poll found that 66 percent of respondents thought "laws intended to stop child abuse have gone too far in limiting parents' rights to discipline their children." In Diane's book, *The American Family*, coauthored with Dan Quayle, the healthy families interviewed all agreed that reasoned spanking is sometimes useful as a last resort in a repertoire of tools for disciplining young children. All this, thankfully, may signal the beginning of the end of a dangerous trend that deprived children of the security and order of a clear delineation of right and wrong.

Barrettes and Bows

At times, parents undermine childhood not only through inattention, but through their own misguided obsessions. When parents push little girls into sexy roles, for instance, they destroy innocence obviously and abhorrently. The pathetic story of JonBenet Ramsey, who pranced down runways in teased hair and mascara, posing seductively for portraits, captured the nation's pity. Instead of pulling her dollies down the street in a red wagon, six-year-old JonBenet spent her time parading before judges, crooning "Cowboy Sweetheart." *Newsweek* magazine described her as "the child-woman in boas and high heels, teeth clenched with the effort of balancing the yin of 'charm' with the yang of 'poise.'"

The culture of child pageantry may be a most crystalline example of parents' scooting their children past childhood into adulthood, but it is by no means unique. Mothers who approve their daughters' sexy prom gowns, towering high heels, and painted-lady makeup do similar damage. Dads who slip their sons condoms with the twenty-dollar bill on their way to a date also make a hurrying statement.

Some parents recognize that sexualizing little ones is not only bizarre but cruel. When several parents in Denton, Texas, objected to their four- to six-year-old daughters singing "Barbie Girl" when cheerleading for a youth football league, they got flak from other moms of the cheerleading squad. Lyrics portraying Ken telling Barbie to "Kiss me here, touch me there, hanky-panky" earned the lame defense that the youngsters should be able to perform the song they'd been practicing all year. The offended moms displayed dirty minds, suggested the coach, for listening to the song in "a sexual kind of way, not in a five- or six-year-old kind of way." Pardon us, do words change their meaning when uttered by a smaller pair of lips?

When little children's clothing is merely miniature imitation of adult styles, children lose their identity as a unique population. Now that women's styles are fairly dowdy and staid (or '70s outrageous), we find the same dead colors or wild prints on the children of trendy parents. Ruffles, bows, petticoats, frills, pastel colors, flowers, and soft little patterns are classic childhood. Anyone wearing these styles appears young, innocent, immature. Puff sleeves. Peter Pan collars. Fluffy hair bows that stick out on either side. The appropriate years for such innocent ornament are all too brief and children (and their parents) should enjoy them while they can. Diane laments that our girls, now nine and eleven, resist wearing these accessories that once adorned them daily. Diane recalls fondly arranging Sarah's hair in multicolored shoelace bows every morning before kindergarten; now the sweet barrettes lie useless in the drawer.

Push and Hurry

The hurried child. Coined by David Elkind in 1981, the term resonates with many exhausted mothers who feel more like chauffeurs and party planners than the affection magnets they want to be. It rings true for two-career couples who program their children from school to bus to gymnastics to play dates to make sure they're tended till the final shuttles round them up at six. The term means something to youngsters who can barely carry their backpacks crammed with textbooks and supplies, and with teachers who post in their classrooms detailed schedules for each student's complicated after-school destinations.

But the hurried child is not necessarily a happy child. Too often, Elkind says, the hurried child becomes a stressed child. That's because *hurry* doesn't just cover daily rushing around. It means something deeper, about the new view of childhood as a race to succeed.

Competitive expectations and economic pressures cause too many parents to put earning money and career advancement ahead of attending to their offspring's development. "For today's parents," writes Elkind, "child rearing may often be in conflict with career, with finding a new mate, with loyalties to children from previous marriages, and with retaining even a modest standard of living." He goes on, "Nonetheless, many parents who are living the new lifestyles still remain invested in the more traditional values of parental nurturing . . ." and feel *guilty* about it. So, Elkind concludes, "The conception of children as competent to deal with, and indeed as benefitting from, everything and anything that life has to offer was an effective rationalization for parents who continue to love their children but who have neither the time, nor the energy for childhood."

No Time for Love

The reason parents feel so guilty about it is because in modern times, the *currency of family is emotion.* The elevation of emotion as the primary product of families came about over the past hundred and fifty years, as the function parents served for children, and children served for their parents, moved from concrete and urgent (helping families earn a living) to soft and elective (love, cuddles, pride in achievement, and continuity to the future). Here's a quick overview of how that change happened.

Historically, children only became valuable when they were old enough for their labor to help the family survive and prosper. As Neil Postman points out in *The Disappearance of Childhood*, agrarians considered little ones, as noncontributors, fairly worthless.

For example, Greeks didn't recognize children as a special age category, and in fact we have no surviving Greek statues of children. At the time, Aristotle was progressive because, though he didn't object to infanticide, he thought there should be some limits to the practice.

Because of high rates of natural infant and juvenile mortality, adults through most of history could not become emotionally attached to their babies. Instead, children dressed as miniature adults in their social class, as pint-sized people, not precious investments in the future. In fact, the first mention of children in wills and testaments wasn't until the late fourteenth century.

During the thousand years of the Dark and Middle Ages, literacy, education, and childhood all disappeared. Adult responsibility began at age seven, the point at which children have a command over speech and can understand the difference between right and wrong. This was evident in the Church's selection of age seven for a child's first communion. People of all ages worked simply to survive.

Only when literacy flourished could parents transcend subsistence occupations and *educate* their children to strive for a superior life. When religious and educational books became widely available, parents "became preoccupied with the task of making their children into God-fearing, literate adults," Postman writes. Parents' concern for transmitting physical survival skills was supplanted by education in abstract concepts borne by symbols and ink. In the twentieth century, as medicine and technology flourished, the primary rewards of parenthood shifted forever from the *material* to the *intangible*.

By the 1960s, parents could assign just about every aspect of their kids' intellectual and moral development to institutions such as schools, day care, church, tutors, enrichment classes—as they refocused their energies into self-fulfillment and earning money. For those on the fast track to career and material success, raising children can now be a compelling hobby rather than an occupation. "Support" institutions cover the child's hours from 7 A.M. to 7 P.M. so that elite parents can turn their Type A personalities to "enrichment" in the evenings.

Here we must acknowledge that the rise in single-parent families leaves many mothers (and a few fathers) with no option but to entrust their children to others while they work, and no doubt most of these parents regret that they cannot be there for their little ones far more.

But elite parents, the ones who truly do push and hurry their children, set a national standard with which all children must compete. With so many teaching aids advertised—including fancy learn-to-read games, educational toys, A-B-C videos, and computer ware—striving parents feel remiss in settling for a normal kid. They stretch their darlings toward the competitive edge, the most advantages; they want *optimal* child development.

David Elkind says that believing our "superkids" competent and flourishing assuages our guilt for leaving them. But parents also seek a payoff in the family's "emotional currency"—they want to feel proud of their children's accomplishments. They love the sports trophies, the scholar-quiz ribbons, the videos they make of their darlings' performances in the school chorus. They want to maximize the cuddly affection exchange of cookies, Girl Scouts, soccer titles, and school plays.

But the one thing parents rue is that they *just don't have the time;* they hurry their children because *they are hurried themselves.* Because they've bought the idea that "having it all" is a worthwhile goal for themselves, tragically, they destroy childhood by pushing their young children to have it all as well. Adults squeeze all of life's facets—marriage, career, working out, church, friendships, "relaxing" with TV, and parenting—into the day. If we see childhood as a time for special nurturing and exploration, we should be protecting our children from the encroachment of too many activities rather than dragging them along into our pursuit of them.

Of course, parents usually think they're doing their kids a favor by accelerating their achievements. But ask the stressed-out kids themselves. "You weren't allowed to be a child," recalls Alex Safford of his elementary years in the late '80s at elite Grace Church School in Greenwich Village. "From the beginning, everything was geared for the future, for getting into the name boarding schools when you finished eighth grade. Kids who didn't get in were so ashamed. Everything was about awards and about coming out on top. There was an unspoken agreement—I know my dad wants me to beat everyone else."

The *New York Times* reports, "In the pressure-cooker atmosphere of Manhattan, there are few rituals that make parents feel quite so ambivalent, anxious, and completely insane as the test to get into Hunter College Elementary School on the Upper East Side." We're talking preschoolers here, prepping for a standardized intelligence test, and parents know their little angels need to score in the 98th percentile to make the cut. Less than 4 percent of the initial applicants ultimately get the nod. "The frenzy has led some parents, and even preschools and consultants, to train children in skills to help them beat the odds," the article notes. "Parents besiege schools and libraries for copies of the test. There are games reputed to improve scores by mimicking intelligence tests and even diets rumored to make children more alert (Frosted Flakes for breakfast)."

Beyond the incredible pressure under which parents place both themselves and their children for the test are the consequences of their reactions to its results. Amanda Rosenberg postponed the exam until the last moment out of fear that if her son scored poorly, she'd view him differently. Parents lie to their friends about their children's scores. "You see all your friends going crazy, and you think, maybe I should go crazy too," admits Dr. Kami Kim, mom of candidate Clayton.

Even in the suburbs, competition can be rough. We know several families who are keeping their kids in preschool an extra year so that when they enter kindergarten, at age six instead of the usual five, their children will have an edge. During a casual conversation at the supermarket, Diane heard that a neighbor planned to hold back one of Danny's classmates, and expressed surprise. "You're new here, so you don't understand," said the mother, her brow furrowed and intense. "I have two older children in the schools, and you don't know how tough it is. It's very competitive. I want Mikey to know how to write and read before he gets to kindergarten." Diane was amazed and inquired further: the teacher in our Danny's preschool confirmed that a third of her charges would be staying on the following year in an effort to assure them a leading place in the grueling, dog-eat-dog public kindergarten where Danny is enrolled right now.

Adding an extra year to preschool is so common that our local paper splashed a huge article across its *front page* warning parents that tykes retained in preschool to gain them that edge fare worse than those allowed to move along with their cohort. It may seem that allowing young ones an extra year of preschool play enhances rather than inhibits childhood. But now, preschools use that five-year-old class to accomplish what peers tackle in a regular kindergarten, and meanwhile, parents can't hide their true underlying motivations and aspirations from their progeny.

On the last day of Danny's preschool—and this is the local Jewish Community Center, not an elite institution—his teacher, wearing an ominous expression, took Diane aside. "I hate to have to tell you this," she began, causing Diane palpitations, "but Danny is the only one left who can't write his name." Relieved, Diane started to laugh. It hadn't *occurred* to her to try to teach Danny to write his name yet. But when Diane mentioned the incident to the family, Danny's sisters took it upon themselves to teach him. They emerged from his bedroom a half-hour later with our then-four-year-old proudly displaying a page full of scrawled "Danny"s.

Everyone knows stories of exclusive preschools where parents register their children as soon as they confirm the pregnancy. We have friends who send their precious ones to private academies where the cost of the primary grades is more than tuition at most top-rated colleges. Lots of families give their kids their own computers, upgraded every year. A preschool teacher quoted in *USA Today* on the anguished competition she observes suggests, "These parents are making young children vehicles for their own unresolved ambitions. It's lunacy." Parents have always nudged their children, but now it's in the context of early competition to top others rather than to fulfill individual mothers' and fathers' dreams.

Pushing children probably *does* give them an edge academically over their peers—at first. Extracurricular lessons effectively teach them all sorts of skills, from computer to karate. But when parents push, they also teach kids a more harmful message: to define success in terms of a good school, a prestigious job, and earning a lot of money, rather than in terms of spirituality or mastering virtues such as charity, honesty, or reliability. Parents would serve their children better if they emphasized happiness over achievement, and goodness over goodies.

Misused Influence

Young boy to his Grandpa:

Boy: Grandpa, can you make the sound of a frog?
Grandpa: I don't think so.
Boy: Come on, just try to make the sound of a frog!
Grandpa: I don't quite know how to do it.
Boy: Please, Grandpa, please make the sound of a frog!
Grandpa: Why is it so important that I should make the sound of a frog?
Boy: Because Daddy said that we could go to Disney World when Grandpa croaked!

This is a true anecdote from a farm family in Searcy, Arkansas, told to Michael and the other participants at the Governor's Conference on the Family in October 1997 by Governor Mike Huckabee. It illustrates two points: the father's disrespect for his parent, and that parents need to watch closely the things they say.

Parents unintentionally assault their children's innocence by carelessly or misguidedly misusing their powerful influence. Children crave their parents' attention, and in most cases gladly somersault to earn it. Sometimes the only way they can grab some parental focus is by acting out; sometimes they ache to please so much that in their stress they harm themselves, most famously via such disorders as anorexia, cutting their bodies, or pulling out their hair. Young children in particular, take to heart what parents say, and in many cases cannot distinguish hyperbole or sarcasm from fact.

Parents don't always understand the power of their words, and more frighteningly, their actions. A University of Michigan study followed families over twenty-five years and found that habits of parents influence their children's futures strongly. Sons of safe fathers—who buckle their seat belts, save money, and insure their cars—make more money as adults. Parents who value education produce kids who display the same priorities. Children living in "very clean" homes are spurred toward higher education levels, and their sons earned 40 percent more than others.

For the Sake of the Children

Divorce is probably the one volitional act that most shatters childhood. What could blast the innocence of a child more than to discover that his parents can no longer live together and, presumably, no longer love each other? What could snatch away childhood more decisively than to crack apart a child's home and leave him vulnerable, caught between adversaries? Parents used to fight in private, and stay together to spare tender sensibilities, but many no longer counter their impulses "for the sake of the children." The numbers show it: in the mid-1990s, there were 509 divorces per thousand marriages, compared to 329 per thousand in 1970, according to a *Time* magazine analysis.

Our confessional culture, celebrated on so many TV talk shows, adds further threats to childhood innocence. Ex-hippies often confide in their children about long-ago use of drugs and their once-enthusiastic pursuit of "free love." "Oh yeah, my kids are not shy about finding good arguments, and when it comes to drugs, they'll say, 'Dad, you did them,'" said Bob Owen, who ran an arts workshop in San Francisco in the late '60s and early '70s. A National Addiction and Substance Abuse study shows that children of parents who admit drug use are more likely to use drugs themselves.

Radio therapist Dr. Laura Schlessinger tells parents to 'fess up, and suggests these words: "I'm ashamed to talk to you today because I can't tell you that I stood on my own without being high and without peer acceptance. I was weak and superficial in my views of life, power and meaning. . . . "

But if you aren't as well-spoken as Dr. Laura, you might not fare as well. Normal parents can't help a few foot-in-mouth slips, but some habitually *choose* to talk about innocence-busting topics (like abortion, marital instability, feelings of anger, lack of trust, or pessimism about the future). Or they use speech that is needlessly graphic or overly sophisticated around their children. You can't expect a youngster not to imitate a dad who peppers his narratives with expletives. Children hear, children do.

Why the Assault: Babies Having Babies

"Alligators drop their eggs, the egg is ready to roll," says anthropologist David Murray, now director of a statistical research center in Washington, D.C. "We hold on to youth more than any other species."

At the heart of parents' unwitting destruction of their youngsters' childhood is their *own* immaturity. They're babies having babies. We don't mean teenage girls who get pregnant out of wedlock, "babies" in chronological age and lack of experience. The parents we're indicting are "babies" in that taunting sense that kids use to insult other kids—they won't grow up and accept their responsibilities. They want to remain perpetual children, selfish, arrogant, the center of attention. For them, having babies is simply one more self-indulgence; they finesse, work around, or ignore any aspect of raising those babies that doesn't fit in with their indulgent and self-serving agenda.

Maybe you remember the rock-'n'-roll oldie "Forever in Blue Jeans." Or the Island of Lost Boys from Peter Pan, where they sing defiantly, "I *won't* grow up!" That's the idea here. Ever since baby boomers legitimized a wide range of pleasure-seeking, parents have been openly and proudly meeting their own needs before those of their children.

"We are the generation that called violent, lust-filled, juvenile fantasies 'adult' entertainment, thereby telling our children explicitly—very explicitly—what our definition of adulthood was," writes Zoe Deen in an insightful article in the *New Oxford Review*. "We are the generation that refuses to face the reality of our own errors even when we see that reality reflected in the misery of our own children."

We rightly worry that those children may grow up too soon, but there is little that is grown-up about the dysfunctional values that threaten them most. The essence of adulthood is self-control, deferred gratification, the understanding that choices and actions involve inevitable consequences. These are hardly attitudes that characterize today's jaded kids: rather than hasty maturity, they run the risk of permanent *immaturity*, falling into the same state of perpetual adolescence that traps too many of their parents. There is nothing adult about an "adult" bookstore, nothing mature about TV or movies designated for "mature" audiences, nothing grown-up about a short-sighted approach to existence that demands constant titillation and instant satisfaction.

Kids are paying the price now for the insanity of touchy-feely ideas that elevate self-esteem above any "rigid" notions of correct and incorrect answers—or correct and incorrect behavior. Children told to go discover mathematical formulas, who never hear that their cockamamie answers are wrong, reflect their elders' innovations, that feelings rule over rationality, and that feelings must rule *immediately*. Mate having a bad-hair day? Get a divorce. Wish the freeway weren't bumper-to-bumper? Help yourself to a little road rage, cut off and cuss out the guy in the next lane. Doesn't matter that your kids are in the car; they might as well learn words that let their feelings "all hang out."

And so our children have learned well the lessons we rule-breakers have taught them. And they've suffered for it. How innocent is the child who watches his dad give the finger to a fellow driver? (And how much worse is the damage if the gesture is made by his mom?) How sweet and unspoiled can a youngster remain when her parents place enormous value on obtaining their own entertainments—cars, stereos, VCRs, electric barbecues for the kitchen—but reserve precious little time for *her*?

Modeling the Need to Collect

Only in the past dozen years have parents acted like fad-driven adolescents in procuring toys—this time we're talking *real* toys—to give their kids for Christmas. Perhaps the first major toy-hunting hysteria emerged over Cabbage Patch dolls; remember those pug-faced, personified, yarn-haired munchkins that came with a birth certificate and a name? When our Sarah was three—long after the Cabbage Patch buying frenzy had passed—her grandparents bought her one, pre-named Phyllis Arlene. Of course, lucky recipients had the option to retain the given name or substitute another. Sarah, in her toddler omniscience, decided to change her doll's moniker to—Arlene Phyllis. Duly, we wrote in the correction and mailed in the birth certificate. We never heard anything from the toy company, but happily Sarah, now eleven, reported that she slept with aging Arlene just last night.

She's an exception. Where are your kids' Ninja Turtles, Power Rangers, Teddy Ruxpins, and Tickle Me Elmos? On the shelf with the now collectible Beanie Babies? Parents don't spend days rooting out Game Boys only for eager squeals of delight and laughter in little ones' eyes; they do it because they themselves are incredibly competitive and haven't ripened past a high schoolish gotta-have-it mentality.

Parents with the misfortune to find their local emporium out of the toy of the moment go to incredible lengths, including fistfights, pulling strings, and camping out in front of stores to nab their booty. And this is not in just a few isolated cases—it's hundreds of *thousands*. "Parents fear that without the toy of their child's Christmas dreams, Dec. 25 will be a bust," says a *USA Today* story on the phenomenon. Yes, but given the adults' maturity levels, a holiday without the *jouet-du-jour* will bust *worse* for them.

In search of an Ariel doll from Disney's *The Little Mermaid* for her six-year-old niece, Susan McCarthy of Carlsbad, California, "tried five stores in San Diego and called four in San Francisco before I found one and had it put on hold," she recalls. She actually got on an airplane and traveled to San Francisco to pick it up, flew back, wrapped it, and with relief presented it to her niece—who then burst into tears. "It was an Ariel doll all right, but it was Ariel in a bride's outfit, not Ariel in her green mermaid's dress," the exhausted Ms. McCarthy muses. "I felt awful."

Don't Blame the Kids

Youngsters suffer from far worse than toy deprivation as a result of their elders' childishness. Mike Males, author of *The Scapegoat Generation: America's War on Adolescence*, says that parents' own behavior is to blame for everything from teen smoking to drug use to out-of-wedlock births. Males' study in Los Angeles County found that more than a third of students lived with parents who smoked—making them three times more likely to smoke regularly by age fifteen than those in nonsmoking households.

A *Los Angeles Times* story asserts that pinning major problems on kids is a scheme to hide adults' culpability. "Basically, this is an undeclared war," said Barry Krisberg, president of San Francisco's National Council on Crime and Delinquency. "In large measure, the blaming of the kids is about covering up what adults are doing."

Babies having babies. James S. Kunen, who wrote the novel *The Strawberry Statement*, which celebrated '60s culture, writes in *Time* magazine, "We knew that when we became parents, with our '60's spontaneity and spirituality intact, our kids would want to be just like us. It hasn't turned out that way. . . . "

No. In some ways, they may turn out better. (College freshmen in 1994 were far more interested in such goals as raising a family and being well off financially than they were in flower-child days.) In other ways, they've turned out worse. (Out-of-wedlock births among whites soared to 25.4 percent in 1993 from 8.2 percent in 1977. Drug use among middle school kids rose beyond even that of the '70s. Ten- to fourteen-year-olds commit suicide twice as often as they did in 1979.) "Indeed, some experts believe the fact that guns have replaced fists and knives as the weapon of choice among some teens is the single most significant change in adolescence today," writes *Wall Street Journal* staffer Cynthia Crossen.

Why do youth have to push the envelope toward greater depravity in order to rebel? Why can't they do something really radical— like wear suits and play classical music?

"When we grew up, it was simple to rebel," says middle-ager Steve Lynn, who was beaten up for wearing a tie-dyed shirt and threatened by a sheriff over his long hair. "There were so many rules to be broken." Well, he may not be breaking rules nowadays, overseeing nine burrito restaurants, but he goes to work in denim overalls and won't say no to teenage daughter Alexandra when it comes to sex, drugs, and rock 'n' roll: "They have to do it to set themselves apart from their parents."

Harry Siegel, nineteen, adds, "The counterculture has been absorbed by the culture. The blue hair and pierced nipples are trite, and so no one pays them any mind. Nothing is outside the fold." That's the influence of parents who won't grow up.

You can't be both authority and perpetual adolescent, so New Agers inadvertently destroy their children's innocence on the way to making them their friends. They structure their families as "egalitarian" because then they don't have to lead: children's and parents' feelings and desires take on equal validity. As part of this strategy, they may proudly assert a "no family secrets" policy and confide the intimate details of their fantasies; they may simply let the child in on worrisome or complex facets of life, like the state of the family finances or nasty office politics.

"Geez, look at that skirt," we overheard a middle-aged father say to the little boy holding his hand, as the two walked down a West Los Angeles street a couple of years ago. The father then stood to rubberneck the young lady, contorting his face in a gawk, as the child, clad in a Barney T-shirt, took it all in.

In her psychology practice, Diane often works with families where both the marriage and adult-child roles break down. Typically, a nonassertive mother expresses her daily frustrations with a domineering husband only to her children. When she finally gains the courage to leave, she's like a volcano, exploding with years of his insults. Her children, who comforted her and kept her confidences as their bond and secret, back the mom, and the dad can't understand what hit him.

It doesn't take a shrink to see that Mom clearly needed an outlet for her feelings and should have worked them through with her husband directly, or at least found a good therapist to help her confront the issue within her marriage. Instead, she burdened her children—reversing roles and forcing them out of childhood.

An editorial in USA Today defends the Rolling Stones' Mick Jagger, fifty-five, Neil Young, fifty-one, and Aerosmith's Steven Tyler, forty-nine, against accusations that they're too old to perform rock music. "You are only young once, rock music reminds us. But you can remain adolescent forever. That's cool."

We're Outta There

One principal reason children lose their innocence is that parents don't care or simply aren't around to know what's going on. Either they're off working long hours, or rarely enter the scene because of divorce. They leave their progeny to the child-rearing of schools, peers, day care, and their TV sets by default, not because they intentionally choose to abandon them.

Since Diane's book *The Case Against Divorce* was published in 1989, hundreds of people have told her that divorce has forced their children to grow up prematurely. Custodial parents may elevate the child to spouse substitute in many ways, or they may work hard to shield their children from new responsibilities. It doesn't matter—when parents divorce, a child inescapably loses the fundamental beliefs of childhood—that the world is good, that the love in his family is genuine, that life is secure and predictable. They're gone with the division of property, with parents' anger or sadness, with a new schedule of visitation. We have no doubt that the enormous increase in divorce over the past quarter-century is a crucial contributor to the caustic edge and aloofness that characterize today's children.

"Every time I see my daughter cry when she goes back to her mother, I cry," the separated father of a four-year-old wrote. "I wish I could get my wife to read your book . . . "

"She doesn't understand that I love her, that I love our children more than the world," said the impassioned dad of five. "I can't bear being in my lousy apartment alone. I used to help them with their homework every night, run their baths, tuck them in bed. Now I'm the bad guy and they have to hate me and hold up their mother emotionally."

From a mother whose husband ran off with a younger associate in his law firm: "We were a family. I always praised Dad to the kids, even when he couldn't be there for their school performances or basketball matches. At least he was working to support us. Now their view of their happy family is ruined and they can't trust their father."

A ten-year-old girl whose parents were newly divorced told Diane, "Now we get to do whatever we want. Dad used to make us do our homework, but Mom lets us take care of it ourselves. I finally get to drop out of piano lessons and I don't have any bedtime." That's because her mother, feeling newly liberated, is out every night dancing. Some improvement.

Judith Wallerstein, who tracked children of divorce for fifteen years, found them wary of marriage, and more prone to divorce. The National Fatherhood Initiative summarized its investigation of the research: "Compared to children in intact families, children whose parents have divorced are much more likely to drop out of school, to engage in premarital sex and to become pregnant themselves outside of marriage. These effects are found even after taking into account parental and marital characteristics before the divorce." And Diane can attest, from many years practicing psychology, that every married person gleans his expectations and initially models his behavior on the marriage of his parents. Young eyes and minds miss very little, and the impact lasts.

Even in intact families, too many parents spend most of their time making a living and in independent activities—so they're absent and ignorant about the content of their children's lives. "Of children age 5 to 14, 1.6 million return from school to a home absent of adults," says a 1994 U.S. Department of Commerce statistical brief.

Parents don't have time to police curricula, interview their children's friends' families, or peruse the magazine rack at the day-care center. They have little opportunity to even talk to their own kids, most of whom don't volunteer much about their lives. Most working parents feel they're doing well to find the kids home, fed, and in their own beds for a goodnight kiss. "Fewer than 25 percent of young boys and girls experience an average of at least one hour a day of relatively individualized contact with their fathers," said Henry B. Biller in a paper presented in White House meetings with Dr. William Galston, Deputy Director of Domestic Policy for President Clinton.

"The Study of Early Child Care," funded by the National Institute of Child Health and Human Development, found that the more time a child spent in child care, the less affectionate and more negative were his interactions with his own mother. Bad news, since "more than half of infants under age one receive care by someone other than their mothers, and most mothers return to work in their child's first three to five months."

Kathleen Parker writes in *USA Today*, "Kids dawdle. They doodle. They dilly-dally. Most of their best learning occurs during those unscheduled moments so few of us seem to have. . . . Parents in previous generations didn't need studies to tell them how to raise kids. Families knew instinctively that babies need focused, loving attention until they're reasonably self-sufficient. Babies haven't changed, but parents have. . . . One might wonder how many children have suffered from society's media-fed delusion that kids are just fine stashed in nurturing warehouses with runny-nosed tykes and too few competent adults." Well, we know the answer: they've *all* suffered.

Little kids need *quantity* time; the myth that a small amount of focused attention is just as good simply because it's labeled *quality* is merely a means to rationalize being away. The only way a parent can know for sure what's influencing his child is to be there while the influence is happening. And the best way to guarantee that the influence is wholesome is to provide it yourself.

Getting Away with It

A final reason why parents allow and even contribute to the assault on their children's innocence is that they can get away with it. Parents in our culture have such leeway in the way they raise their kids that even caring relatives and friends don't dare call them on damaging mistakes. It's true that many parents feel they have to strain to retain control over their children as schools, media, and peers vie to wrest it away. A group called Of the People, based in Arlington, Virginia, strives for parental rights legislation, supported by politicians such as former Governor George F. Allen of Virginia and U.S. Representative Steve Largent of Oklahoma, as well as an array of religious and civic leaders. But their efforts are necessary only because institutions abhor a vacuum, and so many parents have failed to assert their prerogatives that others have simply stepped in. Plenty of government agencies are willing to intrude when it appears parents may have acted in a way physically detrimental to their children; none will notice, though, when parents wound the young by emotionally pulling away.

The problem here is a degeneration in the quality of parenting across the board. Standards of parental responsibility have plummeted along with adults' willingness to live up to them. Few authorities or experts expect parents to provide their children with the moral grounding to resist negative influences in the culture. No one urges them to protect their progeny from encroaching menaces that deprive them of childhood. Nowadays, undermining a six-year-old's self-esteem by spanking him when he deserves it may be considered disgraceful, while taking him to see R-rated fare such as *The Devil's Advocate* or *Starship Troopers*, causing weeks of nightmares, is not. Do you think the ticket-taker at the theater door is going to question another sale? Does the principal scold the parents when he finds they've taken their eight-year-old to see *Silence of the Lambs*? Others may "tsk, tsk" but rarely more.

Evidence that the quality of parenting has declined:

- The *Los Angeles Times* used 75 percent of the space on the front page of its "'90s Family" section for a story on the demise of family dinners.

- A parental responsibility ordinance took effect in October 1996 in McMinnville, Oregon, to compel parents to be responsible for the unlawful acts of their children.

- Parents express mixed feelings about whether they want the v-chip that is supposed to help them monitor their children's television viewing. But when they have it, they're fairly united—in not bothering with it.

- Treasured family rituals have also degenerated: now trips to Target and watching videos have replaced holidays and vacations as sources of closeness.

Even though standards of quality parenting are lower, Moms and Dads feel they can't keep up. "The overwhelming majority of Americans, between 80 and 88 percent, believe that being a parent is much more difficult than it used to be," said Jean Bethke

Elshtain in a panel for a Minneapolis think tank. "Pessimism about the decline of family values is increasing. . . . "

It's not that parents love their children less than in generations past. It's that they no longer receive consistent societal support for the belief that parenting is the highest priority. In times when mobility didn't pry families apart, Grandma was on the scene to help Mother teach the right thing. When Ozzie and Harriet Nelson's life was celebrated rather than scorned, TV messages championed rather than detracted from wholesome ideals. In days when women enjoyed being home for the kids, peers came over for basketball in the driveway and homemade lemonade rather than scattering for unsupervised explorations. Maybe "the old days" before the social changes of the '60s weren't perfect, but they allowed a bevy of family-friendly forces to surround parents with encouragement for their mission: to honor God, country, and family, to use that white picket fence to keep out threats to childhood, and keep loved ones close at hand.

The Defense

A Precious Absence

"There isn't this innocence of childhood among many children, what with broken homes and violence. We can't treat children as if they're all living in tract homes of the 1950s and everyone is happy. That is ridiculous."

—David Vogel, president of Walt Disney Pictures, July 1997

You might recall from our discussion of media this comment by the head of Disney's family films division justifying a harder edge to some of their product. Sentiments like those underscore that the children of our culture have lost something precious. But exactly what *is* "this innocence of childhood"? What is it that Mr. Vogel thinks broken homes and violence stole? What magic brought "tract homes of the 1950's" the happiness he believes is so "ridiculous" today?

We can most easily define innocence as an *absence* of negative qualities, like cynicism, corruption, and degradation. "Innocent, n. a person knowing no evil or sin, as a child," says *Webster's New World Dictionary*. "Lacking in sophistication or worldliness," says our computer's dictionary. Just about everyone would agree that childhood innocence is precious, and that adults should guard it. But how do you protect an absence?

While conducting the research for this book, we found bounteous resources lamenting the pushing, hurrying, and premature sophistication of young people, but we discovered *nothing* analyzing what innocence really is.

Innocence as Gump

Is innocence ignorance? Is it simplicity? Not exactly. The 1994 film *Forrest Gump* emerged as one of the most popular movies of all time, earning more than three hundred million dollars at the box office domestically and winning six Oscars, including those for Best Director (Robert Zemeckis), Best Actor (Tom Hanks), and Best Picture. The powerful appeal of this movie involved more than the accomplishments of a retarded man, or the dazzling re-creation of historical and personal events through which he lived. The character Forrest Gump was neither ignorant nor a fool; he'd observed too much for that. Though he had a limited IQ, viewers embraced him emotionally because of his charming innocence, his unsullied perspective on the world, which was more gentle, more open and accepting than the view of the rest of us.

It always surprised us that the many critics who sought to belittle *Forrest Gump* regularly wrote it off as a simplistic, sappy "feelgood" movie. This sort of characterization makes us wonder if they had even seen it, because the main character goes through a series of almost unimaginable tragedies. He is born with limited intelligence, and he feels it painfully. As a boy, he is forced to wear braces on his legs, and he is incessantly tormented by his peers. Eventually he goes to war and watches his best friend die in his arms, while his courageous command officer loses both legs on the battlefield. His adored mother also dies before his eyes, and the woman he has loved since childhood, after rejecting him time and time again for some twenty years, dies within a few months of their marriage.

Some "feel-good" movie. If Forrest had lived in our crybaby culture, he would have felt entitled to self-pity and victimhood, as "mentally challenged," the son of a single mother, an abandoned Vietnam vet, the husband of an AIDS patient—you name it. But instead of whining, Forrest Gump held fast to his unshakable optimism and felt grateful for what favors he received. That's the deeper meaning of the movie's signature line, when Mama Gump tells Forrest: "Life is like a box of chocolates; you never know what you're gonna get." Sure, you could get a nougat, you could get a covered almond, you could get a cherry cordial, but the most important thing about a box of chocolates is that everything it contains is *sweet*. The film, in other words, suggests that all life's surprises and different tastes amount to treats.

We've described the four sources of the assault on innocence: from media, schools, peers, and parents themselves. But now we want to turn to this basic concept of innocence, the essence of which can be the glory of childhood. Forrest Gump's confidence in a chocolate-box life embodies the three fundamental components of innocence: *security, a sense of wonder*, and *optimism*. We'd like to talk about each of these, and offer families concrete means to maintain and enhance these elements of innocence for their children.

A Gradual Unfolding

Childhood is perhaps the only phase of life when innocence can flourish. But to allow this, parents and others responsible for children's minds need to construct a protective shelter against the painful and frightening facets of life. They need to stand guard at its door, to let the harsher truths of reality *gradually unfold for the child*, in a way and at a pace that allows the child to maintain a positive outlook. Honoring innocence is incompatible with assuming that the earlier children grasp all of the worst aspects of the world, the better prepared they'll be to handle them.

Children are by definition immature: in other words, not ready, not fully developed, unripe. Becoming ready is a process of making sense of the facts and events of immediate daily life; of integrating interactions with people at home, at school, at church, and in the community. In each of these contexts, children encounter both tangible and abstract information—that letters symbolize sounds, that squiggles represent letters, that something invisible, like sound waves, TV signals, and God, can translate into something we see in our concrete world. That kids don't run screaming from information overload is a miracle in itself. Adding scary possibilities that are *not* reality for them just increases the burdens of their development, injecting fear, worry, paranoia, guilt, anger, and pessimism into the other integrative tasks they face. For example, little children don't need to know the details of "what could happen to you," with descriptions specifying that the stranger could grab you and shove you into his car and take off your clothes and . . . It's enough that they learn "Don't talk to strangers," sparing them from injuring images.

We're alarmed at parents' insensitivity about the images they allow into their children's minds and very souls. Parents bring their kids to R-rated films, knowing they'll see close-up dismemberments and sordid sexual encounters. They bring their little ones to John D. Long Lake in Union, South Carolina, to see where Susan Smith drowned her two little boys, and to O. J. Simpson's house on Rockingham Drive in Brentwood. Crimes and tragic events may be part of life, but they were not a big part of *their* young lives until these youngsters' idiotic parents actively chose to make them so.

Most parents consider consequences more fully. Dear friends of ours chose to leave their five young children at home while they attended the funeral of a family member. Though the children knew and loved the deceased man well, the smart mom explained that they were "just kids" and shouldn't have memories of their relatives' grief impressed on their psyches.

The components of innocence—security, a sense of wonder, and optimism—are not just throwaway by-products of the ignorance of youth. They form an important positive basis for the development of the self—which is, after all, the primary task of the early years of life. Childhood is the only time when observations and responses don't have to be accurate, when we expect mistakes and grant leeway. Only children enjoy the luxury of viewing life as unshaped, ill-defined, constantly assembling. Like expressionist art, the world is vague but vibrant. Later, there's plenty of time for the sharp definition of realism.

7

The First Component of Innocence: Security

What is security?

Well, some folks arm their homes with a security system. Security means keeping intruders away—making sure the borders are secure against invasion.

Security, according to our dictionary, includes the ideas of peace, protection, insurance, confidence, self-assurance.

We asked three fathers, and here are their definitions: "Money in the bank and a guarantee that my job's permanent." "Having a house that's paid for and a pension." "Enough put away to live off the interest."

They're pretty typical. Adults usually think of security in financial terms, in terms of making sure that the family stays in comfortable circumstances, free from worries about the basics: a home, the groceries, clothing, transportation, and daily expenses like school field trips, birthday gifts, insurance premiums, downtown parking fees. They think of Social Security, a fall-back assurance that the government will take care of you no matter what happens.

Dads often think they're adding to family security by accelerating in their careers, taking lots of lucrative business trips, working late, pushing to earn bigger bucks by investing more and more time, energy, and focus.

But if you ask most moms and any child, Dad provides *more* security by just being home every night. For kids, security means something completely different from the usual breadwinner or business world definition. It means predictability, routine, expectations never unfulfilled. It means parents right there for them; the opposite of that panic they feel when lost in a huge department store. Children want confidence that their world can be counted upon: consistency, constancy, reliability.

Our house has a somewhat unusual floor plan, with the children's bedrooms upstairs and the master bedroom on the ground floor. It's 3 A.M. Danny wakes up in the night. He's alone in his bedroom. He runs down the stairs: *chonk, chonk, chonk.* We hear him coming toward our bedroom, *chonk, chonk, chonk,* his little feet on the hardwood floor. Even in his stupor, he's trained himself to veer off to the bathroom first, but then that famous *chonk, chonk, chonk* heads our way; he jumps up on our bed, wedges himself between us, and settles in for the rest of the night, one hand on Mommy, the other on Baba. Ahh, security.

He knows we'll be there. As we sleep, if his little foot drifts from contact with Mommy's, he unconsciously reaches out again. He wants to touch us. He wants that reassurance that nothing can harm him, that he's always protected, always desired. His experience has taught him to expect it.

We were delighted when our girls came home from school eager to share the Shakespeare sonnet they had memorized:

> *Shall I compare thee to a summer's day?*
> *Thou art more lovely and more temperate:*
> *Rough winds do shake the darling buds of May,*
> *And summer's lease hath all too short a date;*
> *Sometime too hot the eye of heaven shines,*
> *And often is his gold complexion dimm'd;*
> *And every fair from fair sometime declines,*
> *By chance, or nature's changing course untrimm'd:*

But thy eternal summer shall not fade
Nor lose possession of that fair thou ow'st,
Nor shall Death brag thou wand'rest in his shade,
When in eternal lines to time thou grow'st;
So long as men can breathe, or eyes can see,
So long lives this, and this gives life to thee.

We transcribed Sarah's recitation not to boast of our daughters' accomplishments, though we're certainly proud, or to offer some novel interpretation of the most celebrated poetry in the English language. Listening to our daughter declaim these words, originally intended as a declaration of love, brought to mind exactly what children want—a mild, permanent, consistent, predictable world. One that lives beyond the death of cartoon characters, one that stays firm beyond the darling buds of May. They crave a life lovely and temperate.

In August of 1996, the Medved family settled into a new home in Seattle. For Michael, the rather sudden move, to accept a wonderful offer of his own radio show, came after twenty years living in the same house in a beach community of Los Angeles. For Diane, it represented the first time in her life she had lived outside Los Angeles. As challenging as the move may have been for the two of us, however, it's been much harder for our kids. At ages nine, seven, and four, they left the only home, the only friends, the only world they had ever known.

In our old house, Sarah knew where each of her twenty Barbie dolls sat along the edge of her upper bunk. Shayna knew the location of each of her frilly Sabbath-day dresses in her closet. The girls knew exactly which inches of their shared room were common ground and which were strictly private.

They knew that our baby-sitter, Kristy, would make them eat "one green thing" along with their packaged kosher macaroni and cheese dinner every night. They could walk across the street to their friend Elizabeth's house, or down two houses to the home of Auntie Denise, who had known Diane since junior high. Their grandparents were a short Sunday drive away, Unkey Harry just six blocks from our door. Our religious Jewish community encircled us within a radius of only a few blocks, the children's school and our synagogue together on property within a ten-minute's walk.

Then late one Saturday in August, at the conclusion of our Sabbath, an enormous moving van having emptied our now-cavernous home two days before, we loaded the last of our belongings into our minivan and headed north. Michael was fueled with adrenaline, Diane with exhaustion and trepidation, as we made our way onto Interstate 5 heading toward a home we'd bought in a whirlwind two days and barely remembered. Our children, though, could do little more than moan. "I miss Percy!" Danny wailed about the Springer Spaniel we'd had to place in a new home. "When can I come see Aliza?" Sarah demanded, missing her best friend, who now wore the other half of a split heart-shaped necklace. "What will I sleep on?" Shayna wondered, realizing she'd no longer inhabit her familiar lower bunk.

Michael, enchanted with the Northwest since his first family trip to the 1962 World's Fair, was so excited by the adventure that he drove nonstop—twenty-seven hours—to our new home. Sure, he got lost trying to find our somewhat hidden block, but immediately the thrill of a new life in a safe, unpolluted neighborhood in view of Mt. Rainier brought him deep satisfaction.

The transition was less smooth for the rest of us. Diane kept wondering when the "extended vacation" would be over. Sarah was sullen; Shayna, sunny at heart, kept making long-distance phone calls. Danny pined for Percy and his friends and teacher in the old neighborhood. Our house, not decorated to our taste, took a year's painting, rearranging, and replacing of broken elements to accommodate us comfortably. Only after many months did we final settle in.

The move was definitely worthwhile, and confirmed our strong belief in planting roots—in your home, in your family, in your community. That involves making a commitment, making an investment both physically and emotionally, in your surroundings.

Natural Conservatives

Children's craving for security makes them natural conservatives, meaning they want to conserve, not disturb, everything in their lives. Kids despise change.

They feel most comfortable with a reliable routine, surrounded by familiar people, with few surprises. They don't like rearranging their schedules, as teachers can tell you during that first week of the new school year.

They don't like deviations in their diets. When Michael was young, his perpetual dinner of choice was hot-dogs. Now, our kids demand "mac 'n cheese" every night. And from what we hear, our Shayna is not the first youngster to insist on peanut-butter-and-jelly sandwiches in her lunch box day after day.

Children stick to favorites in clothes, and have to wear them a certain way. Take socks, that most basic of footwear. For our girls, permissible socks have to be stretchy cotton, not pure (flabby) cotton, and the ribs have to be close together. The most contentious aspect of socks is, of course, the seams. Seams must be minimal, inside the sock, and run along the tops of the toes just so. Perhaps the bugaboo in your house is a favorite T-shirt, worn till filthy and torn. If you're Danny Medved, it's a faded green sweatshirt, the same color as Mommy's.

Children incorporate their environments into their identities— "*my* house, *my* school, *my* block." Don't tangle with Danny if he thinks you're after any of *his* toy guns, *his* Legos, or *his* baseball stuff. Moreover, he *becomes* his setups, like the policeman with a dozen accouterments stuck in his belt: a billy club, a walkie-talkie, a plastic Bowie knife, an assortment of fake guns, handcuffs. He wears all black except the sparkle of several badges and the red rickrack on his boots. Or he might become a cowboy, with red bandana, felt hat, and bolo tie. Danny's possessions fuel fodder for his imagination, while allowing him to exert control over his environment.

Children get stubborn if anything deviates from their vision of order regarding material items or just "the way things are supposed to be." Not long ago Diane spoke at the Iowa Governor's Conference on the Family and included an anecdote about our daughters' ponytails. Both Shayna and Sarah adamantly insist that the hair combed back into their rubber-coated holders not have any lumps; it must lie flat against their scalps as it pulls from the roots to the ponytail. Diane remembers countless rushed mornings reconstructing our girls' ponytails because of lumps, real and imagined. Her frustration was a cosmic retribution for exasperating her *own* mother with the same complaint. After Diane's speech, she felt gratified when a circle of mothers gathered to confirm that ponytail bumps were a universal nuisance.

Stop the World, I Want to Grow

The reason all children are natural conservatives and crave external security is that so much in their bodies and minds is changing at an astounding speed. Growth and development in the early years staggers the imagination and reminds us of the miraculous complexity of the human body. From birth to age one, a baby grows more than at any other time of life, tripling in weight, doubling in height, little by little changing from a mouth-centric, instinct-driven blob to a responding, walking, verbal human with a will of his own. And from then on, children confront and adjust to the world differently each day, seeing events and people and themselves from a maturing perspective, building on progress of the day before. Every child is self-absorbed; his first task is to *self-define*, to understand what goes on in his own mind and body. In this context, the environment intrudes.

For children, the world is a puzzle and they try to exchange the pieces that don't fit. Our Danny, at two, heard Michael on the radio and thought that his Baba was inside the little box. He talked back to "Baba in the radio": "Baba!" he yelled, his face against the grille, "when are you coming out of there?" The next year, after much explanation from his sisters, he understood that Baba wasn't wadded up inside the radio, but he thought that, like a tape cassette, his voice was being played from a recording. Only at age four, when Danny actually saw Baba working in the studio, and when Danny himself got to speak into the microphone and "be on the radio," did he understand that the radio is a machine that plays Baba speaking from far away. Neither parent can explain any more than that, so Danny's education about sound waves and radio receiving remains at a standstill. The point is that children constantly reconcile what they believe to be true with new, conflicting knowledge. Couple that with bodily growth, and children experience plenty of change in their lives *without* major external, circumstantial shifts. Anything that anchors them, that offers them comfort and stability to undergird their development, allows them to handle their natural uncertainties more successfully.

Unfortunately, we live in a time notorious for rampant insecurities. Divorce is so common that even children in demonstrative, rock-solid homes ask their parents for reassurances. Since 27 percent of children in America live with only one biological parent, every child in the country is likely to know people touched by divorce. While most children do not directly experience a parent's death while young, they hear enough TV and radio news and headlines of tragedies to make them worry about random accidents or crimes tearing apart their homes. Media bring fears of disruption by all sorts of "bad guys," from tax collectors to burglars to arsonists. Coverage of trials like that of O. J. Simpson leave them doubting even heroes.

Threats to children's sense of security pop up in many forms parents never consider. Even a local supermarket changing its name and redesigning its aisles can disorient little ones. Rearranging household furniture, entering a new school, even Mom's dyeing her hair can cause stress and jar kids' security. Changes adults consider positive—like buying a new car—can bring protests from children, who may view every sort of variation as threatening.

You certainly can't and shouldn't shelter children from *all* change; children need practice to develop flexibility, adaptability, initiative, and a sense of adventure, all characteristics useful during childhood as well as the rest of their lives. But that's the point— expose kids to the skills and information they need to know *now*, to succeed day to day during *this* phase of development. As their needs increase, so can their knowledge and skills.

We know that many people think fifth graders *need* to know about drugs and sixth graders *need* to learn about condoms because they're bound to confront them. We've been fortunate in being able to travel extensively across America, speaking for an array of organizations and meeting thousands of wonderful people. From what we see, the vast majority of children simply do not face significant threats from drugs and sex at such young ages. Look at the studies, like the January 1997 Pew Research survey showing that most parents are happy with their kids and most Americans are satisfied with their lives. They think their own offspring are going to do better than they have, but they also think society at large is a mess, that the family overall is in trouble, and that kids in general are imperiled and likely to do worse than their parents.

So it's a mistaken image, not reality, that leads people to fixate on preparation and to seek to steel our youth. Thanks, media: you guys bring the extremes up-close-and-personal, convincing us that the unusual is dominant and encroaching rapidly—when in truth it's not that bad. Yes, sex education and drug prevention programs have failed miserably, and recent alarming statistics show that children at decreasing ages become exposed to drugs and sex. But these studies only confirm to us the need to abandon the failed model of early preparation, and embrace once more protection and prolonging of childhood. Parents shouldn't fall back on schools and churches to teach values and educate their youngsters—they need to make it their first priority to supervise and communicate with their children, sensitive to the information their particular kids *really* need.

Knowing What to Expect

The way to satisfy kids' craving for predictability, structure, and routine is to give it to them. The basis of security for children is *knowing what to expect.*

If parents made decisions with that in mind, they would probably live quite differently from the norm we observe in our culture now. For example, here's some child-based advice (written with the help of Shayna and Sarah Medved):

"Don't change the house. And don't touch the furniture in my room, especially where I have my bed. I might want to move things around myself, but really, I like the way things are right now. I know exactly where I keep everything. I don't want you to touch it. Come in and read to me, but put the book back on the same shelf.

"Don't ever move. I like my friends. I like our house. It's my home!

"Don't ever get divorced. We belong together. We're a family. Even if you don't like each other. You tell me and my brother to stop fighting, to apologize. Why shouldn't adults stop fighting and apologize too?"

These three items address the most frightening threats to security for children: disorientation, surprise changes, and the end of parental love. Perhaps one of the worst innovations in our selfish divorce culture is shared custody. Forcing upon children two sets of furniture, two closets of toys, an alternating schedule, and tense moments of dropoff and pickup leaves them certain of one thing—that they can't count on anything at all.

The consequences can be hard to see. A seven-year-old boy, arising groggy-eyed at 2 A.M. to go to the bathroom, wasn't sure which home he was in that night, wandered into the kitchen, and made a wet contribution to the pail next to the mop. A five-year-old girl wouldn't part with her overnight bag for even a moment, because it was the only thing she knew would be with her every night of the week.

A firm sense of place is basic to security for anyone. When Diane wrote *The American Family: Discovering the Values That Make Us Strong* with former Vice President Dan Quayle, to her surprise she found that all five featured families credited their successes in large measure to solid links to their immediate environments:

- The farm family in Virginia that together built and maintained a full-service country inn

- The surf shop magnate in Hawaii who got his start as a talented surfboard rider and shaper

- The Mexican-American elders in East Los Angeles who raised their family on the same street where they were born

- The inner-city African-American family in Chicago that, with the camaraderie of neighbors, made their block a safe haven in a rough part of town

- The Irish-American single mother who never gave up on the poor Indianapolis neighborhood where she grew up—living just four doors away from her birthplace

Each of these families enjoyed a connection to the piece of earth where they lived for at least twenty-five years. Their children grew up with a most fundamental security—that relationships in their world remained durable, reliable, and well grounded.

Ceremonially Yours

It amazes us how, by day, many parents stick to the appointments in their Filofaxes, sure to appear for their business meetings punctually. But once they get home, they abandon their organized orientations in favor of "relaxing." That means everyone "grazes" for food, as the evening deteriorates into a maze of parallel activities—two televisions showing competing programs, the computer on, somebody on the phone, and another one out at the gym or a class. Nothing wrong with some "down time," everyone's allowed a night or two per week to "veg out," though most likely afterward the veggees feel they've wasted their time.

But the more routine, ceremony, and fulfilled expectations available to kids, the more secure they feel. Here are some suggestions your family can use to turn everyday, weekly, or seasonal events into specific reminders of ever-present love and stability within your home.

Talk About It

Most families cherish their rituals but can greatly increase their value by *talking* about them, both before (to set up expectations and anticipation) and afterward. Participating in the activity is only half of it; the other half is reinforcing its importance. For example, the bedtime routine of bath, toothbrushing, reading a story, prayer, and a kiss goodnight is terrific—but you can elevate it by, for example, making the selection of a book to read a privilege. Mom can continue to celebrate those moments, by talking at breakfast or to outsiders within the kids' earshot about how precious that time is to her.

Janet Kinosian, writing in the *Los Angeles Times*, described some of the high-tech means by which '90s parents inject ritual and routine into their fast-track schedules. Our first thought when we read her article was that parenthood has sadly deteriorated, because some of these rituals divert the attention of family members in the same room to the TV screen—as does the family that rents a video to watch together every week. But sharing any experience together is valuable, and the process of riding to the video store to jointly choose a movie, and playing amateur critic afterward, all give family members a chance to connect in a personal way.

"Family rituals and all the little warm, intimate behaviors that bind families together grow more important with time," Kinosian writes. "The simpler, the sweeter, the better." She makes an important point—reminiscing about the past is in itself the basis of precious closeness. Looking at photo albums together intensifies the old warm fuzzies. Our daughter Sarah loves the Sabbath morning ritual she shares with Diane of scrutinizing photos from her early childhood. Each photo is an occasion to revisit the original setting, retell stories of happy events, and solidify an ongoing bond.

Fulfilled Expectations Promote Security

Seasons give our lives structure, order, anticipation. Decorating the Christmas tree is a favorite for many families, often with carols, yule log, and the careful unwrapping of homemade ornaments, each a treasured memory of years past. Holidays are natural occasions to personalize because they're already set aside by our culture.

A symptom of dysfunctional families is failure to establish wonderfully hokey traditions. In her psychology practice, Diane often hears clients lamenting that their families couldn't fulfill their expectations or mystique for holidays, leading to the seasonal depression typically trotted out by feature writers every December. But holidays simply emphasize the underlying problem of too little reassurance the rest of the year. Diane's clients felt insecure about the emotional foundations of their families, so they put too much stake in the hope that days designated by the outside culture for demonstrations of love would mend torn closeness. When families incorporate unique traditions into *daily* and *weekly* routine, the holidays don't become an exaggerated focus for the emotional intimacy family members crave.

Rituals offer more than just warm memories. Special behaviors give your family its *identity*, and assure your children a comforting place.

What do we mean by special behaviors? Unselfish efforts demonstrating devotion and commitment. Tucking a loving note into each child's lunch box. Bringing the children chocolate upon returning from a business trip. Playing basketball with the kids every Saturday night. Using pet names for everyone. Serving Daddy cocoa in bed every Sunday. Stopping for pancakes on the way home from church. Leaving a fake flower on a different dinner plate each night, the recipient to describe his day first. Not just little courtesies, but traditions that involve the family members, that reaffirm inclusion. Underscore the idea that family members can justifiably *expect* these niceties. They're not just sweet surprises, but the bedrock of security.

Take birthdays. Everyone has them, and most everyone enjoys the traditions of the birthday cake, singing "Happy Birthday to You," and blowing out the candles. Great start, but it's worthwhile talking about birthdays as a *family* occasion. We collected a few ideas. One family ties helium balloons—one per year of life—to the birthday boy's bedframe during the night—so he wakes up to a profusion of color. Another takes a portrait of each family member on her birthday and puts them in a montage in their entryway. A third family with a cluster of birthdays in the same two-week period throws a joint family party, but one child picks the cake, another picks out the theme and paper goods, and the third selects a piñata.

In our own family at birthday time, Diane goes crazy decorating our dining room with banners and streamers and colored flags—to Michael's chagrin. She makes a cake in the flavor choice of the honoree, lavishly writing greetings on the top in frosting. And she insists on capturing every moment of the festivities with both video and still cameras.

Creating family traditions around birthday celebrations—however silly, sentimental, or substantive those traditions may be—can play a useful role in promoting a child's sense of security and pre-dictability. After all, the underlying message of any birthday is change. Suddenly, the child is older, facing new challenges and an altered reality, learning to provide an entirely fresh answer to that inevitable question, "How old are you?" Familiar patterns in observing such milestones help balance the note of transition and growth with a reassuring emphasis on consistency and reliability.

Religious Ritual as a Source of Security

Each family develops its own unique and sometimes quirky tradi-tions for observing birthdays, meals, bedtime, and other occa-sions. Older rituals, rooted in religious faith, involve more timeless and universal elements, and play an even more significant role in providing children with a secure, solid understanding of their place in the family and in the world. If a child attends services with his parents in a strange place and hears familiar prayers or hymns, that place becomes suddenly less strange. Any youngster will feel more confident and rooted to discover that other members of the same faith throughout the world share behaviors and values that play a part in his life. Best of all, religious practice can connect a child not only with parents who follow the same rules and proce-dures, but even with great-grandparents he never knew and other unseen ancestors. This time-honored observance shows consis-tent patterns going back hundreds (if not thousands) of years, greatly enhancing the security that is an essential element of inno-cence.

We saw religious tradition perform its comforting, protective function with our own kids when they faced the greatest challenge of their young lives: moving to a new home. We have written previ-ously of the anxiety and downright dread that the three children felt as they arrived for the first time in the big, empty house they'd never even seen before. To make the situation all the more stress-ful, the moving van conveying all our possessions from Los Angeles to Seattle faced a series of unexpected delays. After driving north in an exhausting trek in our minivan, we lived for six days in our new home with none of our familiar furniture or other belongings, bedding down in sleeping bags on the floor of the master bedroom where we huddled together for comfort.

We've tried to train the children to avoid pointless complaints and self-pity but in those first days in Seattle they couldn't help themselves. At one time or another, they each gave in to crying jags about their perilous new situation, creating fleeting moments of guilt and doubt for both parents. As we waited each day for the wayward moving van and began to question whether we'd ever feel settled and safe again, we got a phone call from the tardy movers informing us that we'd face our first Sabbath in the Northwest without clean clothes, beds, tables, toys, dishes, or other amenities that we'd always taken for granted.

At Diane's insistence, the Medved family tried to transform this uncomfortable situation into a playful adventure. She secured paper plates, paper cups, a floral bouquet, Sabbath wine, candles, and some fresh, store-bought kosher bread. Even though we still found ourselves camping out in sleeping bags in a bare, echoing, utterly unfurnished house, we prepared to experience our first Friday night in our new home. As the summer light faded and the sun headed for the horizon, Diane lit the traditional candles and our two girls, as always, joined her in the familiar blessing. The family linked arms for the cherished hymn, "Shalom Aleichem," or "Peace Unto You," which emphasizes the protective role of Sabbath angels in sheltering the home. Michael sang the "kiddush," the sanctification of the wine, and then placed his hands on the head of each child, from oldest to youngest, pronouncing the blessing of the children which they'd been hearing since long before they could possibly understand its meaning.

At this point, Sarah, our first born, who'd been sniveling all day, pining over the friends she missed and the room in the old house she always cherished, finally began to brighten. Just before we broke bread for this first makeshift Sabbath meal in the new house, she came over and hugged her father, letting go of her resentment against the parent who'd promoted this wrenching move. "You know," she said with a shy smile, "I think maybe it's going to be okay here."

Her grudging acceptance of our new home at that precious moment related directly to the familiar ritual that enveloped her.

She knew the melodies, the prayers, the tastes, the reassuring Shabbat patterns—Seattle seemed less menacing, less cold, less alien when her immediate environment took on a loving flavor and an ancient essence that she'd known all her life. Religious ritual allows you to re-create aspects of home wherever you happen to be. If children understand that God is everywhere, and if they feel comfortable in their relationship with God, then they can never be far from home.

In Jewish tradition, we begin each day by reciting "*Modeh ani . . . ,*" the Hebrew declaration of personal thanks to the Almighty, "the ever-living King," for allowing us to awaken to a new day. Wherever you happen to arise, this formulation makes the place you've spent the night your own protected bed.

To maximize the role of religious ritual in promoting children's security, that ritual must engage adults as well as kids. This is not only important in order to avoid any sense of hypocrisy or inconsistency, but because children feel inevitably more secure when they see their parents behaving predictably. A pattern of shared religious observance—saying blessings at mealtime, going to church every Sunday, praying together as a family—shows children that the most important adults in their world follow some reliable standards, greatly enhancing their sense that life is orderly and safe.

This sense is especially important when children face situations that might otherwise seem chaotic and threatening—like moving to a new home or, much worse, adjusting to separation or divorce. Unfortunately, many adults will react to the pain of marital breakup by dropping or diluting religious ritual—as if changed circumstances have rendered such gestures empty and meaningless. When a husband and wife face the overwhelming pain of a shattering relationship, it becomes understandably difficult to focus much energy on the little details of day-to-day faith that may suddenly seem irrelevant.

For children, however, problems in their parents' marriage make familiar rituals far more important, not less so. If a mother or father can find the courage to hold on to prayer and other religious behavior as a facet of daily life in the face of family instability, they can send a powerful message to kids that God is still there, even if Daddy (or Mommy) is gone.

Most Americans instinctively understand the crucial importance of faith in equipping their children with a sense of security. As a result, giving thanks for food has become the practice of a majority of American parents: 63 percent of Americans with kids say grace before meals, according to a *USA Today* poll, a notable increase from the 1947 figure of 43 percent. University of California at Santa Barbara professor Wade Clark Roof, who wrote *A Generation of Seekers* about baby boomers and religion, thinks it's an adjunct to the new thrust toward family values. Gratitude to God for meals not only directs children beyond their selfish hunger, it demonstrates that even parents share subservience to authority—motivating kids to respond to parents' directives.

Family Home Evening is a weekly feature for members of the Church of Jesus Christ of Latter Day Saints (the Mormons), with the express purpose of unifying the family around wholesome church-centered activities. This Monday night ritual not only models for children parents' dedication to their faith but, equally important, the priority of their family. Resource books lay out lessons on values from Authority to Work, in which family members focus together on specific activities and thought-provoking questions.

Call Back Later, We're Having Dinner

Americans still consider mealtime togetherness an ideal. For good reason: research shows that a habit of family dinners correlates highly with strong school achievement. Families that make family dinner an inviolate occasion at least four times weekly give their children an advantage—in large measure because kids gain security from their parents' commitment and interest. When Diane was growing up, her family would gather to consume the meal her mother had made—usually a ground beef foil-like spaghetti, stuffed peppers, or "Hamburger Haven," a casserole with noodles, olives, tomatoes, and celery—at 6 P.M when her dad arrived home from work. During that time, no one took phone calls, easily deflecting them with "We're having dinner." Callers universally understood the sanctity of the dinner hour and apologized for intruding on a revered ritual. Diane's dad brought his latest copy of *U.S. News &*

World Report to the table, and as her mother asked each child about the day, her dad would pepper the conversation with exclamations about "shocking" news items. This scene was so common at the time—the 1950s and '60s—that virtually all of Diane's friends enjoyed variants of it simultaneously.

And in our fragmented culture, yearning for those mealtime-based family bonds has returned. An October 1997 cover story in *USA Today* proclaims "Dinner Traditions Nourish Families: A Hunger for Kinship Brings the Ritual Back." The article notes "surveys show that a majority of American families preserve the nightly sit-down dinner—for at least the immediate nuclear family—five to seven nights a week."

Unfortunately, some hurried families dismiss that American ideal of family security. "It's highly overrated," says novelist Carolyn See. "If you like each other it's wonderful to sit down at the dinner table and talk, but where people are not very fond of each other, it's torture." She thinks that one out of five family members is likely to be in such a bad mood that he ruins the experience for everyone else. "Then anything you say is a potential time bomb," she asserts. "Nobody knows what's going to set someone off."

Of course, in more traditional days, the dinner table was a platform to teach manners, and parents chastised unseemly explosions as inappropriate for the table. One Southern California grandmother, acknowledging that her adult children are always on the go, tries to offer her grandchildren some dinner structure. But it's tense: "All I'm doing is telling them to sit up straight, put the napkin in their lap."

The Security of a Napkin in the Lap

That's right, put the napkin in your lap. Don't just grab one of those flimsy ones from the dispenser, dab your drippy lips, and stick it under your plate. When families dropped formal meals, they lost an equally important source of security for kids: *etiquette*. Etiquette represents more than a tradition, more than a crucial means for civilizing people, keeping them conscious of consideration for others.

Etiquette is particularly essential for children because it provides them with perhaps the most powerful source of security: *knowing what's expected of them.*

When we expect a child to behave "like a little lady," she raises her standards for herself. She understands that she can *control* her inclinations, overriding them in order to behave in an admirable, elevated way. One of the books we're especially glad that Uncle Harry gave to our children is the imaginative Sesyle Joslin classic *What Do You Do, Dear?* originally published in 1961, a delightful romp made irresistible with illustrations by Maurice Sendak. Subtitled *A Second Handbook of Etiquette for Young Ladies and Gentlemen to be Used as a Guide for Everyday Social Behavior* (it is the sequel to *What Do You Say, Dear?*), the slim publication derives its humor from the assumption that every child already knows a core of well-worn reminders of proper conduct. A few examples:

> You are at the North Pole, sitting in your igloo eating a bit of blubber, when in comes a huge lady polar bear wearing a white fur coat. What do you do, dear?
> . Help her off with her coat.
> You are riding downtown in a rather crowded howdah. The elephant stops at the corner and a lady climbs aboard, but there is no place for her to sit. What do you do, dear?
> Offer your seat to the lady.
> You have just taken a great mouthful of pudding when into the dining room rides a handsome prince on a white horse. He says, "I am a handsome prince. Would you care to marry me?" What do you do, dear?
> Swallow what you are eating before you speak.

How many parents nowadays teach their young progeny to help ladies off with their coats, offer their seats to elders, or swallow their food before speaking? Probably not many. But in ignoring such rules of kindness, they deprive their children of a sense of order. Children comfortable with etiquette will be at ease in nearly any social setting. Deborah Leyde, mother of Laura, eleven, and Brett, nine, confessed that when her family (with her husband,

Dale, a pilot) were first invited to our home for the formal occasion of a Sabbath meal, she worried that her children wouldn't know their manners. In anticipation, she staged a rehearsal and drilled her already well-behaved youngsters on the courtesies of fork selection and soup-bowl tilting. Her charming children, who have become close pals to the Medveds, needn't have bothered. With parents so concerned about their children's social skills, they already fit in beautifully in the most elegant of settings.

According to a *U.S. News & World Report* poll of April 1996, 89 percent of Americans think incivility is a serious problem. More than three in four said it's gotten worse in the past ten years. Some people, however, are willing to pay to put rude sayings in their homes. Here's a trivial but representative example of how incivility has crept into our daily lives, often under the guise of humor. An item in an upscale Christmas sales catalog—one that under its name proclaims "A World of Gracious Living"—offered among its porcelain candlesticks, monogrammed bridge tablecloths, and gilded cherub music boxes, two wooden plaques: "Dear Lord, If you can't make me skinny, please make my friends fat" and "Be kind to your kids: they pick your nursing homes." Is it only out-of-date sensitivity to perceive an edge of hostility here?

The problem has not escaped the notice of national leaders: retired Senator Sam Nunn of Georgia and *Book of Virtues* author and former Education Secretary William Bennett are heading the National Commission on Civic Renewal, a group in the process of publishing "an inventory of hope" of community efforts to combat impolite behavior. But laudable as neighborhood endeavors are, incivility is only *manifest* in the marketplace or the village; it doesn't originate there. Children whose parents enforce good manners can face glaring rudeness in public and survive with their courtesies intact. They only need three conditions:

1. Parents who model proper behavior (and, ideally, discuss it, politely correcting each other in private when necessary)

2. Parents who openly and consistently *insist* that children practice good manners

3. Friends and associates who reinforce proper behavior

This means that parents must, from their children's earliest ages, place their offspring in environments conducive to these values. Children are going to emulate those around them; smart parents select church, school, extracurricular groups, and friendships wisely, aware of the crucial impact of associations.

"Manners are no more coercive than a dance step is coercive, and indeed they are liberating: seating ladies and opening doors for people, and writing thank-you notes to grandmother, are acts of compliance with a code, but they also facilitate social dealings and the growth and expression of true kindness."

—RICHARD WILBUR, *CHRONICLES*,
SEPTEMBER 1996

These Are the Rules

Etiquette is a recognized form of clear expectations, but rules of etiquette come from strangers. Even more vital to children's security are the rules *parents* set. Sure, every parent sets *some* limits: "Go to the bathroom in a toilet, not at the side of the road." "Brush your teeth." "Wear matching shoes." But many modern parents, in an effort to honor kids' "natural," more primitive instincts, which they consider superior to convention, back off from all but the bare basics. Using the same logic that has kids "discovering" the right answers to addition problems, they think they're doing their youngsters a favor by letting them find their own way, or by letting them express whatever feelings they harbor. But children *need* limits—to balance their selfish, egocentric, megalomaniacal inclinations. Without clear boundaries and consequences, children become spoiled, arrogant, and inconsiderate. And because they get mixed messages about whether they or adults call the shots, they push—and win—in conflicts over authority. In the end, they view adults as incompetent, leaving them mistrustful, jaded, and cynical.

Not long ago, our eleven-year-old Sarah came to us with a look of concern. "It's about Danny," she began. "I think he has too much self-esteem." And indeed, the family joke goes "How many Dannys does it take to screw in a lightbulb? One: Danny holds the bulb and the world revolves around him." Danny needs those boundaries, and sometimes also needs a *potch* (spanking) when he refuses to abide by them.

But every parent knows that the rules mean nothing if they're not applied consistently. And of course, softies buckle. "Consistent consequences": easy to say, difficult to carry out. But here we should mention the benefit of having two parents in the home—one (typically the mother) who is more merciful, and another (typically the father) who metes out justice. The more important of the two, for building security, is the justice giver. In life, people face the consequences of their actions. You're late to work for a week, you get fired. You fail your test, you don't pass the course. You don't pay the rent for your storefront, your business gets the heave-ho. That sense of "If A, then B" is what gives children the freedom not to worry. It gives kids the option to focus on playing the game, because they already know the rules.

William Damon, in *Greater Expectations*, writes that children come equipped with a "drive for competence" and thrive on challenges, so demanding that they follow the rules actually meets a need in them. The reward for succeeding in fulfilling requirements is an innate satisfaction, he suggests. Maintaining high academic standards or posting a bulletin board list enumerating a child's chores exercises that drive, through a structure that trains children to meet subsequent demands.

Delineating rules strongly from the earliest ages—particularly rules emphasizing self-discipline and control—provides your children with two extremely worthwhile benefits:

1. Knowing what is expected of them forms the security children need for innocence.

2. Limits enforced and practiced from early ages pay off later, inoculating your kids with self-discipline against the social problems plaguing teens.

If they master self-control when they're young, then "just say no" will be a concept repeated internally for years, not simply a slogan thrown at them by school authorities.

Limits, Security, and Teen Pregnancy

Individual parents setting and enforcing limits can collectively curb larger social problems. Teen out-of-wedlock pregnancy is not only a misfortune for the girl, thrust into adulthood when entitled to several more years of unencumbered development and exploration, but it's a hardship for the baby, born into unstable financial circumstances and usually raised by only one parent.

But we remember when the concept of sexual abstinence wasn't marred by such a distasteful-sounding term, and teenagers knew clear distinctions between girls with poor reputations and the rest, presumed virtuous. Until the early 1970s, schools didn't even consider discussing condoms, plastic wrap, and birth control options, because students learned from their earliest cognition—through older siblings, in the media, through discussions at home—the common value that sex should be reserved for marriage. In those days, consensus held that unmarried people who indulged their passions acted shamefully.

In most high school classes in that pre–sexual revolution era, one or two girls would leave discreetly before the conclusion of the semester, and their classmates reacted with dismay and shock. Most pregnant teens got married to spare embarrassment, and undoubtedly some of these marriages failed. The stigma placed on premarital sex certainly led to some tragedies—including self-inflicted abortions that were dangerous if not deadly, but the incidence of out-of-wedlock pregnancy overall was significantly lower than the soaring rates of the 1970s and beyond.

When nonmarital pregnancy rates began to escalate, educators looked at the difficulty. Rather than acknowledging that sexual liberation produced problematic results and working to restore the sanity of previous values, they got swept up in the "who are we to judge?" mentality (increasingly as liberationist boomers infiltrated the education establishment). They couldn't say that extramarital sex was bad; they couldn't say that the old values were better than the new ones. They couldn't separate out the idea of civil liberties for minorities from sexual liberties for everyone. Instead of stemming the problem, they chose merely to cope with it: "OK—you've got younger kids having sex and more getting pregnant. It's a fact, so we need to give them information about birth control." In other words, they took on the preparation model, and its permissive underpinnings negated the security of a set of unified standards.

What did we get? Higher rates of illegitimacy. More promiscuity. Did our educators' approach work? No way.

According to Census Bureau statistics, the birth rate for unmarried girls aged fifteen through nineteen was just 5.6 percent in 1950. It climbed steadily from then on: to 6.7 percent in 1960, 12.3 percent in 1965, and 19.4 percent in 1970. It kept rising, to 30.9 percent in 1993. And lest you think that a higher teen birth rate is a personal choice and not a social problem, "by the time their first baby is 5 years old, 72% of white teens and 84% of black teens have received Aid to Families with Dependent Children" (welfare), notes the National Fatherhood Initiative.

So, as the stigma disappeared, more unmarried teens had babies. Or it could be the other way around—as more teens had babies, the stigma disappeared. Hard to tell, because the sexual revolution led more girls to be sexually active, and of course, as a consequence, more got pregnant. And remember, the rise in the out-of-wedlock birthrate occurred simultaneously with an escalating abortion rate. At present, a third of the million teenage pregnancies each year are aborted.

But the main thread here is the sexual revolution, which made formerly strong limits on behavior across the culture break down. With the end of that society-wide security came a burgeoning social problem. Interestingly, official government census terms reflect the demise of the stigma—figures that until the 1970s appeared under the heading "illegitimacy rates" were renamed the less judgmental "births to unmarried women." With the disappearance of the stigma came the decline of the notorious "shotgun" or forced wedding. Young adults today wouldn't even understand the cartoon image of Pa nudging his future son-in-law to the Justice of the Peace with the barrel of a rifle.

The disgrace of illegitimacy became so passé that even some high-achieving older women with a stake in maintaining a positive professional image decided to have babies on their own. Unmarried TV character Murphy Brown set off a controversy in 1992 over appropriate media role models, at a time when a growing number of women chose a similar course. A September 1997 report on 1992 data released by the Census Bureau found that "6% of unmarried women with bachelor's degrees had had children, up from 2.7% 10 years earlier." In another finding, "never-married women with children holding managerial and professional jobs rose from 3.1% in 1982 to 8.6% in 1992." Report author Amara Bachu concluded from the data, "This suggests the out-of-wedlock birth is not viewed as a social stigma any more.

But there's been a sea change. Now, the lack of shame is gaining national attention—as a major problem. "The growing movement towards virginity among the young has been compelling," announced Family Research Council Policy Analyst Gracie Hsu after the Centers for Disease Control and Prevention released data showing a decline in premarital births in October 1996. She cited a raft of mainstream magazines that "have all reported on the new wave of 'smart, sassy and hip' virgins who are proclaiming that they are 'proud to be pure.'" More than half a million teenagers took the Southern Baptists' "True Love Waits" pledge sponsored by many church youth groups; Alma Powell and Elayne Bennett's Best Friends program had expanded to fifty schools in fifteen cities by 1997; evaluations of Chicago's Facing Reality program showed that it changed behavior, even convincing a large majority of sexually active kids to say no to sex. Curricula offered by Teen-Aid in Spokane, Washington; the FACTS Project in Portland, Oregon; and RSVP, based in Cuyahoga Falls, Ohio, all boast figures demonstrating effectiveness.

But for individual parents, the most important news is that this focused effort toward abstinence seems to have turned around the trends. For the first time in twenty-five years, the National Survey of Family growth, an in-depth federal study conducted every five years, showed a decrease in teenage sexuality. In statistics released in May 1997, 50 percent of teenage girls said they'd had intercourse at least once, down 5 percent from the 1990 survey. Previously, girls' sex rates had climbed with every survey since 1970, when 29 percent said they'd had sex. Expecting high personal standards seems to be more beneficial than expecting kids to succumb to temptation.

Security comes from lack of ambiguity. "Sex outside of marriage is wrong" is a lot easier to comprehend than "We'd like you to wait until marriage, but we know you have raging hormones, and given that we don't have the authority or power to stop you, you might as well know about condoms, birth control, and abortion." With that approach, kids get the confusing message that adults really think sex out of marriage is acceptable but are too hypocritical to state it bluntly.

Strong standards not only work to curb societal ills, but also answer a growing call for greater accountability for youth. The New York research organization Public Agenda surveyed adults and concluded, "Americans are convinced that today's adolescents face a crisis—not in their economic or physical well-being but in their values and morals." Nine out of ten adults said that the failure to learn values is widespread, and only 19 percent said that parents are commonly good role models. Half of the adults polled said that it is very common for parents to fail to discipline their children. Asked to describe today's teens, two-thirds offered negative terms, such as *rude, wild,* and *irresponsible.* A full half came up with *spoiled* to describe younger children; nearly a third chose the word *lazy.*

The Public Agenda study suggests that children are not the only ones who need limits on their behavior. *We* need limits on children, to make our *own* lives freer from problems and more refined.

Children's security doesn't come from watered-down values instruction offered in schools (though schools should reinforce and respect the values kids learn from their parents). Kids need the consistency of limits set in their own homes, from their earliest years. They need to know what's expected of them on an array of basics: in terms of respect for elders, in terms of their responsibilities in the family, in terms of courtesies and kindness. "If we wait until they're eight, it's too late," says Bellingham, Washington, Detective Steve Lance, an expert on juvenile habitual offenders. "We've got to get them when they're *two.*"

And we need to be adult enough to actively take on the responsibility of upholding and teaching high standards. Don Eberly of the National Fatherhood Initiative wrote in the *Wall Street Journal*: "Where do empathy, character and self-restraint come from? The primary seedbed of civil society and virtue is the family. This is the toughest truth of all, but refusal to grasp it results in extraordinary hardship for America's children and injury to society."

Standards, Morals, Security ... and Innocence

We're not the first commentators to urge that high moral standards once again become the primary goal of parents for their offspring. But we see it as more than merely a means to create upstanding citizens in an uplifted society—we see standards as essential to an effort to restore childhood *for children.* The security of standards *protects children's innocence,* allowing them to grow up with at least a *glimpse* of an idyllic existence. That glimpse provides them with something to hang on to, something toward which to strive when their lives become fraught with adult worries—or fall to far less than that ideal.

Many middle-aged adults retain a nostalgia for our childhoods because we *enjoyed* that precious space of possibility. We knew we were kids, and we reveled in it. We knew adults were authorities, and we respected it. A surprisingly unified society drew the lines, and our junior status gave us security: security to keep out intrusions from this special unencumbered time and space. Security to lie peacefully in our backyards and watch ladybugs climb blades of grass.

One force preventing today's parents from providing such security for their children is a sense of unworthiness, insecurity, and guilt. We look back on our own mothers and fathers and feel at times that we can't measure up. Statistics show that these earlier generations only rarely divorced, whereas our incidence of marital splits and recombinations has vastly increased. Our parents often lived in the same community and worked at the same job for decades if not lifetimes; now, in a turbocharged global economy, shifts in career and home address occur with unprecedented frequency. No wonder that many mothers and fathers feel powerless to provide the predictability and reliability that they instinctively know their children need.

The important point to keep in mind is that security, like all other aspects of childhood innocence, is a continuum, not an absolute. No parents will either absolutely succeed or absolutely fail when it comes to providing a secure environment for their kids. Conscientious families will do the best they can, even under uncomfortable circumstances.

We acknowledge that parents in personal or financial turmoil may face special problems in following the recommendations in this chapter for predictably patterned adult conduct, religious ritual and clear messages about what we expect from our children. Sometimes, with the best of intentions, you can't avoid a shattering change in family status or an emotionally devastating relocation. Such challenges make attempts to nourish security both more difficult and more necessary. Young people need elements of reassurance, involving both small gestures and major sacrifices, more than ever if their family situation turns worrisome or unstable.

Some measure of uncertainty or doubt will afflict developing youngsters in even the happiest, most secure, most lovingly sheltered home environments; such insecurities are as much a part of childhood as skinning knees or losing baby teeth. Parents can't make the growing years of their offspring perfect, but that doesn't mean that they shouldn't try to protect them. Our own sense of imperfection and insecurity shouldn't prevent a conscientious effort to nourish a sense of security in our kids. We may not succeed in creating a childhood Eden, but we can at least provide a fragrant garden.

8

The Second Component of Innocence: A Sense of Wonder

Why do parents lie to their kids?

Dear Editor: I am 8 years old. Some of my little friends say there is no Santa Claus. Papa says "If you see it in The Sun it's so." Please tell me the truth, is there a Santa Claus?
—Virginia O'Hanlon, 115 West 95th Street
Letter to the *New York Sun*, September 21, 1897

Yes, Virginia, there is a Santa Claus. He exists as certainly as love and generosity and devotion exist, and you know that they abound and give to your life its highest beauty and joy. Alas! How dreary would be the world if there were no Santa Claus! It would be as dreary as if there were no Virginias. There would be no childlike faith then, no poetry, no romance to make tolerable this existence. We should have no enjoyment, except in sense and sight. The eternal light with which childhood fills the world would be extinguished. . . .

The most real things in the world are those that neither children nor men can see. Did you ever see fairies dancing on the lawn? Of course not, but that's no proof that they are not there. Nobody can conceive or imagine all the wonders there are unseen and unseeable in the world.

. . . No Santa Claus! Thank God! he lives, and he lives forever. A thousand years from now, Virginia, nay, ten times ten thousand years from now, he will continue to make glad the heart of childhood.

—Editorial reply by Francis Pharcellus Church

Eloquence in defense of innocence. Why do parents lie to their kids? Because they dearly want innocence to exist in the world—and without children, we have no other source.

And what is more clearly innocent than a child's belief in boundless goodness, even in the face of the physically impossible? Flying reindeer? An overweight senior citizen squeezing down millions of chimneys in a single night? Only in protected childhood can such thrilling fantasies seem possible.

Saving Santa Claus

"What this child is doing is knocking on the door of the adult world and asking to be let in," says *New York Times* editorial page editor Howell Raines of the "Yes, Virginia" editorial. "And what this editor is doing is protecting her—and his adult readers." What does he mean by "protecting his adult readers"? From having to explain their deception to disgruntled youngsters? No, the editor protects them from losing access to children's innocence. *Adults want kids to believe in Santa Claus* because they treasure and crave their own small echo of a child's sense of wonder.

Pulitzer Prize jury chairman for 1997 Bob Haiman asks, "Do you suppose there are any 8-year-olds left in America who still believe in Santa Claus? One can only hope."

Yet the sense of wonder about holidays seems to be slipping in America. Illustrating this point was a January 4, 1998, *New York Times* article headed "There Went the Holidays. Whoopee," accompanied by a photograph with two components: a dull-faced businessman passing a discarded Christmas tree rolling in the gutter of a Manhattan street, and a public trash barrel with a sign admonishing Don't Litter, Put It Here, on which perched an enormous, pathetically denuded wreath. Writer Allen R. Meyerson dubs the dulling of celebrations "Holiday Rot" and points to compacting presidents' birthdays, the end of Easter parades, the near-oblivion of Columbus Day, the downplaying of Memorial and Labor days, and replacing New Year's Eve with First Night in hopes of diminishing drunk driving. Meyerson speculates that festivals are flopping because fewer employers offer the time off with pay, and fewer workers have unions to negotiate holidays for them. Also, as civic organizations, and even bowling leagues, lose members to fast-track schedules, no one's left to stage all these celebrations.

But we don't think that Americans *like* their holidays stolen away. They yearn, of course, for any opportunity to revel, but beyond that, they yearn for ways to bring charm and sentimentality into their lives. Nothing can do that better than sharing flights of fancy with children. Belief in Santa Claus is the premier example of unifying regression to simplicity.

When we speak to groups around the United States about childhood, we encounter near-universal approval of the "adult conspiracy" of Kris Kringle. The sprightly old elf probably has the highest approval rating of any public figure, across every demographic line. After all, retailers, grandparents, and the media all foster the legend. Stores now sell special Night Before Christmas plates for children to leave cookies for their benefactor, with matching milk cups for the man in red. Elaborate stockings, large enough for Bigfoot but delicately edged with family members' names in gold lamé and rickrack, decorate mantelpieces across our nation in anticipation of St. Nick's bounty. Shopping malls discovered generations ago that the jolly fat man lures hoards of shoppers to their emporia, and parents willingly stand in line for hours, waiting as their squirming but eager offspring whisper their cherished desires. Most delighted moms and dads leave the scene clutching a pricey Polaroid of their darlings posed against billows of white beard.

Santa is so ubiquitous that even the Medveds own photos of their Jewish children in Santa's squeeze. Last December, when our brood were ten, seven, and four, we went for a ride on the Mt. Rainier

Scenic Railroad, only to discover that it was the "Santa Train." Our seats were in the front of the car. The train chugged out of the station, and suddenly a trio of lady elves singing "Deck the Halls," one jauntily playing an accordion, burst in, immediately followed by Santa himself. He grabbed our startled Sarah and bounced her onto his plump lap, calling for Mom to take a picture. Diane, intimidated, complied, and our prim daughter's expression of frozen dismay comprises one of our most amusing photos.

Danny and Shayna got the grab next. They were struck dumb with all eyes in the railroad car on them, when portly Santa boomed the question, "And what should Santa bring *you* for Christmas this year?" All three received candy canes to assuage their embarrassment.

Fantasies of Justice in the World

One reason Santa resonates with parents is that we all yearn for justice in the world—and the idea that a kindly being rewards good children and leaves coal to those less deserving is a mystical concept made more concrete in the form of the red-suited reindeer driver. It's *useful* for children to consider that there may be consequences to their behavior. "Have you been a good little girl this year?" every department store Santa intones. And every child nods; but for that split second before the head starts bobbing, the question registers. Yes, you get goodies, but only if you earn them.

We realize that some families downplay Santa because they don't want to make receiving toys rather than the birth of Jesus the center of the holiday. They see the popularized St. Nick as symbolic of the commercialism and selfishness that turn a religious event into a retailing feeding frenzy. While we respect that sentiment, we think parents can present Christmas and Santa Claus in a context that maintains the dignity of the day as well as the joy of the fantasy.

Santa Claus and the Easter Bunny are the *only* subjects around which American adults regularly and collectively salute and exercise their imaginations—for the express purpose of delighting children. In other words, for *the express purpose of creating and maintaining childhood* as a separate experience from adulthood. What a wonderful practice: adults bonding in a positive conspiracy to enhance children's sense of wonder and hope.

Santa Claus as an American Hero

In an era of few real-life heroes, people care even more that Santa remain saintly. And as separation of church and state cases cause cities to downplay many religious aspects of Advent, Santa Claus, seen as secular and nonpartisan, simultaneously rises toward the sacred.

Residents of the Northwest expressed compound horror at the November 1997 case of Lake Forest Park, Washington, shopping mall Santa Ronald C. McDonald, seventy-one, who admitted raping or molesting at least forty-five children over the past sixty years, some as young as *two months* old. McDonald, called Santa year-round because of his white hair and glasses, "was a pedophile who charmed parents with his Santa persona, then charmed their children with dolls and child videos," reported the *Seattle Times*. McDonald's despicable acts evoked special outrage because he murdered innocence on two counts. First, he raped very young children—disgustingly imposing his aberrant adult sexuality—and second, he destroyed victims' trust in adults, especially since he portrayed the universal symbol of benevolence, justice, kindness, and generosity. Any child hearing the TV news or reading of this sordid case suffered that loss as well.

Americans insist on maintaining public trust in this mythical figure partially because they know that only a fictitious character can be trusted completely. As recent history proves, politicians who ostensibly represent their constituents honestly may be dishonest in their personal lives or in the pursuit and protection of public office. Advertisers make big promises and often deliver little results. We cynically expect exaggeration when the contractor says the house add-on will take a month and hold to budget, or when the refrigerator repairman says he'll be there by ten. Everyone recognizes "The check's in the mail!" as a code word for "I don't have the money."

No wonder that in any other context, at any time except Yuletide, institutional authorities squelch any sense of wonder, replacing it with suspicion. Joy Pfaff, a seventy-three-year-old grandfather in Manhattan, Kansas, was a school crossing guard, a job he took for seven dollars an hour to keep busy after retiring as a custodian for the police department. To delight his young charges, he regularly dressed up as Santa at Christmastime, as a Pilgrim at

Thanksgiving, and as the Easter Bunny for the spring holiday. He gave candy and hugs to the children. Though "there was no complaint of criminal misconduct," said police Major Larry Woodyard, Mr. Pfaff was asked to resign because parents were concerned that he was "too close to the children."

The Possibility of Magic

Defining a sense of wonder is as simple as comprehending why *New York Sun* editor Church answered Virginia O'Hanlon's query with his declaration of faith. Wonder is a delightful mix of awe and excitement, an opportunity for the possibility of magic.

For many years, Diane begged her parents to tell her—even at age twelve, fourteen, and twenty—the truth about the Tooth Fairy. Her parents maintain to this day that the sprite who slid dimes under their daughter's pillow is real, proving that a sense of wonder need not be restricted by age. Now both eighty-three, married for fifty-four years, her parents retain that delightful childlike twinkle.

While there's evidence that rushing to prepare children for the harsh possibilities of the world can harm them (in some cases actually encouraging the negative behavior that programs seek to retard), we have no evidence that promoting happy myths like Santa Claus, the Easter Bunny, and the Tooth Fairy brings any harm at all. The only negative result comes when adults or older children too soon expose the delightful fantasy as false, shattering the happy illusion. Diane remembers that in her own childhood, parents of a young playmate decided to disabuse their daughter on the subject of Santa on the girl's seventh birthday. The result: Diane's friend was crushed. Other little friends, whose parents enjoyed Santa's presence, suffered no such letdown when later, at age eleven or twelve, they learned the facts about the Christmas Eve tradition.

Fudging the Truth

Some people just don't get it. Whenever we lecture on the sense of wonder, some angry parent will rise and accuse us of abusing our children's trust. We opened this chapter with the big question: How can we lie to them about mythical beings—tooth fairies and toys with feelings—and then expect them to believe us on more important topics?

We reply that honesty and creativity can coexist, and that parents must strictly delineate the important topics requiring absolute truth from the parallel sphere of artistry and fancy. Kids need to understand the value of integrity, and understand that they must be direct and honest regarding their conduct and reporting events, period. The 1997 film *Liar, Liar* portrays Jim Carrey as a self-serving, manipulative lawyer who can't complete even a single day without lying. When his five-year-old son gets his birthday wish that Dad spend twenty-four hours speaking only the truth, Carrey finally understands the personal consequences of his prevarication. Understanding that both words and ideas have consequences is a lesson everyone must comprehend.

Sensitive people present the truth in a considerate, loving way. We *care* about others' reactions, and so we may speak indirectly in order to spare others' feelings. For example, our tradition commands observant Jews to substitute a kindly comment for the truth when fact would serve to cause only hurt or disappointment—say, when a friend with an ugly haircut asks, "How do you like it?" or one with a crummy new car inquires, "Don't you think it's great?"

The term *white lie* acknowledges the benefit of stretching the truth in order to spare another hurt. When we say the kind thing rather than the most direct truth, we can mend or save friendships, bring harmony to our marriages, and encourage our youngsters. We'd never tell Danny that his crooked scrawl isn't terrific. We wouldn't tell any child that his artwork isn't inspired. Learning to discern the subtleties of the proper time to omit or overlook the truth is a major task of development.

The Wonder of Imagination

But we require only *selective* accuracy from young children. Honesty about real events—describing what actually happened—is the basis of a trusting parent-child relationship, but when a little child invents situations or overlays fanciful distortion on basic facts, we call it something other than lying: *imagination.*

Danny spent an entire three-mile walk to the synagogue one Sabbath describing feats he performed with his "magic powers." Danny swears he can fly, he has superhuman strength, and he can dispense any amount of his powers to whomever he chooses. He uses his astounding gifts to benefit law and order, capturing the bad guys of our town from the most improbable angles. Of course, he combines his derring-do with the liberal use of firearms and weapons, rescuing weaklings like Mommy from the clutches of incompetent robbers. At home, he can spend an hour or so staring into the looking-glassed corner of our bathroom, playing with his "mirror friends." When Danny moves or dances or throws a karate chop, the dutiful friends imitate. They're silent, but they communicate by movement. Danny understands them, and they populate his world. Listening to his inventions, as good parents, do we tell Danny to stop lying? The reason why Officer Danny and the Tooth Fairy are not lies is because they belong to that special time of childhood.

"What's that?" actor Peter Fonda used to say to our Sarah, then about three, snatching an invisible something from the air near her face. "It's your imagination," he'd smile, inspiring her delight. Michael was working with Peter on a book project, and it was in that process that we fully grasped the facile imagination of actors and others whose careers involve complete empathy. Perhaps it is that small corner of imagination in each of us that keeps Santa Claus alive.

The Medved children voted as best film of 1997 *Fairytale*, a magical enchantment based loosely on a true story of two little girls, eight and twelve, who took photographs of the gossamer-winged sprites that inhabited a nearby "beck" (stream-side) in Yorkshire, England, in 1917. The girls' photographs passed muster with photo fraud experts and captured the attention of Sir Arthur Conan Doyle and Harry Houdini. Once Doyle published the photos, hoards descended on the rural town, all yearning to confirm hope and goodness in a dark hour of World War I. The movie is in itself a proclamation of childhood's sense of wonder, but one scene in particular crystallizes the juxtaposition between adult skepticism and innocent belief.

Sitting at the celebrated brook with his daughter, Elsie, the older girl's dad, employed by the local mill, laments the tourists' ruination of the fairy bower. He finds a tiny throne made for the fairies by the girl's older brother before his death from pneumonia just months before. "Why did you make him stop coming to the beck?" asked Elsie.

"He were nearly eleven," her dad responds quietly in his Yorkshire accent. "He would start workin' half-time at the mill when he were twelve. His childhood were nearly over; he just wouldn't let go of it. It was his time to grow up. Yours too, y'know." Sensitive moviegoers felt a collective "Oh no!" at the prospect that these gentle and unsullied children should against their will forfeit their communion with the supernatural. In wartime working-class England, fairies became forbidden once adult responsibility encroached. Have we progressed no farther? Why can't we allow our children a few more years of those gossamer wings?

The Wonder of Children's Literature

Santa Claus and fairies, Easter Bunny and Tooth Fairies—parents can encourage their children's sense of wonder, even in the face of seen-it-all schoolmates and overly frank TV. Other sources of wonder are Aesop's Fables:

The Boy Who Cried "Wolf"

There was once a shepherd boy who kept his flock at a little distance from the village. Once he thought he would play a trick on the villagers and have some fun at their expense. So he ran toward the village crying out, with all his might:

"Wolf! Wolf! Come and help! The wolves are at my lambs!"

The kind villagers left their work and ran to the field to help him. But when they got there, the boy laughed at them for their pains; there was no wolf there.

Still another day the boy tried the same trick and the villagers came running to help and were laughed at again.

Then one day a wolf did break into the fold and began killing the lambs. In great fright, the boy ran back for help. "Wolf! Wolf!" he screamed. "There is a wolf in the flock! Help!"

The villagers heard him, but they thought it was another mean trick; no one paid the least attention, or went near him. And the shepherd boy lost all his sheep.

That is the kind of thing that happens to people who lie: even when they do tell the truth they will not be believed.

Choose books to read to your children specifically with a sense of wonder in mind. Anything that expands their time and space or refocuses their attention can inspire the sense of discovery. One of the books Diane's parents read to her as a child is also beloved by our own children because its tone is one of positive excitement about life's simplicity. When our Sarah was born, we received a new version of the book, updated to a 1983 copyright from its original 1955. It's *The Golden Book of 365 Stories: A Story for Every Day of the Year*, by Kathryn Jackson, illustrated by Richard Scarry. Our daughters like to randomly select the half-page stories, begging Diane to read five, seven, or ten at a sitting. Each charming entry pertains to a particular date and season, so we could start anywhere and continue the cycle. For awhile, we'd read one story a night on the correct day. Then we'd do it again, starting from the end of the book backward because we thought the ones at the end got neglected. They captivate because they redirect our sights from the mega-headlines in the newspaper to the wonder found every day of the year in the smallest of corners:

JULY 10

High in the branches—look at me,
Perched like a bird in the cherry tree—
With the big, black cherries all around,
And the hard, little seeds down on the ground;
Enough for the squirrels—all they please—
And more to grow to be cherry trees,

> *Full of black cherries, warm and sweet,*
> *For the hungry birds—and me—to eat.*

And of course, we spare no sentiment when we read Robert Louis Stevenson's classic definition of childhood, *A Child's Garden of Verses*. When our children come to us complaining of boredom, we simply respond, "The world is so full of a number of things, I'm sure we should all be as happy as kings." Diane remembers her father, born in 1914, reciting "The Land of Counterpane," recalling in luxurious couplets the sick boy's transformation of his bed sheets into the wondrous hills and valleys of his "leaden soldiers'" battle: "I was the giant great and still, / That sits upon the pillow-hill, / And sees before him, dale and plain, / The pleasant land of counterpane."

Professor Mitchell Kalpakgian, in an excellent article in the *New Oxford Review*, argues that "Children who grow up in daycare institutions rather than in homes, children whose main source of pleasure comes from the video culture of television and movies, and children who enjoy no leisure because of over-regimented lives are spiritually starved. . . . " He insists that in order to become intellectually complete adults, kids need "a true childhood [that] provides leisure and light-mindedness—an atmosphere of play that stimulates the creative imagination and nourishes the inner life of the mind and soul."

Bash the Batteries

And how does this come about? Through classic, nonelectric, springs-from-the-mind activities that kids can do alone, with friends, or with you. The kind of play with just a few props, certainly none with batteries. We're not so extreme as to suggest that you throw away all the electronic gadgets—but think about the *drawbacks* of externally powered toys:

- They *do something on their own* rather than requiring the involvement of your child. So the child is more passive and less active.

- *What* they do is predetermined and so retards creativity and discovery and the wonder that accompanies it.

- Most externally powered toys perform *for the user alone*, discouraging play with others. We're becoming a solo culture, sadly free of tea parties, teddy-bear picnics, and kid-staged extemporaneous dramatics.

- *They don't last long.* They break. They need new batteries. Once they've performed, they lose their novelty, and because they're good for one function or action only, they become relegated to the toy cupboard.

Now think of classic toys. The kind you loved as a kid and want to make sure your own children enjoy. A hoola hoop. A basketball. A "play food" set. The *Toy Story* basics: a slinky, toy soldiers, an Etch-A-Sketch. Legos. Lincoln Logs. Why do parents pay Art Fair craftsmen high prices for handmade wooden toys—a smooth-edged choo-choo, a car with bright wheels and a hole in the center for a little hand? Because these are the heirlooms of childhood. These are the raw materials with which children make the most significant developmental strides as well as the warmest memories.

With the approval of our children, we've come up with our idea of—

The Well-Stocked Toy Chest

Crayons and coloring books

Plain paper, pens, scissors

Sports equipment: a bouncy ball, a basketball, a baseball, a bat and glove

Legos and blocks

Small plastic animals or toy soldiers or dinosaurs

Bubbles

A Frisbee

A blanket (to make forts, houses)

Many classic books

A bicycle or tricycle

Puzzles

Stuffed animals and puppets

A bucket and shovel and some gardening tools

"Play food" (cardboard boxes, plastic jars)

Play-Doh

Rope

A few plastic cars

Dress-up clothes

Dolls or "action figures"

After our first pass at a list, we asked our children to add their own suggestions of toys that encourage their imagination. None of our three, ages five, eight, and eleven, mentioned a battery- or electric-powered toy of any kind.

After we composed our list, we came across an announcement of the Toy Hall of Fame of A. C. Gilbert Discovery Village in Salem, Oregon, which inducted its inaugural eleven toys in February 1998. The hall, named for the Salem native who invented the Erector Set, American Flyer trains, and Gilbert chemistry sets, will open in a restored house donated to the city and built in the 1880s. "Nominations [of classic toys] were sought in newspaper advertisements placed around the country," said an Associated Press story, and the winners were culled from sixty-four nominees. More brand-name conscious than the items on the Medved list—though nearly identical—the Hall of Fame honors Barbie, Play-Doh, Etch-A-Sketch, Frisbee, Crayola crayons, Legos, marbles, the Erector Set, the teddy bear, Monopoly, and Tinker Toys.

Professor Kalpakagian says that play enhances intelligence through practice at extrapolating conclusions and uncovering universal truths. "If the young do not enjoy the normal, natural, innocent joys of childhood," he warns, "they will indulge in empty, banal entertainments," patronizing an industry designed "to pander to bored and already jaded youth with ever heavier doses of sex, violence and horror."

TV as the Enemy of Awe

When TV news shows bloody shoot-out scenes, and movies compete in their graphic portrayals of diabolically executed murders, we're insulted that Hollywood dares respond to critics with a shrug of the shoulders and the excuse that they provide merely harmless diversions. We don't buy it. When kids replace their own fantasy and imagination with manufactured images of mutilation, they are victims of harm. Clicking on the remote control leaves children's impressionable minds open to any scene an advertiser or director wants to flash on the screen, and open to any belief system that will titillate an audience enough to increase profits.

Are we saying that TV programmers are purposefully evil? Not at all—to the contrary, most media decision-makers are nice people with personal goals like the rest of us, but professional goals that are anything but ordinary. After spending a generation living in Los Angeles, we can tell you that people in "the industry" are an incredibly inbred clique, out of touch with America, out of touch with most everyone except their own workaholic cronies. Generally, they believe they're making an important contribution to our culture and producing art that adds to the creative mix. We understand that it's not an either/or situation; parents can allow their children moderate amounts of TV and movies and also read to them. But we think the benefits diminish as the balance tips toward the media side—and that's the side that demands the least of parents and that offers parents more of their own autonomy, a prospect difficult for most parents to resist.

Media vs. Reading

Parents who daily read Robert Louis Stevenson to their children and surround them with blocks, plastic animals, and some cardboard boxes or kitchen pots and pans are going to produce a *quali-*

tatively different child from those who spend that time on TV or videos, even if their choices *are* only Winnie the Pooh and Mr. Rogers. How? There are two sets of benefits.

Benefits of parents reading to children: kids who get parents' attention gain greater self-assurance. They increase their communication skills to meet those of the adult, even an adult who intentionally speaks simply. They see their parents *doing* the reading and seemingly enjoying it, a powerful model. They learn that books offer fun stories and pictures, and feel an affinity for reading because they unconsciously associate it with a chance to be close to Daddy.

The reading parents will likely have more control over the direction of their children's values because of role modeling (transmitted idea: "a parent spends time with children") and discussions of stories. Also, when parents read to their kids, they choose or at least influence the books they read—which are more likely to be *Make Way for Ducklings* than a junior edition of an R. L. Stine. And don't forget the ripple effects of reading—two of the factors most highly correlated with academic success are family dinners and parents who read to their children.

Benefits of children playing with simple toys rather than consuming entertainment on TV and videos: children occupied with play rather than the media can more easily look beyond the superficial plot of a story into the messages beneath the surface— because they've practiced analytical thinking rather than passive receiving. Hearing and discussing underlying meanings and depth can counteract the superficiality that's inescapable in our video culture.

Also important, children encouraged and praised for their imaginative explorations gain confidence that will allow them later to take risks. As our five-year-old son dreams of flying over our town to conquer bad guys, we hope he gains the expansiveness of mind that will someday help him plan and dream for more practical, though perhaps at first just as improbable, means of making a positive contribution to the world.

A child with minimal video and TV exposure—and most kids sponge up four hours or more per day—might be more naive about social ills but at the same time more sophisticated in inner direction, self-discipline, and the realities of her actual physical world. And if the child chooses to read, say, *The Book of Virtues*, or one of the classics, she's going to learn something from every story, as well as tap into the great traditions that Americans share.

Unfolding

In opening the second section of our book, we mentioned that a gentle childhood enjoys the gradual unfolding of the truths of adult reality. It starts small: the world of every baby consists of his mouth and his stomach; as he grows, he expands his consciousness and sphere of control to wider and wider reaches. So it is intellectually; a baby is completely self-centered, with the progression of childhood expanding his understanding to eventually encompass both the concrete and the abstract. By sheltering children from the harsh world, parents allow a time when the child does *not yet* know, can*not* understand, and isn't forced to *care* about distant and weighty topics. Childhood is a time when individuals have the luxury to concentrate on the important rather than the urgent because the exigencies of job, finances, and household responsibility don't press. That leaves room for the important explorations that lay the foundation for lifelong learning.

It is in this space that children experience a sense of wonder—wonder about an unfolding world, the excitement of anticipation, freshness, novelty. When our children were quite small, we received a charming music video called *More Baby Songs*, featuring sweet dramatizations of the delightfully touching music of composer Hap Palmer. So many tunes in the *Baby Songs* series express childhood's sense of wonder that the collection is like a video-age *Child's Garden of Verses*. But none can capture the thrill of discovery better than "Baby's First," which celebrates the freshness of an infant's every activity—baby's first rattle, baby's first bottle, baby's first steps, baby's first photograph—each day's "mundane" activities filled with luscious exploration, momentous accomplishment, and awe. We all long for that precious excitement, which imbues each action with freshness and significance.

I've Got a Secret

In order for youngsters to enjoy a sense of wonder, adults must be actively willing to keep certain difficult and complex areas of concern from their children, to allow a process of discovery lighted by amazement. And a critical prerequisite for amazement is *not fully understanding* the scope of what you're seeing. Think about the last time you felt a sense of wonder, perhaps upon viewing a mountain peak or a virgin forest or a magnificent skyscraper or the sea. What was it about the experience that evoked your wonder? Could it be that you felt like an insignificant yet privileged witness to splendor? A child retains the sensitivity to see splendor in a potato bug rolling into a ball around a twig.

Neil Postman in *The Disappearance of Childhood* calls the information that adults keep separate from children "secrets" and says, "the maintenance of childhood depend[s] on the principles of managed information and sequential learning."

But the word *secret* suggests enticing, exciting knowledge that lends its possessor superiority over the ignorant. One who knows the secret has an advantage through his awareness. However, the secrets of *adulthood* are harsh, morbid, oppressive, and seamy. The information that adults reserve for themselves actually brings obligations, troubles, burdens, and the potential for depression and gloom. Adult concerns are *complex*—and carry layers of consequences, often serious ones, contrasted with children's concerns, which are relatively *simple* and incur only limited consequences. When you hear terms like *adult bookstore, adult content, for adults only*, you understand that the difficulty goes beyond the complexity of the vocabulary or the size of the type, to explicit sex, violence, brutality, severe tension, or terror.

Do we consider any of this better or more uplifting or in any way superior to the bliss we ascribe to ignorance? What do we want for our children? An unflinching, straight-on view of hardship, obligation, and every sordid and ugly possibility, or the brief opportunity to approach life unfettered?

Children may seem at times more advanced than grown-ups. Most kids have more computer smarts by age seven than the majority of today's adults will ever fathom. Certainly our children enjoy far more technological advances than any generation in history. But have they advanced spiritually, emotionally, and intellectually any further than youth of, say, a thousand years ago? Computers aside, real wisdom and maturity come only from experience and education.

Sheltering Childhood

So what can parents do to foster their children's sense of wonder? Every day presents opportunities for guarding and enhancing the simple awe that is truly an entitlement of childhood.

The first tool for any parent is sensitivity, to both the positive and the negative. Parents must vigilantly block negative forces that intrude on children's freedom to enjoy their sense of wonder by feeding them a tough, harsh, mature, or frightening view of the world. On the positive side, parents can hone their sensitivity to the small beauties around them and visibly, audibly celebrate them with their children.

Perhaps one of the most valuable benefits of parenthood is the ability to view life through your children's eyes and to recall and relive your own childhood. Parenthood grants a second chance to share the joy and discovery that *only* children can possess. Take advantage of your opportunity; enhance it. Here are several practical suggestions to adopt immediately toward that end.

No News Is Good News

Try to avoid exposing your children to any media news that you can't filter. As we've discussed in our chapter on the assault by media, the news business is really only the *bad* news business. Of course, there's no way to completely shield your children from life's horrifying realities—but repeated reports of gloom and doom will tamp down the residual hope they have.

Don't listen to radio news while carpooling. Don't watch TV news at all. Neither adults nor children need somebody else editing the facts down to the most sensational scenes: hysterical parents discovering dead children, decimated villages in Yugoslavia, ugly thugs led through jailhouse corridors.

We were enormously fortunate to be in West Palm Beach, Florida, at 4:31 in the morning of January 17, 1994, when the Northridge earthquake, later pegged at 6.6 on the Richter scale, slashed through Los Angeles. On the eve of the temblor, after a visit to Disney World, we'd arrived at the Christian college where Michael had agreed to speak. We awoke in the morning to a telephone call from a university vice president asking if our home had been damaged. What? Our home damaged? Yes, he told us, Los Angeles just endured a horrible earthquake.

We quickly turned on the television, our only source of immediate news, and in terror watched aerial views of homes ripped from their foundations and families perched on cliffs awaiting rescue, screaming and crying. We saw streets of apartment buildings cracked apart and pavement opened by three-foot gaping chasms. Distraught, we tried to phone our families, who lived in the area of the devastation, but the lines were jammed, making contact impossible.

Thankfully, Michael's brother knew our whereabouts and caught an outgoing telephone line. He described the chilling jolt and the anxiety during the thirty seconds of shaking. But everyone we knew emerged for the most part with wealth and goods intact. Despite nearby homes with problems—fallen chimneys, walls cracked and misaligned—the houses on our particular block suffered very minor damage, and our own home escaped unscathed but for one fractured window and lots of items fallen from shelves, with only a few breakages. One friend's home was totaled, Michael's mother's house lost part of its chimney and some plaster, other friends found walls severely cracked. That was the extent of visible earthquake aftermath for us and those we know, and we were not unusual.

Such a relief. Certainly many people did suffer, and multitudes more faced prolonged inconvenience. But for weeks, photos in the newspaper and footage on the TV news brought worse aftershocks than the temblor, as they ceaselessly focused on the most vivid devastation and the most severely overwrought victims. Remember the view of the Santa Monica freeway, split across the middle? The San

Fernando Valley on television looked like Dresden after the bombing because the same rubble-strewn street got played over and over until its scene of destruction became firmly cemented in the mind, to the exclusion of the vast majority of the region that remained pretty much as normal, with business as usual.

Visual extremes stick in children's minds and cause fear about their futures. Another Los Angeles product, the Menendez brothers, who ruthlessly shot their parents as they ate ice cream and watched TV in their family room, planted in children's minds the worst possibility—that a parent could die violently at the hands of a child. Youngsters who otherwise would never hear of such topics as oral sex or abortion learn about them from television and radio news. Even without the visuals, the stories that networks choose to highlight bring the fraction of events that are most frightening into clear focus, ignoring the millions and millions of everyday occurrences that would reassure a youngster.

Still need that news fix? Instead of giving up control over the focus of your eyes, ears, and mind via TV and radio, *read newspapers*. In the same amount of time it takes to lie passively in front of a nightly newscast, you can read *two* newspapers fairly thoroughly. You'll get far more in-depth information, can choose articles selectively, and at the same time can model an active interest in community events and a positive attitude toward reading.

Taming the Birds and the Bees

Sex education. If you don't present the facts of life to your children, then your Jennifer and Jacob will learn elsewhere—at school, on the evening news, from poorly informed friends—without the moral context you want to impart. Trouble is, it's difficult enough that your little one is now at the age when he needs this instruction, and it's uncomfortable when you're not sure exactly what to say.

How do you do it? Teach only as much as your child needs to know, little by little. Give simple answers to simple questions—don't jump ahead and assume that the first query about where babies come from means "this is it" and you have to spit out anatomically correct terms and all the details. We told our older daughter, Sarah, about menstruation at age ten and a half, but that's all we told her. We reserved details about sexual performance for two or three years later but emphasized that we were open to any questions and comments. Fortunately, Sarah knows we're available to discuss *any* topic—and physical development, as we called it, is just another one.

One of the more irritating books we've encountered in our research is *Dr. Ruth Talks to Kids*, where the brutally frank pop culture sex expert addresses kids of (based on photos and text level) approximately ten years old. First off, a sensitive parent would offer different lessons to boys and girls—kids don't need to know every mechanical detail of the opposite sex until much later. Second, the array of topics covered, with no effort to soften the presentation, admits the prepubescent completely and suddenly into the adult circle of knowledge. Any innate embarrassment or hesitancy on the part of children to address these issues gets thwarted right off when Dr. Ruth admonishes, "We're going to talk about things that you might feel are too private to discuss with anyone else. But since these things don't make me feel the least bit uncomfortable, there's no reason why you should feel that way, either." In other words, "Your feelings are stupid. Drop your innocence, kid, you're never turning back."

Children who rely on Dr. Ruth for their anatomy lessons are likely to be terrified. For example, they learn that the vagina is "a barrel-shaped opening" and that "testes keep making sperm all the time, until there's no room for it anymore." They learn the specifics of five erogenous zones. And they find out about "myths"—that menstrual "blood comes from the brain, meaning girls and women can't think straight during their periods, or really crazy things, such as if somebody eats food cooked by a menstruating woman, he or she will get sick." They learn that "when the time comes to have sexual intercourse, the size of your penis doesn't have anything to do with how 'good' at it you'll be, any more than the size of your finger does."

Why is this troublesome? Because most kids at ten have not heard the myths. Easing the minds of the few kids frightened by misinformation is certainly laudable, but it comes at the expense of those who never harbored such fears until the good doctor planted them.

When Diane attended college at UCLA, she volunteered for a

year to staff an information booth set up in the student union by the Student Health Center. She received a few hours' training, which qualified her to sit behind a long table displaying condoms, IUDs, birth control pills, and plastic models of human bodies. Pamphlets and books spread out next to the models also lured students over to ask questions. Though this took place in the sexually liberated 1970s, only a few students per day cared to stop, leaving Diane lots of time to read the materials—the content of which was about on the same level as Dr. Ruth's little talk to ten-year-olds!

Does this simply confirm that today's fifth graders mature earlier and thus need information relevant only to college students twenty-five years ago? Not at all. The age of menarche has remained consistent. Physically, children mature at the same time as they have for generations. The change is spiritual and cultural, as we allow new poisons to intrude on childhood. How sad that we protect spotted owls and inch-long blind fish but give no such protection to our own children's endangered innocence.

Ten- or twelve- or even fourteen-year-olds didn't need advanced sexual details a generation ago, and they don't need them now (in most cases). Children certainly should understand their own development—but given the permissive milieu around them, they don't need more sex talk; they need common sense and support for values that encourage self-respect and sexual restraint. To balance our push-the-envelope culture, kids need an environment of people who are strong in their wholesome values. And they need to know to come to their parents—rather than peers or even school personnel—if they desire or require more.

The truth about the world should unfold gradually—the way counting leads to addition and on to subtraction and multiplication—as our expectations change for children of different ages in social situations, and like the universal agreement that younger children and older children may require different content in movies.

Teaching Safety, Not Fear

While the crime rate at long last seems to be ebbing, the need to caution children against potential harm remains. But the way it's taught makes all the difference between implanting fear—which blunts the excitement about the world central to a sense of wonder—and matter-of-factly imparting common sense. Teach children prudence in behavior but without scare stories about what could happen to them. For example, say simply, "Don't talk to strangers unless you're with us," rather than, "Don't talk to strangers because they might want to put their hands in private places or kidnap you. . . . "

One of the most disconcerting aspects of the Drug Awareness Resistence Education (DARE) program our little Danny received in his kindergarten class was the explicit way the kindly officer described potential harm. Anyone who actually reads the fourteen units of the K–3 level of the program can easily become depressed and paranoid because it portrays everyday encounters as threatening. DARE suggests that lurking beneath the most innocuous interchanges could be nefarious aims, and children at age five learn their every nuance. Yes, it is possible that a seemingly normal encounter can turn dangerous, but the likelihood of that happening becomes greatly magnified in the tone and urgency of DARE warnings.

We remember one recent day when we were on a Sunday outing, riding the ferry for a hike in a state park. A father, surrounded by his wife and three young children, watched Danny make eye contact with his little boy and saw Danny, curious and eager for a new friend, come close to where they were sitting, enjoying a snack. When Danny wandered into the family's midst, the father offered a friendly "Hi." Danny's face froze, and he ran away—so abruptly that Diane became embarrassed and called him on it.

"Officer Dreyer told us never to talk to strangers because they could hurt you," Danny reported dutifully. "Wasn't I good—I didn't talk to that man who said 'Hi' to me!" Danny expected us to praise him but instead earned a discussion about rudeness and the simple courtesy of returning a greeting—especially in the safe presence of his parents.

The Courage to Be Different: A Positive Way to Combat Drugs and Gangs

While the DARE program perhaps goes overboard in its explicit admonitions, it at least has gotten one thing right—keeping kids away from drugs and gangs is a process that starts early. But how do you do that without ruining your children's sense of wonder? Without destroying their faith in the goodness of the world that surrounds and awaits them?

The answer is to *avoid* the negative rather than use the approach of most antidrug programs, which rub children's faces in death statistics or illustrate the stupidity of proving their peer membership or rebellion against parental values. Focus instead on arming them with resistence techniques that they begin to practice from their earliest memories. And the most important technique is instilling in your children the courage to be different.

Admittedly, the Medved family cultivates an unusually high number of ways in which we're different from the dominant culture. We have no TV, and our children can't participate in those next-morning bonding sessions comparing notes on particular fad shows. We observe Jewish law, which means that we eat only kosher food and pull back from normal activity every Friday at sunset until the appearance of "three stars" on Saturday night. We celebrate religious holidays that don't often coincide with the dominant culture's holidays, and we place a high priority on our children's Jewish education, meaning that they have different school experiences from our neighbors. Sometimes these differences interfere with our children's connection with peers; most of the time they don't. But since our youngsters just assume that their lives include our observances, they learn as toddlers to "just say no"—a skill that can't be fostered simply by a slogan on a T-shirt.

Any family can emphasize its differences from the generally schlocky media culture around them. Families that go to church on Sundays gain not only reinforcement of solid values, but an opportunity to point out this difference from others. Becoming involved in an activity that involves discipline—the martial arts or ballet, for example—sets your child apart. Working toward a longer term achievement—such as striving to become an Eagle Scout in Boy Scouts, taking pride in staying on the honor roll, playing on the soccer or Little League team through the season—all give youngsters a special niche that can make them feel distinguished from the crowd.

But it's not enough to schedule activities and hope that an

agenda of wholesome pastimes will instill self-confidence. Parents need to repeatedly discuss *why* each of these endeavors makes the child special, and build up the integrity level of the pursuit so that the child feels he must be worthy of it: "A green belt in karate maintains his honor and makes it a point never to lie to authorities, and that means especially parents. . . . "

Another way to give your children the courage to be different is to emphasize the importance of friendships. Make your home a magnet so kids will want to be there from an early age; invite all your children's friends over; screen friends beginning at preschool age, and discuss your criteria for evaluating them.

When we moved to the Northwest, we looked for a house that would meet our needs—and we only had two days to do it. The house that met our criteria also happened to come with an in-ground pool, which we considered an extravagance in a climate where it can be enjoyed only three months a year. Diane much preferred a garden and suggested filling in the concrete rectangle with earth. But Michael prevailed against her with the winning argument that having a pool would attract our kids' friends and keep Sarah, Shayna, and Danny around us during the summer months.

Now, maintaining a pool may not be feasible for you, but when making choices, consider your priorities. Maybe your magnet can be weekly rituals—like Saturday night basketball or a game of charades with popcorn. The message to repeat both implicitly and explicitly is "We stick together," and "Family comes first." If your child genuinely enjoys family times, later, given a choice of peers, she'll gravitate more naturally to friends who validate the values she's lived and her positive memories. Rebellion or simply going along with the crowd have less pull than years of warm fuzzies.

Promote Peter Pan

One way to innoculate your children against the intrusive impact of extrafamily influences is to glorify childhood innocence. Let your children know—straight out—that our culture has lost its universal protection of that special time of youth and that you, as their parent, will do everything you can to preserve that precious opportunity for them.

And then exercise your own sense of wonder. Promote Peter Pan, marvel at magic shows, applaud at seasonal performances of *The Nutcracker* with its dancing toy soldiers. Make sure your children own books like *A Child's Garden of Verses* and read them at bedtime—or at breakfast! That's the key: demonstrating your own appreciation for wondrous stories and events teaches your children most powerfully, by the method of modeling, to savor opportunities for awe and joy. Every American child is entitled to feel that he or she can "grow up with a sense of wonder, a sense of magic." And every adult who shares that gains an enriched life.

We mentioned earlier our family experience a few years ago at the opera *Hansel and Gretel* by Engelbert Humperdinck. It's a wonderful opera for children. Yes, an *opera*—this is one of the truly beautiful works of the nineteenth century, and especially if it's done in English, kids love it. At the very end of Act I is one of the most touching scenes you will ever see on stage—or on video, where it is available for rental.

The two children, Hansel and Gretel, lost in the woods as night falls, desperately want to get home to their father. They know a scary witch is out there, and she's up to no good. Afraid in the forest, as sleep overtakes them, they sing that famous melody of "The Children's Prayer." They ask God's care, and as they fall asleep, fourteen glowing angels with beautiful wings descend to protect them during the night. Guardian angels are part of the sense of wonder for children. Watching our daughters, engrossed in the scene's majesty, we were both moved to tears. Those angels are there to protect *all* children; that sense of wonder and protectiveness needs to be part of the birthright of every child.

Bust the TV

You've read earlier of the myriad ways television assaults children's innocence. In particular, it destroys their sense of wonder. If imagination allows wonder to flourish, then twenty-four hours a week immersed in a medium that spoon-feeds its own sounds and images with mesmerizing urgency and realism dulls and eventually extinguishes the ability to generate and elaborate on fancy.

It's not just the hypnotic, engrossing, and exclusive nature of viewing television that quashes imagination; it's the negative slant of almost all the content—and the constant repetition of this negativity—which eliminate any belief that the world is wondrous.

We suggested that you spare your children exposure to media news, but *television* news in particular hammers into all of us images that show the world is dangerous and crumbling—images that are the polar opposite of a sense of wonder. A *U.S. News & World Report* and Center for Media and Public Affairs study in 1996 "found that in 59.5 hours of coverage, the TV news operations ran 266 stories that by subject matter or on-air interpretation conveyed a sense of risk or peril—an average 4.5 such stories per hour." Center director Robert Lichter summarized the tube's offerings as "an overwhelming portrayal of general misery. The overall picture is that America's in decline." It feels like a losing battle for a parent to maintain a young child's wonder about bugs and snow and stars when every day he's seeing murders, lawsuits, and natural disasters. What's a lady bug in the face of fires in Indonesia? Who cares about the Big Dipper when you can be watching *Star Wars*?

But the problem isn't just watching the actual news shows. On TV, headlines sneak into every type of programming, inserted in the midst of commercials to pique interest in later newscasts. So anything kids watch on the networks produces the damage that watching the news does. That's why our strongest suggestion for maintaining your kids' sense of wonder is *cut out—or cut down on—TV*. Quite simply, the more you allow this antiwonder force into your minds and homes, the more it destroys.

Play this mind game. Imagine a perfect media world, where Bill Bennett or your pastor controls the content of the programs offered on the tube. Imagine that every show your children watch is as tame as Barney, as educational as *Nova*, as informative as the *NewsHour with Jim Lehrer*, like a huge PBS smorgasbord that you actually enjoy watching. Every show suddenly becomes upbeat and sunny, humorous and entertaining. Suddenly, through some amazing magic, everything on TV is worthwhile. Even in this perfect TV world, would you want your child spending twenty-four hours a week glued to the tube? No! The problem is not too much sex or too much sleaze or too much violence, *it's too much TV—period.*

Of course, the ideal situation would be to just stop watching it. Reclaim those twenty-four hours—and that's just the average weekly viewing rate; lots of folks watch far more. But even if you watch far less, the hour or two you forfeit on TV per day could be put to better use. For example, we were talking before about reading to a child. It takes perhaps ten minutes to recite *Green Eggs and Ham*, but the payoff is far greater, significantly increasing her chance of academic success and enriching your mutual bond. Phoning a sick friend might be a five-minute task, but it makes a far greater impact on the morale of the invalid. Some of the most worthwhile activities can be accomplished in an hour—reading part of a novel, playing a game with your children, exercising, even organizing your closet. There's never time. Never time. Except for your old friends *Ally McBeal* or *Suddenly Susan*. You probably know them far better than you know your neighbors. What a pity. Make a batch of muffins, deliver them next door, and see if you feel any differently than if you'd spent that hour lying in front of the TV.

That lovable ad campaign of ABC, with the mustard background and the absurd sentiments, made a hilarious point in one of its back-cover *TV Guide* ads. Touting its November 1997 lineup, ABC hailed its goals "not only to entertain but to bring America together as one happy, TV-watching community." Wonderfully ironic: holing up in bedrooms and dens focusing on a black box, watching fake situations and scripted lines *prevents* people from finding happiness and feeling a sense of community. TV is bad, and we all know it. We're just too tired or too lazy or too slothful to fight it.

The Liberation of Life TV-Free

But in case you'd still like to try, we have a few suggestions. First off, have a family conference and discuss why you want to reduce or eliminate the time invested in TV. If you're willing to go cold turkey and pitch the box, terrific. We often hear from families who consider their decision to pull the plug the best move they ever made. Karl Zinsmeister interviewed parents in TV-free households in the September-October 1997 issue of *American Enterprise* and found the following results:

"Our children don't have desires now for all kinds of stuff."

"The boys got along better. Before, when they would have a squabble, they would stop playing together and one of them would go turn on the TV set. . . . "

"A local Taco Bell offered one taco for every 400 pages a kid read. And it was a big mistake. Molly won 39 tacos."

"She's remaining a child longer. She's the last in her class to continue to be interested in dolls. She lines them up and plays very elaborate games with them. . . . Her taste in clothing is so child-like I've actually intervened a few times. . . . "

"[They're] more innocent. They are introduced to sexual themes in a very different way. I get to do it, instead of having 'Baywatch' do it. And we see less of the coarseness and cynicism. . . . "

Ask any family that has pitched its television if they regret it. Now ask families that spend a good deal of time watching TV if *they* ever regret it. According to the 1997 *America's Watching* longitudinal study of television viewing, 93 percent of Americans watched broadcast network or local TV programs in the week before the survey. That was a 6 percent gain over the 1994 results.

The Medved family has never owned a TV. Well, the senior Medved family, Michael's parents, *certainly* owned one. And it was on constantly. It was Michael's disgust with his early-life TV addiction that spurred him, once away from home in a TV-less dormitory at Yale (according to university rules), to spurn the centerpiece of his youth.

In fact, in 1984, upon proposing to Diane, Michael had one potentially deal-breaking stipulation: no TV. Diane, smitten beyond redemption, acquiesced and has never missed owning this cultural icon. We do own a video monitor, however, though absence of any antenna or cable makes TV reception impossible. We allow our three children to watch selected and approved videos that we own or rent, up to six hours a week. Through videos, they know the identity of Mr. Rogers, Barney, and a few other television characters. But most of their viewing is classic films. Among our girls' favorites are *The Sound of Music, The King and I, Pride and Prejudice, Singin' in the Rain,* and *My Fair Lady.*

When we asked Danny, five, for a list of favorites, he replied without hesitation, "*The Mole* is Number One!" He's referring to a marvelous nonverbal animated Czechoslovakian series created by Zdenek Miler that enchants viewers of all ages. Michael recommended it as a "family find" while cohosting *Sneak Previews* on PBS, and elements from *The Mole* have been woven into the fabric of our family. (To order, phone 1–800–528-TAPE.) Danny also goes for Spot the dog animated videos (with the charming theme music) and then adds that he loves his "scary videos," which include outer-space howlers from the annals of Golden Turkey Awards and a few classics (*Gunga Din*), all of which feature either Duke Wayne or "fighting." That's a boy for you.

All of us agree: what we have is better than the Family Channel. It's the *Medved* Family Channel.

We not only make our own decisions about the programming on this channel, but we also determine its schedule. Rather than arrange our lives according to the whims of some network executive in New York or L.A., we can plan our viewing around our other activities and demands. No one in this household need ever terminate a conversation or chore because *Third Rock from the Sun* is about to come on the tube and we can't afford to miss one precious moment.

One enormous advantage to using a VCR rather than broadcast TV as a source of entertainment is that children learn the lesson that living, breathing people always take precedence over the allure of fantasy. If the phone rings, or someone comes into the room, it's a simple matter to press Stop and to interrupt the tape, then resume the diversion when the real-world interchange is over. Kids who watch their favorite material this way never have to worry about missing key dramatic elements or particularly hilarious bits in order to display common courtesy to their fellow human beings. Moreover, our children learn that watching videos must wait until more significant obligations have been met. Yes, you can enjoy this form of relaxation—but only after you've done your homework and cleaned your room. In this way, you control your own video entertainment—it never controls you.

Listening to Other Messages

One of the many blessings of our life in the Jewish community is the opportunity to observe the Sabbath with other families. The Bible describes how God created the world in six days and rested on the seventh, and we're taught that this means God ceased the thirty-nine creative activities involved in shaping the universe—the same thirty-nine world-changing undertakings that occupy human beings in their impulse to build and shape reality in imitation of the Almighty. In our tradition, every Sabbath we emulate God by pulling back from these activities, enjoying and appreciating the world around us but refraining from changing it. In that context, the Medved household stops its whirlwind of phone calls, kids' CDs, scheduling, and carpooling to focus on more important matters.

For twenty-five hours, we don't write, don't turn on or off electrically powered devices (including lights), don't ride in a car, or cook food. Everything's prepared and set before Diane and the girls say the blessing over the Sabbath candles at sunset. Central to our Sabbath is the lack of videos, sometimes to Danny's chagrin. But what a relief to spend time with friends, walk to the synagogue for services with neighbors, enjoy a meal rich with traditions as well as fancy presentation, and study the wisdom and truth of our forefathers. Once three stars appear in the sky on Saturday night, we can return to our hectic plans and pressures.

"Remember the Sabbath and keep it holy" is one of the Ten Commandments, a basic tenet of Judeo-Christian America. When stores closed on Sundays so their employees could attend church and serve family dinners, our nation, in this sense at least, enjoyed a kinder, gentler time. If your family can't resist the TV for twenty-five hours, why not institute a family policy banning the box for one night per week, or during the day on Sunday? Can't stand the idea of missing a football game? That's a choice and a message. You can always find out the score, or even tape the game for later consumption if you must view every play. As her own religious commitment developed, Diane used to lament losing out on those twenty-four-hour sales that her favorite stores inevitably touted for Saturdays, but it didn't take long before she comforted herself with the truth that there will always be another sale. But will there be another childhood for your little one?

The Sabbath is an opportunity to cease the siren of commercials, to quiet the combat of shoot-'em-ups, and stop the sop of the soaps. That one day a week set aside as special (which is the meaning of the term *holy*) allows you to place the rest of the week in its proper context, as the time to attack with zeal the problems of survival and the beckoning of creative possibility. And if you're able to turn off the tube for just one day a week, you've eliminated at least one-seventh of the assault on childhood and the mind-shaping programming that too strongly influences adults. Take control of your week, and at the same time live a commitment to your values.

Get the TV Out of Your Bedroom

Guess what's among the first questions Diane asks her psychology clients who are having marital problems? "Do you have a TV in your bedroom?" As a clinician, Diane's found that the strange talking heads and moving pictures emanating from the set at your feet constitute a potent antiaphrodisiac. After all, what do women (one-half of the equation) want? Talk. Intimacy, for most women, is defined as talk. Have you ever tried to communicate meaningfully over David Letterman's wisecracks or dumb pet tricks? For men, of course, intimacy is sex. But that, too, is much less likely when you're staring at Jay Leno. One of the basics for couples seeking to increase their closeness is: get the TV out of your bedroom.

Similarly, you retard rather than enhance the business of childhood by allowing your son or daughter to have a TV in his or her bedroom. Sure, private sets prevent disagreements over who watches what when, but think of the real consequences: each of your kids isolated in a bedroom, watching who knows what, doing nothing worthwhile. When you hand the remote to your child, you relinquish any control over his or her TV consumption. For many parents, that's a scary proposition.

According to a *New York Times*–CBS News poll in April 1998, an astounding 66 percent of American teenagers have their own television in their bedrooms. But if you ask kids, they *know* that television is bad for them. They understand that it enslaves them—but at the same time, TV shows are a peer bond, as well as a diversion from more effortful pursuits. Like homework. Do you think your child focuses on and retains the information she studies in front of a TV? Because homework is difficult, it makes sense that she would want the distraction and "reward" of diversion from the task at hand—or would use the TV as an excuse to avoid homework altogether. Take the TV out of kids' bedrooms.

You might consider the same for the kitchen and the living room. (What kind of message does it send guests to sit in a couch facing a wide-screen monstrosity?) Once you've confined your TV to only one room, consider making it harder to watch. Cover it with a tablecloth, and top that with a potted plant to disguise it when not in use. Remember the maxim "Out of sight, out of mind." Anyone' with enough desire to move the plant and uncover the box at least gains thirty seconds to evaluate whether watching is worth the effort.

But maybe you think there are some good shows on TV. That was an argument that Diane used when she first met Michael. His response? "The difference between good and bad TV programming is like the difference between good heroin and bad heroin." In other words, it's the same addiction—the same waste of time— even if some shows are vastly more stylish than others.

We would never suggest that all television programming is sleazy and worthless, but we do argue that it is all inessential. Elegant and substantive productions most certainly turn up from time to time, but missing them when they are first broadcast need not irretrievably impoverish your lfie. For one thing, the most notable TV offerings (say, Ken Burns' epic PBS series *The Civil War*; or the superb *Pride and Prejudice* that aired on A&E) will eventually appear on video, so you can enjoy them at your convenience. This approach can be particularly useful for children, who will want to view the choicest, most enriching programs again and again.

If, on the other hand, kids or parents find it difficult to plan time within a busy schedule to sit down and watch a particular show, that's a strong indication that the show isn't that significant after all. Most hours spent with television are neither scheduled in advance nor even the product of conscious choice: they involve a thoughtless desire to kill time, or to combat loneliness and boredom. Nearly all TV viewers have had the experience of sitting down in front of the tube and restlessly punching at the remote control, jumping from one channel to another and another and another, until two hours later you reach the frustrated conclusion, "Nothing good is on!" Meanwhile, you've lost an irreplacable piece of your life. If you ever took up a childhood dare that led you to place a penny in your mouth, you will never forget the bitter, grimy taste of that coin. That's the same taste left behind for many of us after idly engaged with fidgety, wasted hours in front of the TV.

By spending an hour on *60 Minutes* you may not feel as soiled as you would by using a comparable period to view *The Jerry Springer Show* or *Hard Copy*, but you have still placed yourself in the same passive, inert, and hypnotized position. At the end of a year, facing cheers, champagne, noisemakers, and choruses of *Auld Lang Syne*, few of us look back and wish that we had spent more of the twelve months just passed watching the tube. By the same token, how many Americans will look back from their sickbeds at the end of life and feel remorse that they didn't get a chance to see more television programming? As previously mentioned, the average citizen will allot more than ten uninterrupted years of life—twenty-four-hour days, seven-day weeks, fifty-two-week years—to watching TV.

Would you want this epitaph on your grave stone?

Here Lies Our Beloved Husband and Father, Who Selflessly Devoted
Ten Years of His Life to His TV Set

Your TV set doesn't need it, but your family does, your children do. Their innocence and their sense of wonder demand that you prove a wiser investor of the one precious resource that remains most strictly limited: your time and theirs.

Keep a TV Log

To facilitate that sort of conscious, responsible investment, here's our suggestion: for two weeks, write down every program you see, on a pad you keep near your TV. Write down the name of the show and some kind of reaction. Even better, rate how worthwhile the show was to watch on a scale of 1 to 5 or even 1 to 10. Here's a gem from Stephen Covey's 7 *Habits of Highly Effective Families*: "Adults who complain about being too busy spend 10 hours a week watching TV."

Even as stations and programming options mushroom, Americans express a waning interest: in 1995, 25 percent of those responding to a Louis Harris and Associates poll listed TV watching as a "most favorite" activity; by 1997 the figures had shrunk by 6 to 19 percent, making watching TV a distant second behind the 28 percent who selected reading. Yet the drop in favor doesn't stop people from leaving the television blaring.

On your log, channel-surfing requires an entry for each snippet viewed, or at least write "surfed between . . ." and be honest. If each family member agrees to do that for a week, you'll get a sense of your time allocations as a family, and each person will see in black and white where he devoted his attention.

If, after the two weeks of dedicated logging, everyone is happy with his TV habit, fine. If you're like most people, however, you'll feel horrified by the sheer waste of time involved in your viewing schedule. One of the best ways for you and for your children to tame your addiction to TV is to force an honest confrontation with how much you actually watch. If not, proceed to our next suggestion.

Stick to the Schedule

If you'd like to gain control of your television, rather than letting it control you, why not treat your viewing time the way you do other commitments you choose to make? Sit down as a family one day a week—Sundays, when all major newspapers publish their television broadcast schedules and make a plan. Go through the published schedule, select the programs that are truly important to you, and designate them with yellow highlighting or simple underlining. Chances are overwhelming that you won't come up with twenty-four hours of TV per week you consciously want to see.

Once you've marked the shows worth your investment of time, write out a schedule. Put one copy on the door of your refrigerator as a master guide to your TV time, and other copies taped to the side of every television set in your home. Above all, treat this plan as if it were written in stone, and stick by it. That last step is the crucial one: stick by it. If you can do that, we guarantee a sense of accomplishment. And a heightened sense of wonder.

Many people respond that it's much more difficult to try to stick to a schedule than to simply pitch the box alogether. But they usually come to that conclusion *after* they try abiding by a schedule. And they're probably right: once the TV is no longer a temptation, you just plan other things to do. No more "forbidden fruit" hanging in your living room.

If you're one of those who comes home and uses the TV to decompress after a stressful day or simply to fill up lonely or empty spaces in your life, you're probably watching too much television. Once you turn on that seductive medium, both advertisers and network programmers conspire to keep you tuned in. And with that "enabling" device, the remote control, the only reasons to alight from the sofa are physiological. (Don't forget, "the prevalence of obesity in 12–17-year-olds increases by 2% for each hour of TV viewed daily," according to Dr. William Dietz, New England Medical Center in Boston.)

Instead, find another way to let go of the stress of the day. Shoot baskets. Go for a walk around the block. Listen to a CD and dance. Phone a friend and vent. Read the comics. Take a bubble bath. Ride your bicycle. Listen to talk radio. Why is radio less harmful than TV? Because it requires you to use your imagination. And because you can move freely while listening, it allows you to focus your manual and visual attention on something productive.

Incorporated in the *Shema*, the central Jewish prayer recited in both morning and evening prayers, is this excerpt from the Bible, Numbers 15:40: "you will remember to do all the commands of the Lord, and you will not follow the desires of your heart and your eyes which lead you astray." The essential truth here is that your heart is connected to your eyes—in other words, your emotions and passions arise primarily from what you see, and visual input represents the chief source of destructive behavior. Television, which implants its images in your mind, steals control over what you see and nourishes impulses that originate with advertisers and programmers rather than in your own values and goals. While most of the visual input on TV may be benign, the cumulative impact of those rapidly flashing images will most often lead you—and especially your children—from the directions you hope to travel in life.

Maintaining a Sense of Wonder: Transcendence and a Grander Scheme

I should like to rise and go
Where the golden apples grow;—
Where below another sky
Parrot islands anchored lie
And, watched by cockatoos and goats,
Lonely Crusoes building boats;—
Where in sunshine reaching out
Eastern cities, miles about,
Are with mosque and minaret
Among sandy gardens set,
And the rich goods from near and far
Hang for sale in the bazaar . . .

These sweet verses from Robert Louis Stevenson's "Travel" bring readers wistfully into the imagination of a child with the capacity to view a world broader than his own environment. Children with a sense of wonder rise above the trivialities of crowded agendas, allowing their thoughts to soar to "mosque and minaret among sandy gardens set," and beyond. They look out to the galaxy without pressure to name every constellation, instead speculating on the immensity of the universe, staring long enough to wish on that falling star.

You can inspire your child to appreciate the grandeur of the world, fueling his sense of wonder. Opportunities are as limitless as nature itself. Who can negate the excitement of a sunset, changing colors before your very eyes? Call your children outside to watch the peach-tinged sky turn brilliant magenta, gold, and crimson, and slowly blend to gray and black. Or give them the broader look at time and space that astronomy provides, with fluorescent stars on their ceiling and a telescope at the window. Point out the uniqueness of each snowflake, each leaf, each variety of fruit.

> Moses was shepherding the sheep of Jethro, his father-in-law, the priest of Midian; he guided the sheep far into the wilderness, and he arrived at the Mountain of God, toward Horeb. An angel of God appeared to him in a blaze of fire from amid the bush. He saw and behold! The bush was burning in the fire but the bush was not consumed. Moses thought, "I will turn aside now and look at this great sight—why will the bush not be burned?"
> God saw that he turned aside to see; and God called out to him from amid the bush and said, "Moses, Moses . . ."

This scriptural verse (Exodus 3:1–4) illustrates the rewards of attention to the world around us. The Talmud teaches that God's angel revealed himself only in response to Moses' stopping and marveling at the bush not consumed by fire—in response to his conscious decision to "look at this great sight"—in other words, in response to his sense of wonder. From this we learn to be observant not only of the laws of God but of the *world* of God.

Television producers on PBS sometimes grouse that the only way to guarantee high ratings for their network is to show animals reproducing. Miracles of biology are so compelling because the complexity and diversity among species—who act so strangely by instinct rather than desire—ignite our awe. Upon our move to Seattle, our family joined the Pacific Science Center, where constantly changing exhibits allow children access to technical topics in science. Children watch in fascination the blind, hairless mole rats that scamper through plastic tubing in a ceaseless scramble. They gingerly touch the ocean creatures in the simulated tide pool. At Northwest Trek, an outdoor animal reserve about two hours from our home, they've watched bears gal-umph, owls flutter, and handled horns shed by sheep.

The sense of transcendence also comes from an awareness of time. Considering man's accomplishments over the course of history—Stonehenge, the pyramids, the Easter Island tikis—lets children go beyond their own cultures and centuries. Even talking to grandparents about their childhoods allows youngsters a different perspective. One of Diane's habits is pointing out differences between her own childhood and those of our kids. For example, as our daughters listen to a CD, she'll mention that when she was their age, she listened to 45s. Or when they're typing on the computer, she'll describe her old manual Underwood typewriter.

Perhaps the most important source of transcendence is spiritual awareness, an understanding that there is more to the world than what children can absorb through their senses. One simple way to foster this is by telling Bible stories. You know—David and Goliath, Jonah and the whale, Moses and the splitting of the Red Sea. These stories astound and also bring children to another time. They allow you to describe history that binds Americans culturally, as well as to introduce the source of wonder, the Divine.

Through a religious sensibility, children can blend an awareness of greater power and harmony in the universe with their everyday, childish lives. Children who pray and recite blessings regularly connect their daily activities to God's majesty. For example, observant Jews say separate blessings for seeing a rainbow, the ocean, trees in bloom, an exalted ruler, an electrical storm, a deformed person, and for eating each type of food. Each one-line blessing signals us to stop, step back a moment, and become aware of our time and place.

"Blessed are You, Lord our God, King of the Universe, who has granted us life and sustenance and permitted us to reach this season." This is the English translation of the blessing Jewish people say upon tasting the first fruit of the season, upon lighting candles for holidays, and upon wearing new clothes for the first time. Our children proudly recite it when tying brand-new school shoes or slipping into a new Sabbath dress. It helps them remember to be grateful, but it also expands their view of their new acquisition. No longer is a new skirt merely a taken-for-granted coordinate for the old sweater, but a manifestation of God's generosity through their parents, a reminder of how truly grand and wonderful their world can be.

This is the basis for every child's sense of wonder. Children not yet jaded by the cruelties of life are one step closer to unimpeded spirituality. It is on that spirituality that we should allow them to dwell, not on man's foibles and flaws. Let them revel in the privilege of being alive; let them discover the joy in being human.

This is their birthright. How dare we squander it?

The Third Component of Innocence: Optimism

Our family thoroughly enjoyed the Seattle production of Jerome Kern and Oscar Hammerstein's *Showboat!* and as soon as we got home from the musical, staged at the historic Paramount Theater, our daughters couldn't wait to listen to the sound track. They swayed to "Old Man River," crooned to "Fish gotta swim and birds gotta fly . . . Can't help lovin' dat man o' mine!" And danced to "Life Upon the Wicked Stage." The girls played that CD over and over, no matter what they were doing. As soon as the alarm went off in the morning, those fish gotta swim. As soon as they came in the door from school, those birds gotta fly.

That Sunday, Sarah and Shayna requested we take the sound track with us on our family outing. They sang along joyfully through the first three scenes, but then something peculiar happened. With the first forlorn strains of "Mis'ry's Comin' Aroun'" they both screamed, "Fast-forward! Fast forward!" Though the melody's haunting, they wouldn't even *consider* hearing lyrics that predict sadness or trouble on the horizon.

Kids Are Natural Optimists

Kids can live with many things we adults find distasteful. They often like slimy animals, gross noises, or impossibly messy rooms, because these oddities are interestingly *different* yet pose no threat to their view of the world. But they won't willingly accept anything that disrupts their optimism. Our eight-year-old Shayna vetoed her siblings' video selection of *The Incredible Journey* because she finds it "too sad." Even though the story features a happy conclusion, it's not worth the emotional turmoil of the tense storyline. She is so sensitive that she runs out of the room at any character-endangering plot twist, and prefers not to hear the word *blood.*

Children insist on happy endings. They want to sing "Ding Dong, the Witch Is Dead" and love to see the wicked witch of the West melt into a soggy pile of clothes. You won't find children's successful TV or movies with unresolved or unhappy endings, because producers generally enjoy profits, and kids would stay away in droves.

If reality doesn't conveniently provide a bright outcome, healthy kids will put a neat spin on any situation. When the truth can't be manipulated, they'll create their own realities, with magic powers, time warps, invented characters, and fantastic creatures like Fairy Godmothers and Guardian Angels, in order to make situations fair, safe, and loving.

Psychologists diagnose troubled children by how they play and what they draw, by the inner world projected on the stories they create. Normal children draw flowers and rainbows; distressed kids draw "bad men" and create ominous plots. It's important to note that kids with dour outlooks *learn* their perspectives, from trauma, abuse, or a hammering of ill will and negativity; children in functional homes naturally display an upbeat view of their lives and futures. It's only from twenty-four hours of television a week, combined with harried parents who have little time for them, combined with worldly wise peers, combined with incessant warnings at school, that kids' inherent optimism gets ground down and they lose the charm and delight of childhood.

Everything Will Be All Right

Optimism is founded on hope. Even in the most grim situation, children desperately cling to the bright side. In fact, many divorcing parents count on it, rationalizing their separations with "Kids are resilient." Truth is, kids cope the best they can; they muddle through like the rest of us, learning the recipe for lemonade when their family turns out to be a dimply lemon. Most children clutch onto the possibility that their divorcing parents could reconcile, like Maureen O'Hara and Brian Keith in 1961's *The Parent Trap*. Just sing a few bars of "Let's Get Together," and Mom and Dad will fall in love all over again.

Children reflect optimism about their long-term futures in their earliest career aspirations. They dream of the fanciful—cowboys, ballerinas, or, as our darling Shayna at age three proclaimed, "I'm going to be a clown." They see graceful ladies in tutus (or somersaulting figures in orange hair and white face), and project themselves gliding across a stage, jumping and dancing to applause. Danny insists he's the savior of the world, the cowboy who kills all the bad guys, or the policeman who makes our town perpetually safe. At the youngest ages, healthy children think that not only will everything be all right, but that everything will be perfect.

Dimming the Immigrant Spirit

This inherent optimism has characterized the waves of immigrants to America who often endured arduous journeys buoyed by their hopes for a better life in their new land. However, in recent years, our nation has been torn by fears that immigrants may be bad for America. Citizens worry that they take needed jobs, strain public assistance, and add extra burdens for teachers in public schools.

In April of 1995, a major study at the University of Chicago suggested the profoundly depressing possibility that the reverse could be true: *America just might be bad for immigrants.*

Researchers surveyed more than 25,000 eighth graders and found that in every ethnic group, children with immigrant parents performed significantly better in school than those whose parents were born here: "Their grades are superior, they score higher on standardized tests, and they aspire to college at a greater rate than their third generation peers."

Immigrant mothers and fathers generally "harbor optimism about the advantages of playing by the rules and the benefits that will occur through education ... They have a greater tendency to relieve their children of household chores to give them more study time, encourage older siblings to tutor younger children, and restrict television viewing."

The defining difference, the Chicago report concluded, is "the hopeful attitude of the immigrant parents." Ironically, the longer immigrants live in this society and adjust to contemporary American norms, the more likely it is that they will lose this optimism—and their chances for success suffer accordingly.

The Chicago results are not unique. "Immigrants arrive with tremendous positive energy," said Marcelo Suarez-Orozco, an education professor at Harvard, addressing the prestigious American Association for the Advancement of Science in February 1996. "But the more exposed they are [to American life], the more their dreams fade. The data is very strong on this." Working with his wife, Professor Suarez-Orozco compared middle and high school–age Mexicans, new Mexican immigrants, and second-generation Mexican-Americans with white counterparts near San Diego. While 84 percent of new immigrants agreed that "To me, school is the most important thing," just 40 percent of white students and 55 percent of second-generation Mexican-Americans agreed. While 88 percent of the newcomers used favorable words to describe their schools, just 20 percent of white students and 36 percent of second-generation Mexican-Americans did the same.

A massive longitudinal study of 5,000 Miami and San Diego students by Michigan State University sociologist Ruben G. Rumbaut confirms America's dimming of the immigrant spirit. His results correlate lowering achievement with increased length of time in the United States: "That kind of thing makes you pause," he told the *Los Angeles Times*. "You would think it would be exactly the opposite."

These alarming studies only confirm what thoughtful parents already understand: that our children stand to lose a great deal from prolonged exposure to the dysfunctional elements in our current culture. They lose faith. They lose confidence. And they lose resistence to the most deadly epidemic menacing our youth today—which isn't AIDS, or gang violence, or teen pregnancy but the plague of pessimism, which has infected tens of millions of young Americans.

The plague's main symptom is a crybaby culture, a national orgy of whining and self-pity. Michael routinely visits college campuses in every part of the country, and with only a few notable exceptions, he doesn't see a lot of shining faces or hopeful, enthusiastic students showing the promise of youth as expressed in the wonderful traditional university hymn *Gaudeamus Igitur* ("Let Us Rejoice for We Are Young"). Ivy League student health clinics report that the service they provide most frequently to these privileged young people—aside from dealing with birth control, abortion, and sexually transmitted diseases—involves the treatment of clinical depression.

Adolescent depression is nothing new, of course. Some of us remember the 1950s, when a small handful of sensitive souls dressed in black turtlenecks, drank espresso, strummed guitars, and warbled grim folk songs about the end of the world. Or perhaps memory recalls the 1960s, when Barry McGuire's hit single "Eve of Destruction" provided a litany of dire predicaments faced by a doomed people.

And wringing hands has always been a noble pastime for philosophers. Arthur Herman in *The Idea of Decline in Western History* (1997) traces the apocalyptic tradition through the centuries. But historically, debate over civilization's fate stayed confined to academia and the elite classes, as the vast bulk of humanity struggled for daily bread. Only with the advent of mass communication in this century could rural residents, the uneducated, and every level of employee listen in.

But risks change; prosperity ebbs and flows. The generation with the excuse that "We're living under the shadow of the big bomb" has arrived at arguably the most privileged and carefree stretch of time in our nation's history. The Cold War is over, and the threat of nuclear destruction that Barry McGuire lamented has vastly diminished. Miraculously enough, every country in Europe, even Albania, at the moment boasts a democratically elected government. But instead of the atmosphere of jubilation and celebration we might expect, we instead see a contagious cynicism and bleak visions of the future pervading both the adults and the youth of our nation.

The Crybaby Culture

Whining and self-pity are currently all the rage—to the detriment of our youngsters' optimism and our own well-being. In the spring of 1997, when Hillary and Chelsea Clinton visited Arusha, Tanzania, calling for justice in response to the 1995 genocidal slaughter in Rwanda, Chelsea was taken aside by a group of teenagers to answer questions. In a continent where disease is rampant, where young girls are routinely mutilated to deny them sexual pleasure, starvation and tribal warfare daily lead to uncontrolled death—and in representing the most privileged nation on earth what did she say? "We have big problems with violence in our country, in all spectrums," the First Daughter responded. "We have a big problem with drugs and people not thinking they have a future. There's a lot of hopelessness."

In *Earth in the Balance* (1992), Vice President Al Gore suggests we're all going to perish on a warmed-over globe unless we're saved by swift government action. Robert H. Bork, in his best-seller *Slouching Towards Gomorrah* (1997), spares no hyperbole in enumerating the signposts of destruction, then intones, "for the immediate future, what we probably face is an increasingly vulgar, violent, chaotic, and politicized culture." He adds, "Life in such a culture can come close to seeming intolerable." Writing in the *American Spectator*, Stephen Chapman responds, "Close? Half his readers have probably started eyeing the razor blades by the end of the first chapter."

In our chapters on the media, we discussed how films echo the grim tidings. Promotional material for Kevin Costner's eighty-million-dollar ego trip, *The Postman*, proudly proclaims, "The year is 2013. A war has destroyed the United States of America leaving the country in anarchy, its people defeated and all communications in ruins." According to the movie, life has become so bleak just twenty-five years from now that Costner's character must lead a noble crusade merely to restore mail service.

Other recent films deliver the same message about misery awaiting us in the future. *Waterworld*, Costner's previous apocalyptic epic, shows embittered, primitive, brutalized survivors clinging to life following the melting of the polar ice caps. *Blade Runner*, *Total Recall*, *Johnny Mnemonic*, *Liquid Dreams*, *Brazil*, *Twelve Monkeys*, *The Handmaid's Tale*, *The Running Man*, *Alien Nation*, *Gattaca*, *Strange Days* (set in 1999!), and the popular series *Robocop*, *Mad Max*, *Terminator*, and *Alien* all serve to prepare us for a world of rampaging mobs, rusting machinery, scarce resources, grime, hideous brutality, evil corporations, fascistic governments, and vicious mind control. The only big-budget futuristic films of recent vintage to maintain an even mildly optimistic tone have been entries in the endless *Star Trek* series—which managed to escape the prevailing gloom only because they were so firmly rooted in the fondly remembered 1960s TV show.

For many years, the movie business focused on nightmares about struggling survivors who somehow tried to carry on following the "inescapable" thermonuclear apocalypse; now that the threat of world war looks less credible, it is "environmental holocaust" that provides the fashionable basis for the message of doom.

Earlier we described how television uses its fun-house mirror view of reality as the basis of its sensationalistic and tragic view of the future. What would a Martian think if he tried to draw conclusions about America based on regular watching of daytime talk shows? He'd probably conclude that the population of this country is a collection of weirdos, crazies, and felons, since they seem to constitute the favorite life forms of today's TV programmers. Display of so much sadness and ugliness plants and then relentlessly reinforces a false reality and encourages both self-pity and fear.

In a sense, these pessimistic prognostications fulfill our fundamental craving for challenge, adversity, and valiant struggle. We turn again to 1997's *The Postman*, where the sad state of humanity enables Kevin Costner to ride around on horseback rallying America's pathetic remnants into a grand postal posse to restore their shattered nation. At the moment, the actual state of the country is so comfortable for most of its citizens (despite pockets of poverty and other persistent problems) that we fantasize about future collapse in order to maximize our chances for heroism. Previous generations tamed a wilderness, ended slavery, built the world's strongest economy, conquered fascism and communism, and walked on the moon. How can today's pampered kids possibly compete with this epic past? The underlying sense of boredom and inadequacy helps explain today's yen to rewrite our history as less noble and monumental than it actually was.

We were struck by a stunning example of this during a visit to internationally themed Epcot Center, part of Disneyworld in Orlando, Florida. While the pavilions of Mexico, France, Germany, and even China featured exclusively cheerful, positive views of their countries' pasts and present, with rides through travelogue-worthy scenery and tales of bravery and advancement, the U.S. exhibit presented a bleak picture of our history. Our representation to tourists from around the world featured animatronic effigies of Ben Franklin and Mark Twain taking a troubled tour of the past that emphasized the oppression of Native Americans, blacks, women, and the working classes, the despoliation of the environment, the slaughter of Civil War, and the deprivation of the Great Depression. The overall image gleaned from ten minutes in the U.S. pavilion contrasted mightily with the privileged reality just outside.

During the Clinton-Bush campaign in 1992, Michael gave a speech at a midwestern university in which he praised our nation's resilience and promise. After the speech, a distraught young woman raised her hand to vehemently disagree. "How can you be so upbeat?" she demanded. "Everything is going to pot. We have the worst economy, the worst unemployment, people can't feed their families—things are just getting worse! In fact, it's never been this bad!" Her impassioned protest drew a smattering of applause from the student audience, so Michael decided to ask for a show of hands: How many present agreed with the questioner that unemployment had never been worse in American history? Amazingly, nearly half the crowd at this major academic institution indignantly raised their hands. When Michael pointed out that the unemployment rate in 1933 exceeded 30 percent, while the current rate remained below 8 percent, many listeners stubbornly refused to believe him, or ignorantly insisted that statistics could never accurately reflect suffering. After all, the leading presidential candidate at that time repeatedly (and misleadingly) told the country that "we've got the worst economy in fifty years!" The students could hardly be blamed in extending his remark to conclude that they suffered under the worst economy in two hundred years.

Giving up on trendy nightmares about imminent chaos may deny us the valiant prospect of single-handedly rescuing a fallen world, but we will ultimately benefit from a more hopeful approach to the new century.

Preserving Optimism: A Sense of Context and History

How can you tune out the whining and bolster your children's optimism? Most crucially, you need to balance the grim noise about the present with the reassuring truth of a long-term view.

The "pride" movements of the 1960s empowered minorities by bringing to light the accomplishments and successes of their peoples. African-Americans "discovered" the work of W. E. B. DuBois, Langston Hughes, James Baldwin, and Richard Wright. Women, Mexican-Americans, homosexuals, and other groups gained identities and cohesion by focusing on the achievements of their own. By the time Alex Haley's *Roots* appeared on television in January 1977, the strength of black Americans through context and heritage was so universally accepted that 130 million people eagerly witnessed the fictional story of Kunta Kinte and his legacy, making the series the most watched in all of television history and earning it three dozen Emmy nominations. In order to increase optimism and confidence, foster pride in the achievements of the past.

Teach your children how the United States has been uniquely blessed. Not only were our founding fathers acutely aware of the miraculous events shaping our nation, but through the years since, we have enjoyed extraordinary prosperity and well-being.

At various points in recent history, Americans have joined to celebrate this pride in our good fortune and our promising future. Let your children know this heritage of enthusiasm. David Gelernter, in his fascinating *1939: The Lost World of the Fair*, explains how, at the globally unsteady point between the world wars and after the Great Depression, Americans mounted a farsighted and utopian World's Fair in New York. Attended by 26 million people the first year, it crystalized our nation's hopes and aspirations. Futurama, the General Motors exhibit designed by Norman Bel Geddes, was considered the pièce de résistance of the Fair and offered a glowing look at life in far-off 1960 via a simulated coast-to-coast airplane tour. As riders peered down on glass-domed fruit trees bearing abundantly and multilevel thoroughfares, the narrator noted suddenly, "But, what's this just ahead? An amusement park in full swing . . . Here's fun and merriment in this world of tomorrow!"

The New York World's Fair also featured a model planned community called Democracity, "where children romp in green fields, ride their bikes, and play softball . . . far away from the grind of city traffic . . . " Everything was clean and new, and every sort of employee could enjoy a sparkling fresh home in a green-belt suburb.

The feeling of enthusiasm in our nation continued threading through the century, with the understanding that technology's snowballing advances would bring stunning improvements in every sphere of life.

Like most other baby boomers, Michael grew up on consistently optimistic visions of America's future. His parents contributed significantly to this diet of hopefulness through their enthusiasm for World's Fairs. In 1962, they took their four kids to the exuberant celebration of the space age at the Century 21 Exposition in Seattle—Michael's first-ever visit to the glorious city we now cherish as home. The fair oozed childlike excitement. Writes Don Duncan in *Meet Me at the Center:*

Jackie Souders, 58-year-old director of the official World's Fair band, exemplified the Fair's light tone. Decked out in an all-white uniform with gold braid, radiating happiness with every gesture, Souders led his 37-piece band around the fairgrounds with infectious enthusiasm. When he strutted like Robert Preston in the final scene of *The Music Man*, everyone's step grew a bit lighter. Often, in a playful mood, Souders would hand his baton to some wide-eyed youngster standing nearby.

The band would respond by intentionally speeding up, slowing down or playing off-key.

The Seattle Fair featured a twenty-foot-high cake topped by a large ax-toting figure of Paul Bunyan, an All-Star Tiddly Winks match between Fair employees and Oxford University, astronaut John Glenn and his Project Mercury space capsule Friendship 7, as well as Soviet cosmonaut Gherman Titov, in person. The nation's leading science fiction writers, including *The Twilight Zone*'s Rod Serling, gathering at the Fair for a sold-out panel, complained that "it was becoming increasingly difficult for the imagination to stay ahead of reality."

Two years later, Michael's whole family made the trek to New York City for an even larger World's Fair, where the most popular attraction turned out to be the Carousel of Progress sponsored by General Electric and designed by the Disney Company. This delightful exhibit showed steady improvement in living conditions for a typical American family, including dazzling visions of the decades ahead, accompanied by a catchy theme song, "There's a Great Big Beautiful Tomorrow."

Pop culture offerings amplified this theme of a glamorous, high-tech destiny. Reruns and comic books continued to captivate kids with such seemingly timeless heroes as Flash Gordon, Buck Rogers, and Space Cadets—all zooming toward a future of limitless promise and daring new horizons. *The Jetsons* debuted on prime-time TV in 1962, showing an animated vision of a twenty-first-century family enjoying the blessings of innumerable scientific advancements. Four years later, *Star Trek* appeared on NBC, and two years after that *2001: A Space Odyssey* arrived in theaters, both heralding a new age of adventure, interplanetary travel, and human cooperation.

Rocketlike Trajectory

America has always maintained a rocketlike trajectory, its advances impressive not only in the laboratory, but in our living rooms and the quiet corners of our everyday lives. If you take a look at the long-term gains, you must be encouraged.

On February 8, 1998, humanity lost perhaps its greatest optimist. On that day, Julian L. Simon, professor of business administration at the University of Maryland and distinguished senior fellow of the Cato Institute, passed away of a heart attack at the age of sixty-five. His copious research led him to one major conclusion: that just about everything about life is improving, indefinitely. "Almost every absolute change, and the absolute component of almost every economic and social change or trend, points in a positive direction, as long as we view the matter over a reasonably long period of time," he writes in the introduction to his comprehensive book, *The State of Humanity* (1995).

"Would I bet on it? Sure," he confidently continues. "I'll bet a week's or a month's pay (my winnings go to fund research) that just about any trend pertaining to human welfare will improve, rather than get worse. First come, first served." Professor Simon famously won a bet he made in 1980 with environmentalist Paul Ehrlich, author of *The Population Bomb*, that any five raw materials of Ehrlich's choosing would be less expensive (i.e., more plentiful) in ten years. Sure enough, the prices of all five declined, and Ehrlich paid up $576.07.

The State of Humanity, edited by Professor Simon, brings together the thoroughly documented and balanced work of sixty-four scholars, summarizing knowledge about health, living conditions, natural resources, and the environment. Specialists address all the major social and physical problems, from global warming to soil erosion to loss of species to poverty and unemployment. They look at neutral facts, like longevity, infant mortality, and national productivity. Each expert presents graphs and charts with longitudinal evidence. And Professor Simon, with panoramic interests and clearly a desire for the complete picture, fills out our perspective with additional data in an editor's note at the close of each chapter.

At the conclusion of the book, Dr. Simon dares to forecast the long-term future, based on empirical evidence. His top seven predictions:

1. People will live longer lives than now; fewer will die young.

2. Families all over the world will have higher incomes and better standards of living than now.

3. The costs of natural resources will be lower than at present.

4. Agricultural land will continue to become less and less important as an economic asset, relative to the total value of all other economic assets . . .

5. The environment will be healthier than now—that is, the air and water people consume will be cleaner—because as nations get richer, they will increasingly buy more cleanliness as one of the good things that wealth can purchase. . .

6. Not only will accidents such as fires continue to diminish in number, but losses to natural disasters such as hurricanes and earthquakes will get smaller, as our buildings become stronger and our methods of mitigating disasters improve.

7. Nuclear power from fission will account for a growing proportion of our electricity supply . . . until replaced by some other cheaper source of energy (perhaps fusion).

Your children need a sense of perspective as an inoculation against the plague of pessimism. They need to understand that they are the fortunate beneficiaries of thousands of years of cumulative knowledge, and that they live in a time of accelerated discoveries with near-immediate returns for themselves and their families.

Many of the far-fetched improvements dreamed up by Edward Bellamy and H. G. Wells at the turn of the century are reality. John Tierney, in a piece titled "The Optimists Are Right" in the *New York Times Magazine*, notes:

The air-conditioned house, predicted in a 1915 article in *Ladies' Home Journal* headlined "You Will Think This a Dream," is here. We have the dishwashers imagined by Wells and the "electronic ovens" featured in the old RCA/Whirlpool "Miracle Kitchen."

People enjoy long retirements and routinely live to their 80's, as Bellamy dreamed, and they have even more cultural wonders than the citizens of his utopia. In *Looking Backward*, a visitor to Boston in 2000 is astonished to discover he can lis-

ten to any of *four* concerts being transmitted by wires from
distant halls.

And the strides seen in just the lifetime of today's parents are
astounding. Diane's list for her daughters of lifestyle improvements
since she was a child include panty hose, CD players, touch-tone
telephones, and calculators. Color televisions. Automobile seat
belts. Automated teller machines. Blow dryers. In 1970, 28 percent
of families had two cars; in the mid-1990s, 54 percent did. In the
'70s, 45 percent of homes had a clothes dryer; in the mid-'90s, 69
percent did. In 1977, the percentage of households with a VCR was
zero; by 1997, 44.8 percent owned one.
   Medical advances have increased life expectancies at astounding
rates. In 1960, American men could expect to live to age 66.6;
American women to age 73.1. By 1990, men could expect to live to
73.1, a gain of 6.5 years. Women could expect to live to 78.8, up 5.7
years. "The most spectacular development, and by far the most
meaningful in both human and economic terms," wrote Julian L.
Simon, "is the revolution in health that we are witnessing in the
second part of the twentieth century." Techniques to stave off the
most prevalent killers, heart disease, and cancer, have proliferated,
while medicines, such as vaccines for polio, mumps, measles,
rubella, smallpox, and a host of other debilitators, have made risks
plummet. A wide range of antibiotics have shortened or stopped
infections, from children's strep throat through venereal diseases
that once maimed and ultimately killed. Though we face new
scourges such as AIDS, medical technology, compounding the
knowledge of earlier scientists, can relatively quickly discover useful treatments if not cures.

Land of Abundance

Another perspective on the immense good fortune we enjoy in the
United States comes from viewing our lifestyle cross-culturally.
Even the poor in American live well compared to the general popu-
lation (not necessarily poor) among our European counterparts.
Figures from 1991 and 1992 show that the U.S. poor own such luxu-

ries as VCRs, microwave ovens, dishwashers, and clothes dryers far more often than residents of the most well-to-do nations, such as Switzerland, the United Kingdom, Denmark, the Netherlands, and Sweden. For example, 60 percent of the U.S. *poor* own a microwave; just 15 percent of all Swiss, 36 percent of all Germans, 37 percent of all Swedes, and 6 percent of all Italians are so equipped. And 60 percent of the U.S. *poor* own a VCR, compared to 50 percent of the Dutch, 48 percent of the Swedes, 39 percent of the Danes, and 35 percent of the French.

"A poor American is 40 or 50 percent more likely to own a car than the *average* Japanese, twice as likely as the average Saudi Arabian, eight times as likely as the average Russian, 18 times as likely as the average Turk, and 215 times as likely as the average Indian," finds Robert Rector, senior policy analyst for the Heritage Foundation. These measures of our everyday conveniences are easy, concrete means to give your youngster a context for our good fortune in this blessed land.

Progress in the Spiritual Realm

"As to the non-material aspects of human existence—good luck to us."

—JULIAN L. SIMON, FINAL SENTENCE OF *THE STATE OF HUMANITY*

According to nearly all indicators of improvement in the physical quality of life, Americans enjoy the rewards of ongoing progress. The only areas where doomsayers can charge that we've slipped reflect *personal behavior*, such as divorce, ethics, out-of-wedlock births, drug use. With eager journalists to inform us, we are all too conscious of the way social problems seem to wax and wane.

Even here, we've seen progress over the past several years. William J. Bennett's August 1997 update for his *Index of Leading Cultural Indicators* shows abortion declining, violent crime decreasing, welfare caseloads shrinking, teenage sexual activity lessening, AIDS deaths slowing. Fewer teenagers drop out of high school, more elementary students attain basic skills, and fewer marriages end in divorce. Out-of-wedlock births remain high, but these, too, "recorded a drop in the most recent annual statistics from the Centers for Disease Control, after rising for the previous 16 years," reported the *Wall Street Journal*. Wonderful news, especially in a Murphy Brown culture without consensus about whether or not out-of-wedlock birth *is* a problem.

While scientists, inventors, and technicians fuel the ongoing rocketlike trajectory of progress in better health and a higher standard of living, Americans' status in the spiritual and social realm retreats and returns to certain fundamentals, centering around Judeo-Christian principles.

The influence of religion "is growing in their own lives," said 62 percent of respondents to a December 1996 *U.S. News & World Report* poll. No one can doubt that religion is rebounding as a major force in our country, with 87 percent of Americans considering themselves Christian. "And most of them attend church, at least sometimes," says a *New York Times Magazine* story on the strength of religion. Ninety-three percent of American homes have at least one Bible. And the percentage of our countrymen belonging to a church or synagogue is high: 68 percent in 1997, up from 50 percent in 1900, 37 percent in 1861, and a surprisingly low 17 percent in 1776.

Counter the Headlines

We clearly live in a privileged and prosperous land in a miraculous time, and facts historically and cross-culturally support this. Teach your children the broader view. Keep in mind that most Americans feel terrific about their own lives, but due to the media's relentless hammering on the negative, think that the country as a whole is a lot worse off. This is a distortion, and kids need to know it.

Julian L. Simon tells this anecdote about the deleterious effect of the media on our view of the world. His mother, born in 1900, understood that she had been witness to a dazzling wealth of advancements. "In her eighties she knew that her friends had mostly lived extraordinarily long lives. She recognized the convenience and comfort provided by such modern inventions as the telephone, air conditioning, and airplanes. And yet she disagreed when I said the conditions of life had markedly improved." His punch line: "When I asked Mother why she still thought things have gotten worse, she replied: 'The headlines in the newspapers are all bad.'"

A 1996 *U.S. News & World Report* article, "I'm OK, You're Not," notes that "About 40 percent to 50 percent of Americans think the nation is currently moving in the wrong direction. But 88 percent think their own lives and families are moving in the right direction."

Americans' beliefs that their individual higher levels of well-being are unrepresentative informs many of their behaviors. For example, "Although 64 percent of Americans give the nation's public schools a grade of C or D, 66 percent give the public school attended by their oldest child an A or B." Given this disparity, some people would call for all sorts of national remedial educational programs because they think everyone else can't read or add, but at the same time see their own children as the superior exceptions.

Another example: Americans feel safe in their own homes and neighborhoods, but express fears about the general problem of crime. A survey released in December 1997, conducted by the Harvard School of Public Health and the University of Maryland, found that 24 percent of Americans considered crime a major concern, more than in previous years—which is unwarranted, given declining crime rates, according to study director Robert Blendon. "People really are anxious about things that should be going down on the list," he commented.

A study by the Pew Research Center confirmed this difference between perception and reality. Asking people to assess our progress nationally, they found that 61 percent of respondents said the country is losing ground on crime; 15 percent said we're making progress, and the rest said we're staying the same. Yet "six in 10 say there's no area within a mile of their homes where they would feel unsafe to walk alone at night—the most positive assessment in three decades," notes *USA Today*.

When it comes to their families, Americans emphatically report they fare better than their fellow citizens: "Almost 90 percent of Americans think that a major problem with society is that people don't live up to their commitments," says *U.S. News & World Report*. "But more than 75 percent say they don't find it difficult to meet their own commitments to their families, kids and employers." A December 1996 Gallup poll found that almost three-quarters (73 percent) of Americans said they're happy with their family lives, and four out of five (79 percent) described their families as extremely or very close. But when it came to assessing the larger picture, adults turned glum: 66 percent believed families are less happy today than when they were kids growing up.

Whining may be the pastime of philosophers, pundits, and pollsters, but don't allow your children or yourself to be sucked under. Focus on your family and community. Remember that what you see in the media is likely sensationalized and unrepresentative (another reason to dump your TV); be aware and vigilant about electronic journalism's depressing and frightening effect.

If you'd like to maintain your youngster's optimism, *talk* about the contradictions between experienced reality and the negativity in the media. Discuss the day's news at the dinner table, asking questions designed to let your child see a positive balance to the unnerving headlines. Interject your values and *label* them as your values. Pride in principles that depart from the mainstream is the basis of the courage to be different, the psychological tool that provides inner resources to counter temptations.

Make it a family project to understand history and the historical context for current events. And don't just leave it to the kids; provide that crucial modeling so that your children catch your view that history is exciting rather than homework. Create a family scrapbook with clippings and the reactions of each child to major events. This can be a wonderful means to document the activities and thoughts of your children while they are young. Include mementoes of vacations, school achievements, and holidays chronologically so that every year stands out as special.

Keep an encyclopedia handy to instantly look up background on any topic—and use it together. Diane remembers her frustration as a teenager when she'd raise a question, hoping for a quick and easy answer, and her mother would sing, with a glint in her eye, "Let's go look it up!" The entire set of the old *World Book Encyclopedia*, on its wooden rack, sat within two feet of her family dinner table. She remembers her dad sitting in his brown Naugahyde easy chair in the living room, reading those volumes for relaxation in the evenings.

Pardon our bias, but we consider a real book, with a cloth cover and pages to turn, pulled from a nearby shelf, a superior family unifier. But if you're an Internet family, gather 'round the monitor and surf the web for the information you crave. The important message you want to instill is the importance of the search for balanced and context-rich information. Teach your kids to be perceptive media consumers, inquisitive listeners, eager learners. It's a Jewish principle to have confidence that all is well, and it makes ultimate sense over the long run. In Hebrew, we say *Gam zu la tova* ("This, too, is for the best").

Happy

Be heartened that our culture seems to be lifting from its gloomy perspective toward a more positive outlook. "Sullen Got Old. The Attitude Now Is Fabulous," asserts a *New York Times* headline. Accompanying the article is a reproduction of a magazine advertising layout for a new fragrance, an ad that Diane had actually clipped earlier because of its striking exuberance. A young woman, seemingly dancing for joy, is overlaid with the phrase "C'mon get happy. Clinique happy." The caption reads, "Before, there was Obsession and Poison and Opium [names of other perfumes]. But that was then. Now there's Happy . . . " According to the article, signposts in the media indicate that "a brighter, sunnier and, yes, happier attitude seems to be emerging. MCI's latest campaign asks, 'Is this a great time, or what?' Network prime-time televison offers more than 60 situation comedies. In music, up-tempo tunes sung by fresh-faced groups . . . are climbing the charts." Calvin Klein, radically changing his fashion advertising campaign from brooding and dark to upbeat and social, said, "The real big change for me is that I feel everything is prettier, healthier, cleaner, attractive. It's no longer the downtown, hip kind of thing. . . . I think it's a fresh and clean kind of sexy, which seems sexier now than another dirty-looking model."

That positive messages are gradually making their way back into the culture was underscored at—of all places—the New York Film Festival. "A couple of years ago," said Richard Pena, chairman of the selection committee for the September 1997 event, "I looked at the films in the festival and there was something connecting a lot of them, something about the notion of family." An article by Rick Lyman in the *New York Times* touting this discovery notes, "If a theme does emerge . . . it is not because of planning but because the selection committee has inadvertently stumbled onto something that is happening in the global culture and is reflected in its cinema."

The Antidote to Pessimism: Gratitude

Though optimism is a major factor in childhood innocence, and though media, schools, peers, and even parents may assault children's natural upbeat outlook, it's not enough to oppose self-pity and pessimism with the simple directive "Chipper up." To tell parents and children to become optimistic is like asking the classic glass-is-half-empty observer to just turn over the glass. More usefully, the most powerful antidote to the crybaby culture, with its relentless complaining and doomsaying is one very simple and practical concept: *gratitude*.

Most of us know from personal experience what happens if we owe a debt of thanks to an individual—a parent, a spouse, a business colleague—but for some reason find ourselves blocked from expressing our appreciation. Thankfulness that is stifled can quickly turn bitter and poisonous. It becomes an acid that corrodes our very soul. At this moment in history, ingratitude is the acid that is eating away at the soul of America.

Even as we absorb the depressing message of the news media, we realize that living in this remarkable country, we are the envy of the world. We've just mentioned a dazzling range of opportunities that should make us the envy, in fact, of all previous generations. That doesn't mean we should ignore the ferociously complex problems that confront our country every day. But dwelling on the negative, and neglecting the debt of gratitude that is so obviously due, makes it harder, not easier, to summon the will to find solutions to our most serious dilemmas.

Children need to be taught gratitude. Being egocentric, showing appreciation is not something that comes naturally to them. Every mother teaches her toddler to say thank you when given something—a cookie, a toy, a new suit. These are the tangibles, a logical and necessary place to start. But along with this, parents can point out opportunities to express gratitude for *intangibles:* the people who help and protect the child (teachers, heroes, armed service personnel, police officers, fire fighters) for their services, and for laudable behavior, such as honesty, perseverence, kindness, and even demonstrations of affection—by the child or by other people. "Thank you for that hug! It means so much to me when you hug me because I love you so much!" Or, "It was so nice to see you hug Grandma—I saw how happy she was that you showed her you love her." "Look at that boy picking up that piece of litter. What a wonderful thing he's doing—he's showing that he cares about our neighborhood."

Gratitude not only reinforces children's optimism, allowing them to retain their childhood, but it makes them into happy adults, glass-is-half-full people, who quite simply enjoy a better life than their dismal counterparts. When Diane was in graduate school, one of her professors, Linda Beckman, conducted a study comparing the life satisfaction of elderly women, half of whom had children and half of whom did not, though not by choice. The hypothesis of the study was that those without children would claim less satisfaction, but the results did not confirm this. Instead, the crucial factor in life satisfaction was attitude—optimistic or pessimistic. The self-pitying pessimists who were not mothers blamed their infertility for their misfortune; those with children said their plight was due to rude or troublesome offspring. The optimists who had children called them the "light of their lives"; optimists who never became parents, while disappointed, cited all the accomplishments they enjoyed that might have been impossible with the responsibility of parenthood.

In addition, an optimistic attitude, gained only by an upbeat upbringing, increases the likelihood of a happy marriage. In Diane's clinical experience, the prognosis for ailing marriages drops con-

siderably when one or both spouses classify themselves as pessimists. Foster gratitude from your child's earliest moments, and
we guarantee that it will be returned.

Honor Thy Father and Thy Mother

"Honor thy father and thy mother" is not only one of the biblical
Ten Commandments, it is also the most fundamental precept of all
human decency and right behavior. But as you've read in our previous chapters, our media, our government, and our schools work
together to undermine that imperative. In Dana Mack's persuasive
documentation of our "family-hating culture" (*The Assault on
Parenthood*), she describes a raft of freshly published books with
the theme "parent as pariah," all suggesting that instead of honoring, we should chastise and overrule parents because, though they
may be well-meaning, they don't know what's best for their children, and may even prove "toxic."

This dismal situation requires nothing less than a revolution in
American education. The first priority of every school, of every curriculum, of every teacher should be to bring children and parents
closer together, not drive them farther apart. With disillusioned
members of the younger generation so palpably hungry for heroes,
our educators should make it clear that they need look no farther
than their own homes—where so many hard-working American
parents clearly qualify as everyday heroes. One of the reasons we
dislike the institutions of Mother's Day and Father's Day is that
these holidays carry with them the implication that we can pay our
debt to our parents one day each year and forget about them the
rest of the time. Instead, every day should be Mother's Day, every
day should be Father's Day—particularly in our schools.

Monitor your child's school curriculum, especially history and
social studies, to ensure balanced messages. Most teachers and
administrators eagerly work with parents who approach them
respectfully with constructive ideas. Your child's school is not an
intentional adversary, though media, in reporting the most severe
skirmishes, help us believe so. Get to know your child's teachers at
the beginning of the year, be sure to offer abundant praise when

deserved, and in that context, you will most likely encounter a receptive ear should you notice questionable material.

Children best learn every essential value at home, *especially* gratitude to parents. Again, modeling is perhaps the most potent tool. If children see their parents treating *their* parents—the grandparents—with respect and consideration, they will learn the same. If you speak about your parents when they are not present with admiration and gratitude, youngsters will pick up the cue. Just as important as freely praising is *refraining* from criticizing. Even when you dislike or disagree with your parents' behavior, keep your discussion about these issues between adults. And if you must comment negatively on your parents near or to your children, we advise using terms that acknowledge the good and, if possible, minimize the bad.

The Ten Commandments, one of the foundations of our culture, were given, according to the Bible, on two tablets. Why? Couldn't God have fit ten brief ideas—in Hebrew, ten "statements"—on one piece of stone? The answer provided by Jewish teaching is that the commandments are arranged to make the point that obligations of man to God and obligations of man to man are equally important. Had the directives appeared on a single piece of stone, from one through ten, there would be the clear implication that man's duties to God, enumerated in the first commandments, take precedence. As it is, the two sets of instructions have been listed side by side, stressing their parallel nature and similar importance.

The most puzzling aspect of this explanation is the placement of "Honor thy father and thy mother." In the traditional Hebrew counting it turns up as number five, at the end of the tablet concerning our duties to God. It is, in fact, at the precise point of transition.

Striking the Serpent

Patriotism. Beyond acknowledging a historical and cross-cultural context that proves America uniquely blessed, our children's optimism will thrive if we openly and joyfully express our pride in our country. Though most public schools still begin the day with the Pledge of Allegiance, our educational system should celebrate our country as if every day were the Fourth of July. We lament the hokey and "uncool" image that patriotism has attained over the past decades, though we certainly see the origins of this disturbing trend.

Nothing contributes so powerfully to the present plague of pessimism than the despicable attempt to smear the extraordinary and honorable history of the United States of America. This form of ingratitude strikes us as especially grotesque because, like the students with increasingly dimmed spirits, Michael is the son of an immigrant. His mother came to America with her family in 1934 to escape Nazi Germany. On Michael's father's side, it was his grandfather who made the trip from a little village in the Ukraine in 1910. He worked all his life as a barrel-maker, and Michael's dad recalls that his father used to come home every day with sore and sometimes bloody hands. Beginning at the age of five, Michael's father used to help his exhausted "Pop" take out the sharp wood splinters, one by one.

This immigrant laborer never made much financial progress in his life and died in 1958 in the same gritty South Philadelphia neighborhood where he had lived for nearly forty years. Did he feel bitter? Did he suffer from clinical depression? No, he felt grateful for the opportunities America had given him, and he lived long enough to see his son, Michael's father, win a full scholarship to attend the University of Pennsylvania and earn a Ph.D. in physics.

We mention this family story not because it is so unusual, but because it is so typical. When Michael's grandfather died, his father went through his things and brought back something that Michael will always remember. It was an American history book, written in Yiddish with Hebrew characters, that Michael's grandfather used to study for his citizenship exam; he always took pride in the fact that he finally managed to become a naturalized American. This book was filled with inspiring stories about our nation's great achievements and noble heroes, and if anyone would bother to translate it back from Yiddish to English, it would teach our children more effectively than any of the officially "enlightened" textbooks used in public schools today.

How could we ever repay this country—this island of sanity and goodwill in the vast, turbulent ocean of historic human misery—for all the gifts it has showered on us so freely, so open-handedly, and with such an uplifting and generous spirit?

There is a strange twist at the very beginning of our national experience in the fact that George Washington, the justly beloved father of our country, never had children of his own. One can almost see the hand of Providence in this, because it means that to this very day, our children and your children are just as much Washington's descendants as anyone else. In effect, we have all been adopted into a noble family line.

That is why it is so essential that we celebrate not the mulicultural contributions of our various ancestors in Eastern Europe or West Africa or Asia, but the achievements of our common forefathers, our national ancestors, who launched this country and changed humanity's fate forever. Too many courageous people have sacrificed their lives or their health for the principles that allow us the life we enjoy. Too many people continue to revere and uphold this nation's honorable standards for us to forget them and take our privileges for granted. We want our children to claim that noble heritage and to celebrate it as their precious birthright as Americans.

James Madison's "Advice to My Country," written to be read after his death in 1834:

"The advice dearest to my heart and deepest in my convictions is that the Union of the States be cherished and perpetuated. Let the open enemy to it be regarded as a Pandora with her box opened; and the disguised one, as the Serpent creeping with his deadly wiles into paradise."

We fear the creeping serpent, a disunion of the spirit, a dissention of common identity. We must not let our children succumb.

Encourage patriotism. Fly the flag. Sing patriotic songs in your home. Read history as a family, and recite the great words of heroes, such as those in William J. Bennett's *Our Sacred Honor: Words of Advice from the Founders in Stories, Letters, Poems, and Speeches*. Hang a map of the United States and teach your children geography and state capitals. Plan a visit to our nation's capital and feel the grandeur and pride for which so many have fought and died.

Gratitude to God

Perhaps the most basic explanation for the illogical epidemic of self-pity in this country is that too many of us, especially among our academic and media elites, refuse to recognize the great Benefactor who most richly deserves our thanks. When schools distort the purpose of the first Thanksgiving into a thanks to the Indians, when civic leaders must remove every public remembrance of the origin of Christmas, when television programs and movies show the bars and discount stores of Everytown America without glancing at a single church—our culture discourages gratitude. We cannot fully express gratitude to our fellow humans while embarrassed about our gratitude to God.

Prayer is perhaps the most common means of expressing gratitude to God, but in addition, saying in words to your family the gratitude you feel will make these positive articulations a part of everyday life. For centuries the *Shulchan Aruch*, the precisely detailed "Code of Jewish Law," has regulated the behavior of the religiously observant in every aspect of life. The enumeration of obligations opens with a single commandment, which we are supposed to keep in mind on each new day as we open our eyes from sleep: "Rise up like a lion for the service of the Lord!" In his impoverished village in the Ukraine, Michael's grandfather fought to follow that demand, and in later years its theme helped him, under difficult circumstances, to continue dreaming his American dream.

One could hardly ask for a more forceful—or empowering—response to the attitude of gloomy impotence fostered by the mass media, or the chronic ingratitude that saps the confidence from our national culture. Let that be the message to America's parents, to our children, to our schools, to all those who feel overwhelmed by problems, who feel their patience tried, their faith challenged, and their hope undermined. Whenever our vision may be clouded by the fog of pessimism, we should recall that we have deeper reasons for confidence and joy. Rise up like a lion for the service of the Lord!

Gratitude for Our Children

It is through the experience of parenthood that we mortals come closest to understanding the divine. As parents, we are privileged to have these miraculous souls, these reflections of God, entrusted to our care for such a brief time. We must guard and extol this precious opportunity, and commit ourselves to providing our children with the most advantageous means to enjoy the few years of their development.

Last year on Shayna's eighth birthday we celebrated with a Sabbath meal party. Our guests all helped serenade her with the traditional "Happy Birthday" over the cake (without candles, since we refrain from creating fire on the Sabbath) and our delighted daughter beamed. Toward the end of the day, as the Sabbath was ending and the sun was going down, Shayna came over to Michael to cuddle. "Well, I want to say good-bye," she said sweetly and solemnly.

"Why?" Michael asked with some surprise.

"Because," she explained, "after today, you're never going to see a seven-year-old daughter again." And of course, she was exactly right. After today, the gift of your child at this precious moment of time is gone forever.

May we conclude with a story from the Talmud about Beruriah, the wife of Rabbi Meir, considered the most learned woman in our tradition:

> While Rabbi Meir was teaching in the house of study on a Sabbath afternoon, his two sons died. What did Beruriah, their mother, do? She left them lying on their couch and spread a sheet over them. When the Sabbath ended, Rabbi Meir returned. "Where are my two sons?" he asked.
>
> "They went to the house of study," Beruriah answered.
>
> "I looked for them but I did not see them."
>
> She gave him the cup of wine for *havdalah* [the prayer ushering out the Sabbath and other holy days] and he pronounced the blessing. Again he asked, "Where are my two sons?"
>
> "They must have gone elsewhere and will return soon."

She brought food for him, and after he ate, she said, "I have a question to ask you."

"Ask it," he said.

"A while ago, a man came and left with me an item to watch for him. Now he has returned to claim what he left. Shall I return it to him or not?"

"Is not one who holds a deposit required to return it to its owner?" Rabbi Meir asked.

"Still, without your opinion," Beruriah said, "I would not give it back to him."

What did she do then?

She took him by the hand, led him up to the children's room, and brought him to the couch. She pulled off the sheet, and he saw that both boys were dead. He burst into tears . . .

Then Beruriah said to him, "Did you not tell me that we are required to restore a pledge to the owner?"

To which he replied, "'The Lord has given, and the Lord has taken away; Blessed be the name of the Lord.'"

It is with gratitude that we now return ourselves to parenthood, to our darling Sarah, Shayna, and Danny, still interested in Barbies and toy soldiers and learning to ride bicycles and plan slumber parties. They've waited so patiently while their parents toiled, the three of them sitting together with their glorious books of childhood. We see them open the first page of Robert Louis Stevenson's *A Child's Garden of Verses*, and hear Shayna's melodic little voice read the very first poem, reminding us again of this fleeting, special gift—

> *To Any Reader*
>
> *As from the house your mother sees*
> *You playing round the garden trees,*
> *So you may see, if you will look*
> *Through the windows of this book,*
> *Another child, far, far away;*
> *And in another garden play.*
> *But do not think you can at all,*

By knocking on the window, call
That child to hear you. He intent
Is all on his play-business bent.
He does not hear; he will not look,
Nor yet be lured out of this book.
For, long ago, the truth to say,
He has grown up and gone away,
And it is but a child of air
That lingers in the garden there.

May all our children linger in the garden.

Notes

Chapter One

1. Marie Winn, *Children Without Childhood* (New York: Pantheon Books, 1981), p. 5.
2. William Bennett, "What to Do About the Children," *Commentary*, March 1995, pp. 23–28.
3. C. Edward Hall, ed., *A Matter of Fact* (Ann Arbor, Mich.: Pierian Press, 1995), p. 651.
4. National Center for Health Statistics, 1995.
5. Bennett, "What to Do About the Children."
6. Debra Goldentryer, *Gangs* (Austin, Tex.: Raintree Steck-Vaughn Publishers, 1994).
7. "Clinton's War on Drugs?," *Entertainment Today*, 4 June 1996.
8. Drug-Free Southern California, Los Angeles County survey, April 1995.
9. Ibid.
10. Alan Guttmacher Institute, "Teenage Reproductive Health in the United States," *Facts in Brief*, 31 August 1994.
11. Wade Horn, Ph.D., *Father Facts* (Lancaster, Penn.: National Fatherhood Initiative, 1995), p. iii.
12. Wendy Shalit, "The Death of Girlhood," *Weekly Standard*, 29 April 1996.
13. Carla Hall and Max Arax, "7-Year-Old Flier, Father, Instructor Die in Crash," *Los Angeles Times*, 12 April 1996, pp. A1, A32.
14. Lisa Hathaway, interview by Katie Couric, *Today Show*, NBC, 12 April 1996.
15. Jerry Adler, "The Strange World of JonBenet," *Newsweek*, 20 January 1997, pp. 43–47.
16. Steve Dunleavy, "Lil Miss' Persona May Have Made Her the Target of Sicko," *New York Post*, 19 January 1997.
17. Neil Postman, *The Disappearance of Childhood* (New York: Vintage Books, 1994); first published 1982.
18. David Elkind, *The Hurried Child: Growing Up Too Fast Too Soon*, rev. ed. (Reading, Mass.: Addison-Wesley, 1988); first published 1981.

19. Dana Mack, *The Assault on Parenthood* (New York: Simon and Schuster, 1997).
20. John W. Wright, ed., *The New York Times Almanac* (New York: Penguin Reference Books, 1997), p. 284.
21. Goldentryer, *Gangs*

Chapter Two

1. Tim Brooks and Earle Marsh, *The Complete Directory to Prime Time Network and Cable TV Shows* (New York: Ballantine, 1995), p. 1083.
2. Television Bureau of Advertising, New York, Summer 1997.
3. Ibid.
4. Neilson Ratings Co. figures for 1996. From Cherie S. Harder, "Are We Better Off? An Index to Our Not-So-Civil Society," *Policy Review*, July-August 1997, p. 58.
5. Bruce Fellman, "Taking the Measure of Children's TV," *Yale Alumni Magazine*, April 1995, p. 49.
6. Calvin Woodward, "Where People Gather, TV Sets Are Not Far Behind," Associated Press, 7 April 1997.
7. Robert Kubey, *Television and the Quality of Life: How Viewing Shapes Everyday Life* (Hillsdale, N.J.: L. Erlbaum Associates, 1990).
8. Many thanks to Chiat Day Advertising for supplying their advertising slogans for ABC Television.
9. Brian Lowry, Jane Hall, and Greg Braxton, "There's a Moral to This: The Times Poll Finds That Most Americans Say TV Has Too Much Sex and Violence, and Many Question the Industry's Values . . . ," from AP Entertainment, published in the *Los Angeles Times*, 21 September 1997.
10. Dan Olmstead and Gigi Anders, "Turned Off: Special TV Survey: Sex and Vulgarity," *USA Weekend*, 2–4 June 1995, pp. 4–6.
11. Jim Impoco with Robin M. Bennefield, Kenan Pollack, Richard Bierck, Karen Schmidt, and Stephen Gregory, "TV's Frisky Family Values," *U.S. News & World Report*, 15 April 1996, p. 62.
12. Brian Lowry, "TV on Decline, but Few Back U.S. Regulation," *Los Angeles Times*, 21 September 1997.
13. Impoco et al., "TV's Frisky Family Values," pp. 58–62.
14. Robert L. Jamieson, Jr., "Boy Burned Trying TV Fire Stunt with

Friends," *Seattle Post-Intelligencer*, 19 September 1997, p. C1.

15. S. Robert Lichter, "Bam! Whoosh! Crack! TV Worth Squelching," *Insight Magazine*, 19 December 1994, p. 19.

16. Katia Hetter, "A Kinder, Gentler Hollywood," *U.S. News & World Report*, 4 May 1994, p. 40.

17. Ibid., p. 41.

18. Lichter, "Bam! Whoosh! Crack!," p. 20.

19. Brandon S. Centerwall, "Television and Violent Crime," *The Public Interest*, Spring 1993, excerpted in *American Enterprise*, September/October 1997, p. 62.

20. S. Robert Lichter, Linda Lichter, and Stanley Rothman, *Prime Time: How TV Portrays American Culture* (Washington, D.C.: Regnery Publishing, 1994), p. 299.

21. Greg Braxton, "TV Violence Poses Risk to Viewers, Study Says," *Los Angeles Times*, 7 February 1996, p. F1. The article reports on the National Television Violence Study conducted by researchers from the University of California at Santa Barbara, the University of North Carolina, the University of Texas, and the University of Wisconsin, analyzing approximately 2,500 hours of programming on twenty-three cable and network channels.

22. Laura Outerbridge, "TV's Lesson: Kick First, Talk Later," *Insight Magazine*, 25 March 1996, p. 40.

23. Nanci Hellmich, "Power Rangers: Negative or Empowering?" *USA Today*, 21 July 1995, p. 4D.

24. Joe Chidley with Showwei Chu, Sharon Doyle Driedger, and Dan Hawaleshka, *Maclean's* [Canada], June 1996.

25. Laurence Jarvik, "Violence in Pursuit of Justice Is No Vice," *Insight Magazine*, 19 December 1994, p. 21.

26. Sherry Boschert, "Socially Harmful Violence Spans TV," *Pediatric News*, March 1996, p. 34.

27. Robert Putnam, "On the Decline of Our Civic Life," *American Prospect*, Winter 1996.

28. Frazier Moore, "Survey Finds TV Newscasts Focused on Crime More than Ever," Associated Press, 12 August 1997; also "TV Violence Survey-List," Associated Press, 12 August 1997.

29. Don Feder, "Good News, Bad News, the Trouble with Network News," *American Enterprise*, September/October 1997, p. 45.

30. Lichter, "Bam! Whoosh! Crack!," p. 18.

31. Hetter, "A Kinder, Gentler Hollywood," p. 39.
32. Laurie Goodstein with Marjorie Connelly, "Teen Age Poll Finds Support for Tradition," *New York Times*, 30 April 1998, p. A18.
33. "Glued to the Tube: Facts and Figures on U.S. Television Ownership and Viewing Habits," *Washington Post*, 14 September 1997, p. 29. Source: TV Free America.
34. Web site by woman who "hangs out" at Mediarama, authors the *'zine Inquisitor*, and receives messages at P.O. Box 123, New York, N.Y. 10024. Summary of *Beverly Hills 90210* for 21 May 1997.
35. Chidley et al., *Maclean's*.
36. Susan Crabtree, "Trash TV Pulls America Down the Tubes," *Insight Magazine*, 4 December 1995, p. 8.
37. Frazier Moore, "'Jenny Jones' Still Travels the Low Road," Associated Press, 25 November 1996.
38. Crabtree, "Trash TV," p. 9.
39. Thomas Johnson, "Television's Slime Time," *TV Etc.*, May 1995, p. 2.
40. James Gleick, "Addicted to Speed," *New York Times Magazine*, 28 September 1997, pp. 58–59.
41. Media Research Center, "A Vanishing Haven: The Decline of the Family Hour," Special Report No. 6, 8 February 1996.
42. Cheryl Weitzstein, "Children Hooked on TV's Stimulus Find School Dull," *Washington Times*, 14 September 1997, p. 29.
43. Kay S. Hymowitz, "On Sesame Street, It's All Show," *City Journal* [Manhattan Institute], Autumn 1995.
44. Ibid.

Chapter Three

1. Michael Medved, *Hollywood vs. America* (New York: HarperCollins, 1992).
2. Evan Gahr, "Religion on TV Doesn't Have a Prayer," *American Enterprise*, September/October 1997, pp. 58–59.
3. Media Research Center, "A Vanishing Haven: The Decline of the Family Hour," Special Report No. 6, 8 February 1996.
4. Lichter et al., *Prime Time*, pp. 384 and 388.
5. Betsy Sharkey, "Sexy Orphans with Great Demographics," *New York Times*, 14 September 1997, p. AR31.

6. Harder, "Are We Better Off?," p. 58.

7. Patrick F. Fagan and Dorothy B. Hanks, "The Child Abuse Crisis: The Disintegration of Marriage, Family, and the American Community," report from the Cultural Policy Studies Project, the Heritage Foundation, published in *Backgrounder*, 3 June 1997, p. 10.

8. Susan Page, "The Mood at Inauguration," *USA Today*, 17 January 1997, p. 1A, reporting on a Pew Research Center poll.

9. Alvin F. Poussaint, "R-Rated Child Abuse," *New York Times*, 2 April 1996, p. A23.

10. John Evans, "Foul Language and Sex Content, 1996, All Films," *Preview Family Movie and TV Review*, 25 April 1997.

11. "USA Snapshots: Movies R Us," *USA Today*, Source: Motion Picture Association of America, 31 January 1997.

12. Judith A. Reisman, Ph.D., *Soft Porn Plays Hardball* (Lafayette, La.: Huntington House Publishers, 1991), p. 102.

13. Bernard Weinraub, "Fun for the Whole Family: Movies for Children, and Their Parents, Are Far From 'Pollyanna,'" *New York Times*, 22 July 1997, p. B1.

14. Bruce Orwall, "Cut the Cute Stuff: Kids Flock to Adult Flicks," *Wall Street Journal*, 29 August 1997, p. B1.

15. Oliver Stone, "Full Circle: Movie Violence—What I Tell My Kids," *Family Circle*, 1 November 1995, p. 140.

16. Weinraub, "Fun for the Whole Family."

17. Bernard Weinraub, "Entertainment Biz Is Girl Crazy About a Surging Consumer Market," *New York Times*, 3 March 1998, p. E1.

18. Richard Corliss, "Rated X," *Time*, 7 May 1990, p. 92.

19. Robert G. DeMoss, Jr., *Learn to Discern* (Grand Rapids, Mich.: Zondervan Publishing House, 1992), p. 69.

20. Soren Baker, "A Beat Becomes a Profitable Fashion," *New York Times*, 18 August 1997, p. C7.

21. Christopher John Farley, "Rocking the Cradle," *Time*, 19 May 1997, p. 84.

22. Judy Blume, *Deenie* (New York: Dell Publishing, 1973).

23. Lisa W. Foderaro, "2 Children's Books Depicting Digestion Become Best Sellers: What Appeals to 4-Year-Olds Grabs Adult Readers Too," *New York Times*, 16 July 1997, p. A14.

24. Diana West, "The Horror of R. L. Stine," *Weekly Standard*, 25 September 1995, p. 43.

25. Karen S. Schneider, "Mission Impossible," *People*, 3 June 1996, p. 65.

26. Mary Pipher, Ph.D., *Reviving Ophelia: Saving the Selves of Adolescent Girls* (New York: Ballantine Books, 1994), p. 12.

27. Marketing and Research Resources [Frederick, Maryland], poll conducted for *People* magazine 16–19 May 1996, reported in the 3 June 1996 issue, p. 70.

28. Bill Hewitt, Gabrielle Saveri, Ken Baker, Lyndon Stambler, Julie Jordan, and Nancy Day, "Last Dance," *People*, 28 July 1997, p. 48.

29. L. M. Vincent, M.D., *Competing with the Sylph: The Pursuit of the Ideal Body Form* (New York: Berkley Books, 1981).

30. Holly Brubach, "Beyond Shocking," *New York Times Magazine*, 18 May 1997, pp. 24–26.

31. Ibid, p. 28.

32. "Be Cool, Be Glamorous, Be Dead," *Los Angeles Times*, 24 July 1995.

33. Richard Klein, "After the Preaching, the Lure of the Taboo," *New York Times*, Arts and Leisure section, 24 August 1997, p. 1.

34. Joe Rehfeld, "Overexposed: Cyberspace Pornography and Our Families," *Washington Citizen* [Washington Family Council], July 1996, p. 1.

35. Enough Is Enough, P.O. Box 888, Fairfax, Virginia, mailing dated 15 July 1997, p. 2.

36. Steven L. Kent, "Darkplay: Why So Many Computer Games Have Violence and Devil Imagery," *Seattle Times*, 18 May 1997, p. C1.

37. David Shaw, "Critics of Media Cynicism Point a Finger at Television," *Los Angeles Times*, 19 April 1997, p. A1.

38. Mitchell Kalpakgian, "Why the Entertainment Industry Is Bad for Children," *New Oxford Review*, March 1996, pp. 12–16.

Chapter Four

1. Mack, *Assault on Parenthood*, p. 150.

2. "AIDS ... and Lesbians" (a brochure), San Francisco AIDS Foundation, P.O. Box 426182, San Francisco, CA 94142–4182, July 1995.

3. Carol Innerst, "'He Was Learning Everything but Academics' in Class," *Washington Times*, 2 November 1997, p. 15.

4. Jeff Jacoby, "When the Lesson Is Sensitive, Parents Should Be in Charge," *Boston Globe*, 7 March 1995.

5. Eric Buehrer, *The Public Orphanage: How Public Schools Are Making Parents Irrelevant* (Dallas: Word Publishing, 1995)

6. Carol Innerst, "Look Where Teachers Are Sending Their Kids," *Insight Magazine*, 17 July 1995, p. 31.

7. Harder, "Are We Better Off?," p. 58.

8. Christopher S. Wren, "Fewer Youths Report Smoking Marijuana," *New York Times*, 7 August 1997, p. A10.

9. Joseph Adelson, "Exaggerated Esteem: How the 'Self-Esteem' Fad Undermines Educational Achievement" (speech given at the Center of the American Experiment's annual convention, Minneapolis, Minn., 8 November 1995).

10. William Damon, *Greater Expectations: Overcoming the Culture of Indulgence in America's Homes and Schools* (New York: The Free Press, 1995), p. 96.

11. Darrell Glover, "Teacher Tells Court of a Day of Terror," *Seattle Post-Intelligencer*, 5 September 1997, p. C8.

12. William Kilpatrick, *Why Johnny Can't Tell Right From Wrong* (New York: Simon and Schuster, 1992), p. 17.

13. John Leo, "A No-Fault Holocaust," *U.S. News & World Report*, 21 July 1997, p. 14.

14. Charles J. Sykes, *Dumbing Down Our Kids: Why American Children Feel Good About Themselves but Can't Read, Write or Add* (New York: St. Martin's Press, 1995), p. 21.

15. Ibid., p. 93.

16. "Nation Faces a Bad Spell," *Los Angeles Times*, reprinted in *Seattle Post-Intelligencer*, 22 June 1997, p. A1.

17. Sykes, *Dumbing Down Our Kids*, p. 6.

18. Carol Innerst, "No Challenge for Growing Minds," *Washington Times*, 2 November 1997, p. 1.

19. Lynne V. Cheney, "Exam Scam: The Latest Education Disaster: Whole Math," *Weekly Standard*, 4 August 1997, p. 25.

20. Matthew Robinson, "Who's Teaching the Teachers? Education Schools Mold More Than Instructors," *Investor's Business Daily*, 6 November 1997, p. 1.

21. Judith Martin, *Miss Manners' Guide to Excruciatingly Correct Behavior* (New York: Warner Books, 1984).

22. Innerst, "'He Was Learning Everything but Academics.'"

23. Mack, *Assault on Parenthood*, p. 119.

24. Carol Innerst, "P.C. Pressures May Shape Teaching of U.S. History," *Insight Magazine*, 21 November 1994, p. 15.

25. Dan Quayle, "Bias in the New U.S. History Standards," unpublished article, 5 November 1995.

26. Peter Steinfels, "Beliefs: A Survey of Americans Shows That They Mostly Agree on the 'Framing Narratives' of the Nation's History, but That There Is a Lot of Gloom," *New York Times*, 2 November 1996, p. 7.

27. Eric Buehrer, "Let's Talk Turkey," *Focus on the Family Magazine*, November 1995, p. 3.

28. Ibid.

29. Innerst, "No Challenge for Growing Minds," p. 15.

30. Michael Sanera and Jane S. Shaw, *Facts Not Fear: A Parent's Guide to Teaching Children About the Environment* (Washington, D.C.: Regnery Publishing, 1996), p. 64.

31. "Good Pollution News," *USA Today* "Nationline" report, 22 May 1997, p. A3.

32. Craig Easterbrook, *A Moment on the Earth* (New York: Viking, 1995), and John Elvin, "Easterbrook's Book Sparks Environmentalist Warning," *Insight Magazine*, 14 August 1995, p. 27.

33. John H. Cushman, Jr., "Critics Rise Up Against Environmental Education," *New York Times*, 22 April 1997, p. A8.

34. Michael Sanera, Ph.D., "Environmental Education in Wisconsin: What the Textbooks Teach," *Wisconsin Policy Research Institute Report*, June 1996.

35. Robert Greene, "Environmental Textbooks Weak on Science," Associated Press, 2 April 1997.

36. School District of Kettle Moraine, Wisconsin, K–5 Protective Behaviors Curricula, 1992, as cited in Sykes, *Dumbing Down Our Kids*, p. 177.

37. Sykes, *Dumbing Down Our Kids*, pp. 177–78.

38. Chi Chi Sileo, "As Kids Accuse Teachers, Society Learns a Lesson," *Insight Magazine*, 3 October 1994, pp. 14–15.

39. "Teacher Hugs," Associated Press, 20 November 1997.

40. Mack, *Assault on Parenthood*, pp. 50–51.

41. Innerst, "No Challenge for Growing Minds," pp. 1 and 15.

42. Personal communication from Dana Mack, 12 October 1997. She reviewed the curricular materials in depth for her book *The Assault on Parenthood*.

43. Jacoby, "When the Lesson Is Sensitive."

44. "Out, Proud and Very Young," *Time*, 8 December 1997, p. 82.

45. Jacoby, "When the Lesson Is Sensitive."

46. Paul Bedard, "Provincetown Preschoolers to Learn ABCs of Being Gay," *Washington Times*, National Weekly Edition, 31 August 1997, pp. 1 and 15.

47. Leslea Newman and Diana Souza, *Heather Has Two Mommies* (Boston: Alyson Wonderland, 1989).

48. Mary Jordon, "Angry New York Parents Protest First Grade Class on Gay Lifestyle," *Washington Post*, 8 December 1992.

49. Erin Texeira, "Study Assails School-Based Drug Programs," *Los Angeles Times*, 21 October 1995, p. 81.

50. Robert Greene, "School Drug Prevention Programs Have Little Impact on Use," Associated Press, 25 February 1997.

51. Richard Lee Colvin, "L.A. Children More Open to Drug Use, Study Finds," *Los Angeles Times*, 28 September 1995, pp. A1, A16–17.

52. Tim Friend, "Report Shows That More Preteens Are Trying Drugs," *USA Today*, 5 March 1997, p. 1A.

53. Christopher Wren, "Survey Finds More Children Being Offered Marijuana," *New York Times*, 5 March 1997, p. A10.

54. "Study: Marijuana Use Doubles for Kids Ages 9–12," Associated Press, 4 March 1997.

55. Christopher Wren, "Drugs Common in Schools, Survey Shows," *New York Times*, 9 September 1997.

56. Barbara DaFoe Whitehead, "The Failure of Sex Education," *Atlantic Monthly*, October 1994, pp. 55–90.

57. Richard A. Panzer, *Condom Nation: Blind Faith, Bad Science* (Westwood, N.J.: Center for Educational Media, 1997), p. 44.

58. Jacqueline R. Kasun, "Condom Nation," *Policy Review*, Spring 1994, pp. 79–82.

59. Glen C. Griffin, M.D., "Condoms and Contraceptives in Junior High and High School Clinics," *Postgraduate Medicine*, April 1993.

60. Lynda Richardson, "Condoms in School Said Not to Affect Teen-Age Sex Rate," *New York Times*, 30 September 1997, p. A1.

61. David Murray, private conversation, 6 May 1998.

62. "Youth Risk Behavior Surveillance—United States, 1993," *Morbidity and Mortality Weekly Report—CDC Surveillance Summaries*, 24 March 1995.

63. Leighton Ku, Freyn Sonenstein, and Joseph Pleck, "Factors Influencing First Intercourse for Teenage Men," *Public Health Reports*, November/December 1993, reported in Richard Nadler, "Abstaining from Sex Education," *National Review*, 15 September 1997, p. 51.

64. M. Howard and J. B. McCabe, "Helping Teenagers Postpone Sexual Involvement," *Family Planning Perspectives*, January/February 1990, pp. 21–26, reported in "Do School-Based Clinics Work?" *Family Policy*, March 1991, p. 5.

65. Associate Press, 29 October 1996.

66. "5-Year-Old Suspended for Taking Beeper to School," Associated Press, 29 October 1996.

67. "Cough Drop Suspension," Associated Press, 6 November 1997.

68. "Lemon Drop–Pusher: First Grader Busted for Sharing Lemon Drops," Associated Press, 19 November 1997.

69. "Alka-punks," Associated Press, 10 October 1997.

70. Dee Norton and Jennifer Bjorhus, "School Lessens Punishment When Parents Appeal," *Seattle Times*, 8 January 1997.

71. Chi Chi Sileo, "As Kids Accuse Teachers," p. 14.

72. Ibid., p. 15.

Chapter Five

1. Spur Posse information gathered from three stories by Janet Wiscombe in the *Los Angeles Times*, 22 March 1996, p. E1 and E3, all under the major headline "An American Tragedy": "One Spur Posse Mother Struggles to Understand," "Some Never Got Back on Track," and "She Paid a Price for Speaking Out."

2. Kate Pavich, "Clueless About the Secret Lives of Teenagers: What Parents Need to Know," *Los Angeles Times*, 30 July 1996, p. 82.

3. William J. Bennett, *The Index of Leading Cultural Indicators: Cultural Trends in the 1990's*, draft updated 28 August 1997.

4. Texeira, "Study Assails School-Based Drug Programs," p. B1.

5. "Life in Lockup, Three True Stories," *Teen Magazine*, June 1994, pp. 44–50.

6. Sey Chassler, "What Teenage Girls Say About Pregnancy," *Parade*, 2 February 1997, pp. 4–5.

7. Catherine Fitzpatrick, "Girls Just Want to Fit In, But the Dresses Many Are Donning Aren't Very Fitting," *Seattle Post-Intelligencer*, 25 June 1997, pp. D1–D5, syndicated from the *Milwaukee Journal Sentinel*.

8. David Elkind, "Teenagers Under Pressure," *Boston Globe Magazine* Special Issue, December 1989, p. 24.

9. Laura Meckler, "Teen Sex Rate Drops for First Time in 25 Years," *Seattle Times*, 1 May 1997, p. A1.

10. Associated Press, "U.S. Juvenile Crime Growing Swiftly, Report Warns," *Los Angeles Times*, 8 September 1995, p. A35.

11. Ibid.

12. U.S. Government, *Sourcebook of Criminal Justice Statistics*, 1995.

13. Bill Hewitt, Joseph Harmes, and Bob Stewart, "The Avenger," *People*, 3 November 1997, pp. 116–22.

14. Dan Quayle and Diane Medved, Ph.D., *The American Family: Discovering the Values That Make Us Strong* (New York: HarperCollins, 1996), p. 57.

15. Nick Gillespie, "Arrested Development," *Reason Magazine*, December 1994, pp. 6–7.

16. Elizabeth Mehren, "As Bad as They Wanna Be," *Los Angeles Times*, 17 May 1996, p. E1.

17. Dan Korem, *Suburban Gangs: The Affluent Rebels* (Richardson, Tex.: International Focus Press, 1994), p. 127.

18. Bettijane Levine, "A New Wave of Mayhem," *Los Angeles Times*, 6 September 1995, p. E1.

19. Elizabeth Mehren, "Her Story: Tamara," sidebar to "As Bad as They Wanna Be," *Los Angeles Times*, 17 May 1996, p. E1.

20. Janet M. Simons, Belva Finlay, and Alice Yang, *The Adolescent and Young Adult Fact Book* (Washington, D.C.: Children's Defense Fund, 1991), p. 85.

21. Mehren, "Bad as They Wanna Be," p. E1. "Girls aren't immune to the cycle of violence afflicting many homes. When the family falls, they turn to delinquency," Mehren writes.

22. Maria Puente, "Teens' Tattoos Getting Under Parents' Skin," *USA Today*, 24 March 1997, p. 11A.

23. Robyn Meredith, "Tattoo Art Gains Color and Appeal, Despite Risk," *New York Times*, 17 February 1997, p. A10.

24. Richard Johnson, *New York Post*, 10 March 1998, p. 6.

25. Puente, "Teens' Tattoos Getting Under Parents' Skin."

26. Mary Wentz, "After Tattoos and Piercing Comes Branding," *Los Angeles Times*, 9 September 1995, p. B7.

27. Jordon Elgrably, "In Your Faith," *Los Angeles Times*, 13 May 1996, p. E1.

28. Ian Fisher, "The No Complaints Generation," *New York Times Magazine*, 5 October 1997, p. 71.

29. Shari Roan, "The Problems with Piercing," *Los Angeles Times*, 21 November 1995, p. E1.

30. Meredith, "Tattoo Art Gains Color and Appeal."

31. "2nd Teen Arrested in Family Slayings," *Seattle Times*, 15 January 1997.

32. Emelyn Cruz Lat, "Unlikely Friends Key to Bellevue Slayings?" *Seattle Times*, 12 January 1997.

33. Mark Edmundson, *Nightmare on Main Street: Angels, Sadomasochism, and the Culture of Gothic* (Cambridge, Mass.: Harvard University Press, 1997).

34. Korem, *Suburban Gangs*, p. 174.

35. Melanie Wells, "76ers' Iverson Still Starting for Reebok," *USA Today*, 25 September 1997.

36. Nanci Hellmich, "Today's Schools Cursed by an Increase in Swearing," *USA Today*, 20 May 1997, p. 4D.

37. "Kids Often Cuss for Emphasis," *USA Today*, 20 May 1997, p. 4D.

38. Mike Singletary, *Daddy's Home at Last* (Grand Rapids, Mich.: Zondervan Publishers, 1997).

39. Gordy Holt, "Yearbooks Are a Sign of the Times," *Seattle Post-Intelligencer*, 29 May 1997, p. B1.

40. "Younger and Younger," editorial, *New York Times*, 5 March 1997, reporting on an annual survey by Partnership for a Drug-Free America.

41. Bennett, *Index of Leading Cultural Indicators*, p. 6.

42. Chassler, "What Teenage Girls Say about Pregnancy," p. 5.

43. Korem, *Suburban Gangs*, p. 63.

44. "Educational Commitment Affected by Families, Peers," item in "Research Highlights," *Assets Magazine* [Search Institute, Minneapolis], Autumn 1996.

45. *Seattle Post-Intelligencer*, 19 September 1997, p. A3.

Chapter Six

1. Fitzpatrick, "Girls Just Want to Fit In," pp. D1–D5

2. Julian Guthrie, "Ex-Hippies Feel Turmoil of Parenting," *Seattle Post-Intelligencer*, 26 August 1997, p. E1, syndicated from the *San Francisco Examiner*.

3. Hathaway, interview.

4. Lynn Smith, "Parents Should Just Say 'No,' Too," *Los Angeles Times*, 11 October 1995, p. E3.

5. Cal Thomas, "'Marilyn Manson' and Milquetoast Parents Abet Minors' Delinquency," *Seattle Post-Intelligencer*, May 1997.

6. Maggie Gallagher, "Parents Without Authority Aren't Parents," *USA Today*, 9 July 1997, p. 17A.

7. "Elias," *Newsweek*, 17 July 1995, p. 49.

8. Damon, *Greater Expectations*, pp. 85–86.

9. Seth Hettena, "Schoolyard Dispute Goes to Court; Judge Orders Girls to Play Nice," Associated Press, 1 December 1997.

10. Peter Applebome, "Children Score Low in Adults' Esteem, a Study Finds," *New York Times*, 26 June 1997, p. A12. The study is titled "Kids These Days: What Americans Really Think About the Next Generation" and was conducted by the nonpartisan group Public Agenda for the Advertising Council and Ronald McDonald House Charities in June 1997.

11. Eric Pryne, "Moral Breakdown: It's Real, Most Say," *Seattle Times*, 13 October 1996, p. A1. The poll, titled "Front Porch Forum," was conducted by Elway Research of Seattle for the *Seattle Times*, KCTS-TV, KPLU-FM, and KUOW-FM in October 1996.

12. Paul Gottfried, "Decoding the Rhetoric about Shame," *Insight Magazine*, 19 June 1995, p. 36.

13. Kilpatrick, *Why Johnny Can't Tell Right From Wrong*, pp. 248–49.

14. Gottfried, "Decoding the Rhetoric."

15. Kilpatrick, *Why Johnny Can't Tell Right From Wrong*, p. 247.

16. Katherine Dowling, "The 'Village' Is a Moral Slum," *Los Angeles Times*, 21 February 1996, p. B9.

17. Julie V. Iovine, "When Parents Decide to Take Charge Again," *New York Times*, 7 November 1996, p. A17.

18. Quayle and Medved, *The American Family*.

19. Adler, "Strange World of JonBenet," p. 43.
20. "Youth Football League Finds Lyrics of Barbie Song Too Racy," Associated Press, 12 November 1997.
21. Elkind, preface to *The Hurried Child: Growing Up Too Fast Too Soon*, Revised Edition, p. xiii.
22. Postman, *The Disappearance of Childhood*.
23. Ibid., p. 44.
24. Patrick Welsh, "Parents, Why Do You Push So Hard?," *USA Today*, 9 June 1997, p. 19A.
25. Anemona Hartocollis, "The Big Test Comes Early," *New York Times*, 15 December 1997, p. A17.
26. Welsh, "Parents, Why Do You Push So Hard?," p. 19A.
27. "Clean Beginnings Lift Children to Affluence, Researchers Say," *Washington Times*, 25 May 1997, p. 12. The study was by Jean Yeung and Martha Hill (University of Michigan) and Greg Duncan (Northwestern University), results announced 13 May 1997.
28. George Church, "Are We Better Off?," *Time*, 29 January 1996, p. 38.
29. Guthrie, "Ex-Hippies Feel Turmoil of Parenting."
30. Laura Schlessinger, "Kids and Drugs: What Boomer Parents Should Say," syndicated column appearing in the *Seattle Times*, 10 November 1996, p. M1.
31. Cynthia Crossen, "Growing Up Goes On and On and On," *Wall Street Journal*, 24 March 1997, p. B1.
32. Zoe Deen, "Why the Feel-Good Generation Should Feel Rotten," *New Oxford Review*, December 1995, pp. 19–23.
33. Beth Ashley, "Gotta-Get-It Gifts Send Parents into Seasonal Frenzy," *USA Today*, 10 December 1996, p. D1.
34. Mike Males, *The Scapegoat Generation: America's War on Adolescence* (Monroe, Me.: Common Courage Press, 1996).
35. Lynn Smith and Dennis Romero, "Could the Blame on Kids Be Misdirected?," *Los Angeles Times*, 18 October 1995, p. E1.
36. James S. Kunin, "It Ain't Us, Babe," *Time*, 1 September 1997, p. 66.
37. Alexander W. Astin, "1994 Report of the Cooperative Institutional Research Program for the American Council on Education and the Graduate School of Education and Information, University of California at Los Angeles," published in *American Enterprise*, September/October 1995, p. 101.

38. National Center for Health Final Natality Statistics (1997, 1994), cited in Harder, "Are We Better Off?," p. 58.
39. "Great Transitions: Preparing Adolescents for a New Century," Carnegie Corporation report, October 1995.
40. Crossen, "Growing Up Goes On and On and On."
41. Kunin, "It Ain't Us, Babe."
42. Ibid.
43. "Old Is for Old Folks," *USA Today*, 24 September 1997.
44. Judith Wallerstein and Sandra Blakeslee, *Second Chances: Men, Women and Children a Decade after Divorce* (New York: Ticknor and Fields, 1989).
45. Horn, *Father Facts*, p. 6; source listed is Frank F. Furstenberg, Jr., and Julien O. Teitler, "Reconsidering the Effects of Marital Disruption: What Happens to Children of Divorce in Early Adulthood?," *Journal of Family Issues* 15 (1994), pp. 173–190.
46. Ibid., p. 19; source listed is "Who's Minding the Kids?" U.S. Dept. of Commerce Statistical Brief, Bureau of the Census, April 1994.
47. Ibid., p. 20; source listed is Henry B. Biller, "The Father Factor and the Two Parent Advantage: Reducing the Paternal Deficit," paper based on the author's presentations during 12/17/93 and 4/15/94 meetings with Dr. William Galston, Deputy Director of Domestic Policy for President Clinton, Washington, D.C.
48. Carey Quan Gelernter, "The Impact of Child Care," *Seattle Times*, 4 April 1997, p. E1.
49. Kathleen Parker, "Forget Day-Care Research—Trust Your Instincts," *USA Today*, 17 July 1997, p. 15A.
50. Ann Shields, "Turning the Tables," *Los Angeles Times*, 2 August 1995, p. E3.
51. "McMinnville's Parental Responsibility Law Takes Effect," Associated Press, 14 October 1996.
52. Janet Kinosian, "The Times That Bind," *Los Angeles Times*, 6 September 1995, p. E3.
53. Jean Bethke Elshtain, Tim Penny, and Vin Weber, "Families and Citizens, Why the Stakes for Democracy Are So High," Center of the American Experiment, Radisson Plaza Hotel, Minneapolis, 16 February 1995.

Section 2

1. Weinraub, "Fun for the Whole Family," p. B1.

Chapter Seven

1. U.S. Bureau of the Census, *Marital Status and Living Arrangements*, March 1995.
2. Page, "The Mood at Inauguration," p. 1A.
3. Kinosian, "The Ties That Bind," p. E3.
4. Gregg Zoroya, "Uncovering a Surprising State of Mealtime Grace," *USA Today*, 21 April 1997, p. 1D.
5. *Family Home Evening Resource Book* (Salt Lake City: Church of Jesus Christ of Latter-day Saints, 1983).
6. Gregg Zoroya, "Dinner Traditions Nourish Families: A Hunger for Kinship Brings the Ritual Back," *USA Today*, 15 October 1997, p. D1.
7. Shields, "Turning the Tables," p. E3.
8. Ibid.
9. Sesyle Joslin, *What Do You Do, Dear?* (New York: HarperTrophy, 1989).
10. Jill Lawrence, "Wanted: Good Citizens, Close Communities," *USA Today*, 16 December 1996, p. 1A.
11. Damon, *Greater Expectations*, p. 85.
12. Horn, *Father Facts*, p. 16. Source listed is Jayne Garrison, *Seminar Summary: Sexuality, Poverty, and the Inner City* (Menlo Park, Calif.: Henry J. Kaiser Family Foundation, 1994).
13. Amara Bachu, "Unwed Moms: Fewer Blacks and Teens, More College Grads," *USA Today*, 4 September 1997, Science section.
14. Information on sexual abstinence programs gleaned from Kristine Napier, "Chastity Programs Shatter Sex-Ed Myths," *Policy Review*, May/June 1997, pp. 12–15, and the Press Information Kit of Best Friends, Washington, D.C.
15. Applebome, "Children Score Low," p. A12, and Gina Chon, "Today's Adults Don't Put Much Faith in Today's Kids," *Seattle Post-Intelligencer*, 27 June 1997, p. A3.
16. Eugene H. Methvin, "Mugged by Reality," *Policy Review*, July/August 1997, p. 37.

17. Don Eberly, "Toward Civil Society," *Wall Street Journal*, 3 February 1995.

Chapter Eight

1. Thomas Vinciguerra, "Yes, Virginia, a Thousand Times Yes," *New York Times*, August 1997.

2. Ibid.

3. Allen R. Meyerson, "There Went the Holidays. Whoopee," *New York Times*, 4 January 1998, Week in Review section, pp. 1 and 6.

4. Ronald K. Fitlen, "Shopping Mall 'Santa' Pleads Guilty to Rape," *Seattle Times*, 10 November 1997, p. B2.

5. "BC—Odds and Ends," Associated Press, 28 November 1997.

6. William J. Bennett, *The Book of Virtues* (New York: Simon and Schuster, 1993), p. 602.

7. Kathryn Jackson, *The Golden Book of 365 Stories: A Story for Each Day of the Year*, (Racine, Wis.: Western Publishing Co., 1995), p. 129

8. Robert Louis Stevenson, *A Child's Garden of Verses*, ill. Alice and Martin Provensen (New York: Golden Books, 1979), p. 56.

9. Kalpakgian, "Why the Entertainment Industry Is Bad for Children," pp. 12–16.

10. "Eleven Toys Join Oregon Pantheon of Playthings," *Seattle Times*, 22 February 1998, p. B10.

11. Kalpakgian, "Why the Entertainment Industry Is Bad for Children."

12. Postman, *The Disappearance of Childhood*, p. 72.

13. Ruth Westheimer, *Dr. Ruth Talks to Kids: Where You Came From, How Your Body Changes, and What Sex Is All About* (New York: Macmillan, 1993), p. 10.

14. Officer Dreyer is a pseudonym for the DARE officer who made weekly visits to Danny's half-day kindergarten class during the fall of 1997.

15. David Whitman with Timothy M. Ito and Amy Kost, "A Bad Case of the Blues," *U.S. News & World Report*, 4 March 1996, pp. 54–62.

16. Karl Zinsmeister, "TV-Free: Real Families Describe Life Without the Tube," *American Enterprise*, September/October 1997, pp. 63–71.

17. Roper Starch Worldwide, *America's Watching: Public Attitudes Toward Television* (New York: Roper Starch Worldwide, 1997), p. 9.

18. Goodstein and Connelly, "Teen Age Poll," p. A18.

19. Stephen Covey, "How Any Family Can be Happy," *USA Weekend*, 26–28 September 1997, p. 10.
20. "Snapshots, a Look at Statistics That Shape the Nation: Free Time Choices," *USA Today*, 22 September 1997, p. A1.
21. Joyce Brothers, "The Reasons Children, Adults Tend to Overeat," *Los Angeles Times*, 8 November 1995, p. E5. Similar results were found in a Harvard study reported in the *Seattle Times:* "The strongest predictor for gaining weight was watching television: For each hour of TV viewed each week, subjects averaged ½ pound gained." (Molly Martin, "On Fitness" column, *Pacific Magazine*, 26 October 1997, p. 6.)
22. Translation of Exodus 3:1–4 from Rabbi Nosson Scherman, *The Chumash*, Stone Edition, Artscroll Series (Brooklyn, N.Y.: Mesorah Publications, 1993), p. 301.

Chapter Nine

1. University of Chicago, April 1995.
2. Elaine Woo, "Immigrants, US Peers Differ Starkly on Schools," *Los Angeles Times*, 22 February 1996, pp. A1 and A19.
3. Ibid., p. 19.
4. Arthur Herman, *The Idea of Decline in Western History* (New York: The Free Press, 1997).
5. Robert H. Bork, *Slouching Towards Gomorrah: Modern Liberalism and American Decline* (New York: Regan Books, 1996), p. 342.
6. Stephen Chapman, "The Sky Is Always Falling—Even When It's Blue," *American Spectator*, May 1997, p. 75.
7. David Gelernter, *1939: The Lost World of the Fair* (New York: The Free Press, 1995), p. 24.
8. Don Duncan, *Meet Me at the Center: The Story of Seattle Center From the Beginnings to the 1962 World's Fair to the 21st Century* (Seattle: Seattle Center Foundation, 1992).
9. Julian L. Simon, ed., *The State of Humanity* (Cambridge, Mass.: Blackwell Publishers, 1995), p. 7.
10. Julian Simon eulogy, from Cato Institute, 10 February 1998.
11. Simon, *State of Humanity*, pp. 644–45.
12. John Tierney, "The Optimists Are Right," *New York Times Magazine*, 29 September 1996, pp. 91–97.

13. Figures for cars and clothes dryers from a table, "America, Then and Now," *Time*, 29 January 1966, p. 38.

14. Figures on VCR ownership from a table in *Policy Review*, July/August 1997, p. 58.

15. Life expectancy at birth figures from National Center for Health Statistics, reported in *USA Today*, 19 June 1996, p. 2B.

16. Simon, *State of Humanity*, p. 650.

17. Table "Percent of Households Owning Selected Appliances" from Euromonitor, 1991, and U.S. Bureau of the Census, 1992, accompanying an article by Bruce Bartlett, "How Poor Are the Poor?," *American Enterprise*, January/February 1996, p. 58.

18. Robert Rector, "How 'Poor' Are America's Poor?" in Simon, *State of Humanity*, p. 247.

19. Alan Murray, "Riding a Wave: It Looks Like Good News Ahead," *Wall Street Journal*, 10 February 1997, p. A1.

20. David Whitman, "I'm OK, You're Not," *U.S. News & World Report*, 16 December 1996, p. 26.

21. Russell Shorto, "Belief by the Numbers," *New York Times Magazine*, 7 December 1997, pp. 60–61.

22. Simon, *State of Humanity*, p. 655.

23. Whitman, "I'm OK, You're Not," pp. 24–30.

24. Laura Meckler, "Drugs, Crime, Family Life Top American Concerns about Children," Associated Press, 8 December 1997.

25. Page, "The Mood at Inauguration," p. 1A.

26. Whitman, "I'm OK, You're Not."

27. Gallup poll results on American family life from "Families Say Their Own Lives Are Good," *USA Today*, 18 December 1996.

28. Stuart Elliott, "Sullen Got Old. The Attitude Now Is Fabulous," *New York Times*, 5 October 1997.

29. Stuart Elliott, "Advertising" column, *New York Times*, 4 February 1998, p. C9.

30. Rick Lyman, "Film Festival Has a Theme This Year: It's Family," *New York Times*, 22 September 1997, p. B1.

31. Mack, *Assault on Parenthood*, pp. 29–50.

32. James Madison, "Advice to My Country," quoted in William J. Bennett, *Our Sacred Honor* (New York: Simon and Schuster, 1997), p. 92.

33. Story of Beruriah from the translation of Burton Visotzky, *The Midrash on Proverbs*, p. 121, quoted in Rabbi Joseph Telushkin, *Jewish Wisdom* (New York: William Morrow, 1994), pp. 265–66.

Index